D1525217

THE INTELLECTUAL IMAGINATION

THE
INTELLECTUAL
IMAGINATION

Knowledge and Aesthetics in North Atlantic
and African Philosophy

OMEDI OCHIENG

University of Notre Dame Press

Notre Dame, Indiana

University of Notre Dame Press
Notre Dame, Indiana 46556
undpress.nd.edu
All Rights Reserved

Published in the United States of America

Library of Congress Cataloging-in-Publication Data

Names: Ochieng, Omedi, author.
Title: The intellectual imagination : knowledge and aesthetics in North
    Atlantic and African philosophy / Omedi Ochieng.
Description: Notre Dame : University of Notre Dame Press, 2018. | Includes
    bibliographical references and index. |
Identifiers: LCCN 2018012507 (print) | LCCN 2018012636 (ebook) | ISBN
    9780268103316 (pdf) | ISBN 9780268103323 (epub) | ISBN 9780268103293
    (hardcover : alk. paper) | ISBN 0268103291 (hardcover : alk. paper)
Subjects: LCSH: Imagination (Philosophy) | Aesthetics, African. |
    Africa—Intellectual life. | North Atlantic Region—Intellectual life.
Classification: LCC BH301.I53 (ebook) | LCC BH301.I53 O24 2018 (print) | DDC
    121—dc23
LC record available at https://lccn.loc.gov/2018012507

∞ *This paper meets the requirements of ANSI/NISO Z39.48-1992*
(Permanence of Paper).

CONTENTS

ACKNOWLEDGMENTS

———————————

Antonio Gramsci writes that history is deposited "as an infinity of traces" within us "without leaving an inventory." This book on the intellectual imagination is also the story of the constellation of thinkers, teachers, mentors, friends, writers, readers, and publics whose thought and practice gave flavor to my intellectual sensibility. As Gramsci also points out, of course, whereas everyone is an intellectual, not everyone is designated as such by national and geopolitical institutions of canonization and credentialing. Thus this book also acknowledges the fugitive intellectuals who invited me to their moveable feasts, who taught me that there are more knowledges than are yet dreamt of in the philosophies of power and pedigree. I cannot hope to do justice to these diverse publics and persons, but if particular lines of thought are in the end fruitful, certain analytic distinctions turn out precisely, and a few idiomatic accents prove resonant, they are no more than the polyphonic echoes of those who, in allowing me to be, also invited me to become.

My deepest thanks to the University of Notre Dame Press for keeping a tradition open to vigorous contestation on the biggest and most meaningful questions in the humanities. I'm grateful to Charles Van Hof for his enthusiasm and boundless encouragement when I first suggested this project and to Stephen Wrinn for his overall stewardship of a flourishing academic press. Many, many thanks to Eli Bortz for keeping faith with the project. Special thanks to Stephen Little for his vision and integrity. I am also deeply grateful to many in the Notre Dame Press team that ushered this book to production: to Matt Dowd, for the precision of his editing; to Wendy McMillen, for her aesthetic judgment; and to Kathryn Pitts for her work in making this book known to the world. Special thanks as well to many more in the Notre Dame team whom I have yet to meet but whose labor made this book possible.

At Denison University, I am invited every day to a community of exacting rigor, boundless generosity, and vibrant friendship. My deepest thanks to Olivia Aguilar, Sky Anderson, Lauren Araiza, Andy Barenberg, Stafford Berry, Dan Blim, Tabitha Chester, Hsun-Yu Chuang, Suzanne Condray, Kim Coplin, John Davis, Karen Graves, Julia Grawemeyer, Hollis Griffin, Fareeda Griffith, Amanda Gunn, Alina Haliliuc, Ayana Hinton, John L. Jackson, Zarrina Juraqulova, Toni King, Bill Kirkpatrick, Susan Kosling, Linda Krumholz, Sangeet Kumar, Jeff Kurtz, Veve Lele, Anna Lim, Jeehyun Lim, Lisbeth Lipari, Diana Mafe, Regina Martin, Andy McCall, May Mei, Nausica Marcos Miguel, Yvonne-Marie Mokam, Anna Nekola, Emily Nemeth, Isis Nusair, Heather Pool, Fred Porcheddu, Laura Russell, Ron Santoni, Sally Scheiderer, Jesse Schlotterbeck, Karen Powell Sears, Jack Shuler, Margot Singer, Catherine Stuer, Jo Tague, Megan Threlkeld, PJ Torres, Johan Uribe, Luis Villanueva, Wes Walter, Anita Waters, Alison Williams, Adam Weinberg, Sarah Wolff, and many, many more.

Students have often been my first publics—their questions are the Ariadne's thread braiding through this book. Thank you Yusuf Ahmed, Nordia Bennett, Arlesha Cospy, Deirdre Debrah, Bailey Fitzgerald, Kaitlyn Folkers, Niyah Gonzalez, Ellie Hasan, Haley Jones, Sianneh Jensen, Cierra King, William LaGrone, Megan Lovely, Susana Meza, Francis Kalombo Ngoy, Marlén Ortiz, Andrianna Peterson, Jose Rodriguez, Sharlyn Ruiz, George Steckbeck, Thomas Stephenson, Amilia Tsegai, Richard Van Voorhis, and George Webster. Special thanks to the communication department fellows—Asesha Vivek Dayal, Erin Dunlap, Connor Dunn, Ashlyn Flaherty, Carolin Frias, MJ Gewalt, Sianneh Jensen, and Sophie Lee—to whom I owe the world for meticulous work on the bibliography and notes. MJ, I miss your leadership, laugh, and razor-wit. Thank you.

I can scarcely believe my fortune in having encountered thinkers who offer intimations of what a fully realized intellectual life would look like if we lived in a world that valued sustained and intense critical inquiry. My deepest thanks to Barry Brummett, Radhika Gajjala, Matthew Heinz, Segun Ige, Lisbeth Lipari, Thaddeus Metz, Derek Peterson, and Gail Presbey for your extraordinary imagination, your exemplary scholarship, and your wondrous friendship.

In the close-knit and yet deeply vibrant community of African philosophers, I have encountered thinkers whose brilliance and rigor are only matched by their generosity and hospitality. Thank you to Sam Imbo, Bruce Janz, Kai Kresse, D. A. Masolo, Ronke Oke, Uchenna Okeja, John Ouko, Gail Presbey, and Olufemi O. Taiwo.

To friends, for breathing joy and beauty into this book. Thank you Chris Bollinger, Kermit Campbell, Julianna Carlson, Hsin-I Cheng, Jack Cho, Deborah Dunn, Jamie Friedman, Kaho Futagami, Lincoln Hanks, Rachel Harril, Carson Hensarling, Erin Herring, Amy Heuman, Felix Huang, Segun Ige, Ako Inuzuka, Daniel Johnsen, Savannah Kelly, Kelsey Lahr, Brennan Lanphear, Andrea Larez, Peter Matthews, Lauren McGee, Kaci Mexico, Michael T. McGill, Jr., Denise Menchaca, Mallory Mitchell, Clemency Nabushawo, Aki Nakamura, Diana Navarrete, Emily Pagano, Matt Pace, Jamie Poteete, Sara Reinis, Kelly Schon, Sarah Yoder Skripsky, Greg Spencer, Lesa Stern, Madison Taylor, Samantha Tevis, Elizabeth Touneh, Brittany Tuscan, Melissa Vogley Woods, Elijah Walubuka, Ping Yang, and Alison Yeh. Jeff Aquilon, I remain in awe at your sheer genius, but most of all, your kindness and compassion. Thank you. Elena Yee, your hope and courage and intelligence is a light that keeps me going. Bruce L. Edwards and Mary Kizito, loving teachers and mentors, your memory holds me.

To my family, whose sustenance—intellectual, affective, and ethical—has been life-giving. Thank you to my dearest parents—Joyce Vosenge and Noah Ayim—and my deepest gratitude and love to Ben, Caro, Isaac, Goddy, Jennifer, Chris, Rachel, Joel, Halima, Doryanne, Steve, Rachel, and my treasured nephews and nieces.

This book is dedicated to Ania Arleta Las and Milosz Jan—for discoveries profound with wonder, mystery, and wisdom; and for adventures rich in grace, warmth, and beauty. *Dzikuj, moi kochani.*

Groundwork for the Intellectual Life

Ontology, Imagination, and Praxis

In winter's twilight, when the red sun glows, I can see the dark figures pass between the halls to the music of the night-bell. In the morning, when the sun is golden, the clang of the day-bell brings the hurry and laughter of three hundred young hearts from hall and street, and from the busy city below,—children all dark and heavy-haired,—to join their clear young voices in the music of the morning sacrifice. In a half-dozen class-rooms they gather then,— here to follow the love-song of Dido, here to listen to the tale of Troy divine; there to wander among the stars, there to wander among men and nations—and elsewhere other well-worn ways of knowing this queer world. Nothing new, no time-saving device—simply old time-glorified methods of delving for Truth, and searching out the hidden beauties of life, and learning the good of living. The riddle of existence is the college curriculum that was laid before the Pharaohs, that was taught in the groves by Plato, that formed the *trivium* and *quadrivium,* and is to-day laid before the freedmen's sons by Atlanta University. And this course of study will not change; its methods will grow more deft and effectual, its content richer by toil of scholar and sight of seer; but the true college will ever have one goal—not to earn meat, but to know the end and aim of that life which meat nourishes.

—W. E. B. Du Bois, The Souls of Black Folk

2 The Intellectual Imagination

"What constitutes intellectual practice? Where are intellectual spaces? When is intellectual work produced? Who is an intellectual? Why intellectualism?" These questions—about the definition, meaning, scope, justification, and normativity of intellectual practice—are the insistent, urgent questions animating this book. The overarching ambition of this book holds that robust and rigorous thought about the form and contours of intellectual practices are best envisioned in light of a comprehensive *critical contextual ontology*—that is, a systematic account of the context, forms, and dimensions in and through which knowledge and aesthetic practices are created, discovered, embodied, performed, disseminated, translated, learned, and critiqued.

Three implications immediately emerge if this is granted. First, that intellectual practice is best understood only against the background of a deep and thick social ontology. Second, that questions about the what, where, when, who, and why of intellectual practice— that is, about the definition, form, objects, methods, embodiments, and justification of intellection—are best engaged as inextricably entangled questions rather than separate, scattered investigations. It follows, then, that the manifold forms of knowledge—historical, performative, empirical, rational, and imaginative—are interanimated. Third, that the normative horizon of intellectual practice consists in their flourishing as ways of life. Accordingly, intellectual practices—when acknowledged as ways of life—are dialectically constitutive of the good life and the good society.

These theses, undoubtedly controversial within the dominant philosophical systems of the moment, continue to find resonance in lost, defeated, or otherwise attenuated practices. From the Mediterranean to Melanesia, Africa to the Americas, intellectual practices— from critical inquiry to the making and performance of the arts—were seen as all of a piece with the fabric of everyday life.[1] If, within these societies, particular intellectual schools emerged, this was to the end of articulating a comprehensive vision of the good life. In ancient Greece, for example, various schools of philosophy conceived of the intellectual life as precisely a way of life. But, as the renowned French scholar Pierre Hadot argues persuasively, this conception of the intellectual life underwent a thoroughgoing transformation when Christianity's hegemony in antiquity reduced philosophy to a theoretical study.[2] Modernity both completed and cemented this transformation with the transmutation of wisdom into epistemology,[3] ethics into morality,[4] and aesthetics into taste.[5]

The technology that alchemized intellectual practice into propositional knowledge was the establishment of disciplinary faculties, perhaps the singular most consequential invention of the North Atlantic research university. Within these disciplines, two developments in particular were notable. First, the ascendance and, later, dominance of scientific paradigms of knowledge—and, crucially, their adoption in the social sciences—resulted in the widespread conviction that legitimate epistemological practices were those that were value-neutral or objective. Second, and closely related to the first, was the notion that aesthetic artifacts and performances—that is, literature, music, paintings, dance, film, and so on—increasingly came to be seen not only as lacking in knowledge content but also as fully realizable only if they were apolitical.

These developments did not take place in a historical vacuum. The North Atlantic university was embedded in a political economy furrowed and seeded with the proceeds of imperialist conquest, human trafficking, and colonial subjugation.[6] These proceeds in turn established the endowments that funded far-flung anthropological forays in search of the "savage" other, which fired philosophical speculation on the irrationality of the "primitive" native, and which flourished in an elaborate taxonomy of human racial classification in the biological sciences. The upshot, then, was not only the seizure of the commanding heights of global politics and economics by the ruling powers in the North Atlantic world but also the violent appropriation and erasure of knowledges and imaginations of the global south.

A significant task of the present project, then, consists in proffering an alternative account of the intellectual life that is critical of this modern *episteme*. Against the compartmentalization of knowledge encouraged by the machinery of disciplines and departments in the modern research university, I want to offer an outline of what I shall refer to as an *articulated* practice of the intellectual life. Such an account, I will argue, not only endeavors to break the oppositional binarisms of modern knowledge—fact versus value, science versus the humanities, truth versus art, politics versus aesthetics—but also seeks attunement with fugitive forms of knowledge pulsing below the frequencies of supremacist discourses.

To be sure, this project takes its distance from other discourses that have sought to challenge the ruling presumptions of modernity. It holds no brief for a nostalgic return to autochthonous *epistemes*—be that, for example, an Aryanist[7] discourse that claims ancient Greece as the origin of "Western" civilization, or an Afrocentrist[8] discourse that traces its lineage back to ancient Egypt. Quite apart from the dubious historiographical decisionism involved in declaring origins by fiat, prelapsarian projects (Philhellenism and Egyptophilia being prime examples) are awash in an untowardly romanticism. Nor—as I shall argue at length in later chapters—do I find especially convincing recent spirited neoclassical and medieval retrievals of lost intellectual practices.[9] For one, ancient philosophies such as the famed oeuvres of Plato and Aristotle presuppose an elaborate metaphysics that have not stood up well to the deliverances of the best scientific and humanistic critique. Moreover, for all that ancient philosophies conceived of intellectual work as a way of life, they ultimately proffer a far too narrow account of the life of the mind. As John M. Cooper has argued in his *Pursuits of Wisdom,* for the ancients "only reason, and what reason could discover and establish as the truth, could be ultimately an acceptable basis on which to live a life—and for them, philosophy is nothing more, but also nothing less, than the art or discipline that develops and perfects the human capacity of reason."[10] Against this impoverished account of rationality, I want to proffer a layered and richly woven intervention that conceives of the intellectual life as the realization of knowledges in all their spectacular diversity—historical, performative, empirical, rational, and imaginative.

But the most pressing reason why I want to depart from ancient, modern, and postmodern accounts of the intellectual life has to do with my alternative understanding of what an intellectual ontology consists in. In my account, the intellectual life is inextricably embedded, entangled, and engendering of a *social ontology.* There is thus a dialectic between larger social structures—politics, economics, and culture—and the ideas, arguments, and reasons that are constitutive of intellectual flourishing. This argument cuts against both ancient accounts of intellectual ontology—which I characterize as "inflationary"—and modern accounts of intellectual ontology—which I consider to be "deflationary." Plato, to pick one canonical ancient, posits the philosophical life as the best form of life because it involves the pursuit of the knowledge of Forms. Given his belief that philosophers are alone guided by reason, he advances as ideal a social ontology in which the *philosophoi* are a permanent ruling strata. I characterize Plato's account as "inflationary," not only because its extravagant metaphysical presuppositions are held as determinative of an earthly social ontology but also because of the inflationary role it assigns the philosopher over and above other forms of life.

But if the Platonic account is inflationary, the research program in the sociology of knowledge that emerged in the modern university is determinedly deflationary. For the sociologist Emile Durkheim, "social life must be explained not by the conception of it formed by those who participate in it, but by the profound causes which escape their consciousness."[11] What is particularly problematic about this account is the manner in which it casts the realm of consciousness—ideas, arguments, representations, mentalities—as reflective of an anterior social structure. In doing so, it offers a reductionist account of the intellectual life. Ideas in this account are seen as little more than post hoc rationalizations.

It shall be part of this book's goal, then, to critique both the "inflationary" idealism and the "reductive" materialism that characterize dominant accounts of knowledge articulation. Against ancient inflationary intellectual traditions, modern deflationary disciplinary divisions, and postmodern social constructionist conflations, this project endeavors to proffer a vision of the intellectual life as precisely a critical contextual practice. In doing so, it advances a critical contextual account that does justice to the political, economic, and cultural structures within which intellectual life is embedded as well as to the ideas, reasons, and imaginations that in turn constitute and illuminate the structural formations of society.

As pointed out above, this book intends to situate itself as a dialogue in global philosophy. As such, it is undergirded by a critical stance toward the parochial perspective that now reigns dominant in North Atlantic philosophical discourse. To be sure, this book does not seek to offer a comparative account of how North Atlantic philosophy contrasts with philosophical worldviews in other parts of the world. Such efforts at comparative philosophies, I hold, too often falsely assume a view of the world as neatly divided into civilizational or cultural blocs. Against this view, I begin from a stance that takes philosophies and the societies they are embedded in as entangled and responsive to one another. I focus most insistently in two philosophical traditions that I have most familiarity with—that of African and North Atlantic philosophical discourses. The implicit argument of this book is to invite readers to consider how a close critique of intellectual practices in Africa and the North Atlantic world may serve as a propaedeutic toward a robust account of a truly global vision of intellectual practices as ways of life. The upshot of such efforts, this book contends, is nothing less than planetary practices on what makes for good societies and good lives in the twenty-first century.

OUTLINE OF THE BOOK

Chapter 1 outlines the constitutive context within which the intellectual life is embedded. The chapter begins by mapping what I shall refer to as a critically contextual ontology—a systematic, comprehensive account of knowledge as emergent in actually existing contexts as opposed to idealized scenarios. Specifically, I argue for an ontology of knowledge as irreducibly contextual, embodied, rhetorical, social, interpretive, and critical. The thick account of intellectual ontology is advanced with an eye to a broader argument that an adequate account of knowledge can only be possible if we take seriously the nonideal conditions under which humans create knowledge. That is, insofar as humans are embodied creatures, who, moreover, live and think in historical contexts riven with power and violence, a robust account of the meaning and value of knowledge ought to begin not with the ideals striven for in articulating knowledge but rather with actually existing practices of knowledge articulation. It is only against this background that I proffer a normative account of knowledge articulation. The upshot, I aver, is that knowledge articulation is best conceived of as a way of life—indeed, as constitutive of the good life.

If chapter 1 is concerned with the ontology of knowledge articulation, chapter 2 takes a turn toward fleshing out archetypal embodiments of the intellectual in the twenty-first century. This chapter neither intends to offer an exhaustive listing of all existing intellectual embodiments nor is it aimed at advancing the ideal type of the intellectual. Rather, I aim to sketch the potentialities and limits of various dominant practices of intellectual life in the current historical moment. By doing so, I gesture at the utopian horizon that every particular intellectual practice intimates.

Chapter 3 articulates an aesthetic ontology—that is, a comprehensive, systematic account of the context, nature, and form of aesthetic invention, performance, dissemination, and reception. I argue that a fully realized aesthetic ontology involves the structuration of form toward the robust exploration of a four-dimensional asymptotic hori-zon: *participatory embodiment, knowledge, politics,* and *meaning.* Such an account of aesthetic praxis, I argue, suggests a thoroughgoing critique of the binary oppositions that are currently dominant in the understanding of aesthetics—specifically, those that pit aesthetics against participatory embodiment, against knowledge or truth, against politics, and against existential meaning. One upshot of this argument is that aesthetic practice goes beyond the creation and critique of artworks. Rather, a robust aesthetic ontology reveals that aesthetic practice is constitutive of the well lived life.

Chapter 4 then takes a turn toward the concrete by engaging with contemporary aesthetic practices. I do so through a close reading of five major aesthetic theories: a *communalist aesthetic,* characteristic of the long African quincentenary marking precolonial, colonial, and postcolonial encounters on the continent; an *elemental aesthetic,* largely the result of North Atlantic discourses about Africa; a *pedagogical aesthetic,* with a particular focus on the doyen of African letters, Chinua Achebe; a *mythopoeic aesthetic,* championed by the Nobel laureate Wole Soyinka; and a *late modernist aesthetic*, which I shall illustrate through a critique of J. M. Coetzee's oeuvre. My goal in this chapter consists in testing the aesthetic theory articulated in chapter 3 by bringing it into dialogue with some of the most acclaimed bodies of artistic work emergent from the African continent. This is toward a broader goal of engendering a global aesthetics oriented by the question of how aesthetic embodiment, practice, and realization can contribute to robust practices of the good life and the good society.

Finally, this book concludes by turning to the rhetorical genre of the theses to distill the irreducible commitments and the imaginative horizons of this book. In forty pungent, succinct theses, I offer a call for a radical practice of intellectual life. That radical practice, I aver, invites an acknowledgment of the social ontology from which intellectual practices are embedded. But it also demands a rigorous appreciation of the constitutive power and potentiality of intellectual production. Ultimately, what I hope to accomplish by these theses is to unfold what is critically at stake in knowledge and aesthetic production. To wit—that intellectual practice at its most realized enacts the life of the mind as a way of life.

What are the ends of intellectual practice? What ought critical thought aspire to, hold itself accountable for, harness its energies toward? The ambition of this book consists in an inquiry into the contexts, forms, and practices of thinking. By thinking, I want to foreground a mode of intellection and kinesthetics that is irreducibly speculative—that is, one that dialectically articulates the relationship between the actual and the modal, the evental and the ordinary, the uncanny and the sublime. It is to this adventure in speculative thinking to which I invite readers in the chapters that follow.

CHAPTER 1

Radical Knowledge

Toward a Critical Contextual Ontology
of Intellectual Practice

Intelligent practice is not a step-child of theory. On the contrary theorizing is one practice amongst others and is itself intelligently or stupidly conducted.

—Gilbert Ryle, *The Concept of Mind*

This chapter articulates a *critical contextual ontology*—that is, a systematic, comprehensive account of the nature and lineaments of knowledge articulation in actually existing contexts. As such, the idea of a critical contextual ontology offers a significant inflection on traditional epistemology. If epistemology is often understood to be the study of knowledge and justified belief in abstraction from actually existing contexts, a contextual ontology situates knowledge articulation as a practice embedded in political, economic, and cultural structures. At the same time, however, it is precisely critical not only insofar as it advances a resolute critique of the idealizing currents in standard epistemological accounts but also because it seeks to reimagine—but not discard—normative theorizing. The argument, rather, holds that normative theorizing should proceed only against the background of a thick social ontology.

In an earlier work, I proffered a critical account of what such a social ontology ought to look like.[1] This chapter will therefore not restate these arguments. Instead, it pushes further to investigate the contours and forms that intellectual practice would take if embeddedness, embodiment, entanglement, encounter, and engenderment were given serious consideration. In what follows, I proffer an account of knowledge as irreducibly contextual, embodied, rhetorical, and social. Such an account, I go on to argue, yields a critically normative revisioning of knowledge as the interanimation of historical, performative, empirical, rational, and imaginative practices.

Mapping an Ontology of Knowledge

Knowledge Is Embedded Contextually

> We have got on to slippery ice where there is no friction and so in a certain sense the conditions are ideal, but also, just because of that, we are unable to walk. We want to walk: so we need friction. Back to the rough ground!
> —Ludwig Wittgenstein, *Philosophical Investigation*

To speak of knowledge as embedded contextually is to affirm its emergence within a natural ontology—that is, that the world is a spatiotemporal entity that contains no sentient disembodied beings such as spirits or gods. Within such a naturalistic ontology, knowledge is contextual insofar as it is constituted in and by time, space, language, and practice.

The notion of knowledge as contextual cuts against Plato's epistemological legacy. Plato proffered a conception of knowledge as that which is possessed when the *nous* achieves an identical, unmediated contemplation of the Forms, eternal and changeless reality. In the *Phaedrus,* Plato vividly paints his vision of the lover of wisdom (the philosopher) who possesses absolute truth. He tells Phaedrus:

> Now a god's mind is nourished by intelligence and pure knowledge, as is the mind of any soul that is concerned to take in what is appropriate to it, and so it is delighted at last to be seeing what is real and watching

what is true, feeding on all this and feeling wonderful, until the circular motion brings it around to where it started. On the way around it has a view of Justice as it is; it has a view of Self-control; it has a view of Knowledge, not the knowledge that is close to change, that becomes different as it knows the different things which we consider real down here. No, it is the knowledge of what really is what it is.[2]

Plato's view is straightforwardly transcendental and absolutist. The absolutist ontology proffers at least three propositions about ontology. First, it conceives of ontology as *singular*, in the sense that it claims that the being of the world is ultimately foundational on a single thing, in this case the Forms. Second, the substance posited as ultimate being is *transcendental*. It denotes an entity that not only is completely divorced from matter and human activity but that in some forms is beyond human comprehension or understanding.[3] Third, the absolutist ontologist claims that the substance underlying reality can never *change* and, insofar as it can ever be discovered, it renders the epistemic discovery itself unchangeable, certain, absolutely true. Plato's absolutist ontology bears a weighty legacy in the epistemologies that have been claimed or appropriated by North Atlantic philosophers.

But to say that knowledge is "contextual" does not also mean a fall into willy-nilly relativism. The very notion of context means that there exist contours and constraints to knowledge articulation. Moreover, there is a mind-independent context—call it "the brute world"—that would exist without humans. This of course does not mean that the world is simply "given" and is thus passively absorbed by humans. Knowledge, within this account, is ineluctably entangled with agency.

Knowledge Is Embodied

If someone says, "I have a body," he can be asked, "Who is speaking here with this mouth?"
—Ludwig Wittgenstein, *On Certainty*

Among humans, sentient awareness has often—but not always—found extension in three inextricably intertwined *embodied* capacities: that of language, emotion, and rationality. Language emerges from a human faculty to generate and develop auditory and visual symbols and signs for communication, expression, and action. Emotions, on the other hand, are embodied (conscious and nonconscious) qualitative states of being (which include sensations, feelings, and desires) that are experienced relationally and institutionally and that in certain cases yield particular forms of knowledge about the objective world (judgments). Humans share with other creatures certain emotions such as fear, anger, and revulsion. Moreover, some kinds of emotions are also intentional and cognitive, that is, involve evaluations about external states of affairs and, moreover, orient humans to the state of the world.

Emotions are deeply intertwined with another capacity within the human, that of rationality. Rationality is conceptualized in this context as the ability of humans to make inferences of logical and empirical entailment, implicature, and presupposition; inferences about probability and possibility; and inferences about cause and effect. Emotion is necessary to rationality insofar as certain inferences about creaturely intentionality can only be made on the basis of affective attunement to other creatures' emotional status. Conversely, humans can significantly modify their emotional responses by means of reason and argumentation. As such, emotions are subject to rational critique as to whether they are warranted or unwarranted.

There are several salient implications that follow from taking seriously the embodiment of knowledge articulation and the capacities constituted by embodiment. Reckoning with embodiment—and the full panoply of embodied capacities—explodes the idealism/materialism dualism that has vexed the larger part of North Atlantic philosophy. It will be recalled that Descartes argues that the *cogito* ("I think, therefore I am") is the indubitable foundation upon which the superstructure of knowledge is to be built. The mind, in Descartes' view, is self-transparent, yielding representations of innate ideas. Though Descartes is anxious to find an absolute foundation to prop up every other knowledge claim about the external world, in the end he has no answer for the thought experiment that an evil demon may be manipulating his thoughts. He therefore resorts to the claim that God guarantees correct access to his thoughts. In its appeal to God as

the guarantor of external reality, the Cartesian project—though idealist in its starting place—rearticulates Plato's transcendental ontology.

Cartesian ontology bears a weighty legacy in debates about epistemology in philosophical discourse. Even those who did without his
appeal to God clung to his *cogito* as the irreducible starting point
for epistemology. Moreover, it is not simply that North Atlantic
philosophy—exemplified, for example, by Kant's transcendental unity
of apperception and Fichte's will—clings tenaciously to a residual
idealism. It bolstered the "epistemology first" mythos that now domi-
nates the discipline of philosophy; the assumption, within traditional
North Atlantic philosophy, that epistemology constitutes the privileged core of philosophy.

The flaws of the Cartesian project, however, remain as glaring as
ever. The mind, according to the Cartesian formulation, is posited as
the executive "cause" of bodily behavior or actions. The first problem
is that, insofar as the mind is posited by Descartes as a substance or
entity of some sort, it remains a mysteriously ghostly cause that seemingly has no position in physical space.[4] Gilbert Ryle famously diagnoses one possible source of Descartes' error as a "category mistake"
—the erroneous classification of a term or phrase that belongs in one
logical category by classifying it in another category. From the fact that
there exist "mental processes" and "bodily processes," it does not follow that these are references to "two different species of existence." Rather, the sense in which a person speaks of *existence* when referring to
the mind differs from that in which she or he speaks of the *existence* of
bodies.[5] Consider, Ryle points out, a foreigner who, when watching his
first game of cricket and having learned the functions of the bowlers,
the batsmen, the fielders, the umpires, and the scorers, goes on to ask:
"But there is no one left on the field to contribute the famous element
of team-spirit. I see who does the bowling, the batting, and the wicket-
keeping; but I do not see whose role it is to exercise *esprit de corps*."[6] As
Ryle points out, the foreigner's mistake is in supposing that team spirit
is another thing or entity that one can point to as supplementary to all
of the other special tasks performed by each player on the field. Rather,
it is "the keenness with which each of the special tasks is performed,
and performing a task keenly is not performing two tasks."[7] Descartes,

Ryle argues, commits a similar category-mistake: "The belief that there is a polar opposition between Mind and Matter is the belief that they are terms of the same logical type."[8]

Of course, it does not follow that the problematic aspects of dualism thereby render an eliminativist reductionism attractive either. A physicalism that denies *qualia*—that there is such a thing as being a certain sort of organism that feels or experiences *in an irreducibly particular manner*—fails to engage with such a large dimension of the organic world that it loses any claim to naturalism, whatever its pretensions. Against then the inflationary claims of dualism and the reductionism of mechanistic physicalism, a critical perspective would argue for an *emergent physicalism* wherein the mental is emergent but not reducible to the physical. Such a theory has the virtue of indicating that the mind and the body are not two substances but one—a physical substance—but without denying the unique dimensions of the brain that make it central to consciousness.

Moreover, reckoning with embodiment also means complicating the dualism between an "internal," "private," and "individual" mental realm and an "external," "public," and "social" realm. Knowledge is thoroughly social because the mind is embodied. Because the brain does not subsist in a vat, the mind is shaped by the social world within which it is embedded. Through the processes of socialization, any talk of "external" social structures and "internal" phenomenological consciousness is rendered moot through the formation of a *habitus*. A *habitus* denotes a complex of dispositions that are durable—that is, that designate a person's predisposition, tendency, propensity, inclination, and liability; a habitual bodily comportment; a way of being. Moreover, a *habitus* designates a complex of generative, transponsable dispositions.[9]

Thus understood, a robust and expansive conception of knowledge articulation as an irreducible dialectic of *knowledge that* (propositional knowledge) and *knowledge how* (performative knowledge) comes into view. Of all the legacies of Cartesian thought, perhaps none has been as dominant within the modern mind as the "intellectualist legend," the supposition "that the primary exercise of minds consists in finding answers to questions and that their other occupations are merely applications of considered truths or even regrettable distractions from their consideration."[10] This model of the intellect casts theorizing as a private "internal monologue or silent soliloquy."[11] The upshot is "the absurd assumption . . . that a performance of any sort inherits all its title to intelligence from some anterior internal operation of planning what to do."[12]

The notion that intelligent performance is merely the application by the agent of particular regulative propositions runs aground under the scrutiny of logical and empirical critique. The first objection is that the claim that a private criterion or rule is ostensibly adverted to before any action can be undertaken raises conundrums of an infinite regress or vicious cycle: there's an infinite regress in the claim that to act intelligently, one must master particular regulative propositions, but since such mastery of regulative propositions are in themselves intelligent or stupid acts, one must have had particular propositions about this mastery of intelligent acts, thus triggering another trailing off to the next propositions of propositions, or, looked at from another perspective, spinning the wheel of a vicious cycle. "The consideration of propositions is itself an operation the execution of which can be more or less intelligent, less or more stupid. But if, for any operation to be intelligently executed, a prior theoretical operation had first to be performed and performed intelligently, it would be a logical impossibility for anyone ever to break into the circle."[13] The upshot is that "when I do something intelligently, i.e. thinking what I am doing, I am doing one thing and not two. My performance has a special procedure or manner, not special antecedents."[14]

Thus, against the notion that practices are simply the application of rules, they are best conceived of as articulated performances. That is, competence involves less the mastery of propositions and more what Bourdieu calls a "feel for the game," a holistic "flow" of conscious and unconscious bodily practices. Practices are textured competences, existing at the intersection of beliefs, perception, memory, and style. For that reason, they seem at once utterly familiar because they are repetitive, and completely new because they are innovative. Competent performance of a practice appears as a seamless flow of exigence, the *kairotic* seizure of time, and the perfect alignment of bodily comportment, gesture, expression, and tone. A paradigmatic example is the art and practice of telling jokes. There is many a wit who, when challenged to cite the maxims or canons for constructing and appreciating jokes, is at a loss of what to say. A person's actions are a seamless "flow" of the conscious and the unconscious. Mental concepts such as heeding and minding involve, not the two-worlds legend of a mechanical doing and a spiritual or mental heeding, but rather the activation of a disposition to do one thing in a particular way.[15] A "grocer is not described as 'grocing' now, but only as selling sugar now, or weighing tea now, or wrapping up butter now."[16]

For all the verve, however, with which Ryle devastates Cartesian dualism, his positive theory of consciousness lends itself to charges of a weak behaviorism. His account largely focuses on giving a semantic account of dispositions—that is, what it means to state that a person is acting in a particular way. He argues that while dispositional statements are not categorical, witnessable facts, they are nevertheless "testable, open hypothetical and what I shall call 'semi-hypothetical' statements."[17] Ryle rightly wants to reject the notion that one has to peep into a subject's "secret grotto" of a mind in order to explain her behavior. But it is possible to offer an account that rejects the notion that behavior is ultimately mysterious because one has no access to the inner workings of a person's mind, while still insisting that there is indeed such a thing as phenomenology—not only in the form of qualia but also in accounting for the importance of belief and the efficacy with which belief often, though not always, structures behavior.

Knowledge that and *knowledge how* are articulated and inextricably entangled, but not reducible to one or the other. It is arguable that most forms of knowledge have a dimension of knowledge that and knowledge how. Rather than reducing knowledge that to knowledge how (as Ryle's account is often tempted to do), or retreating to the ghostly machinations of the Cartesian philosophy of mind, or simply opposing these forms of knowledge (as some Heideggerian and Bourdieusian epigones have been inclined to do), a nonreductionist account stresses the interanimation of cognitive, affective, and kinesthetic capacities. Within such an account, propositional knowledges are no longer seen as isolable facts but rather are understood only against the background of a social ontology. On the other hand, various competences—such as swimming or riding a bicycle—while not reducible to conceptual representations are for all of that sensory-motor capacities that are inflected by agents' abstract conceptions of size, speed, distance, volume, force, weight, and so on.

Moreover, the embeddedness of bodies in time and space should shatter any notion of knowledge how as arationally instinctual or irrationally habitual. According to Bourdieu, models of action must pay attention to the notion that practice is always enacted in *time*: "To restore to practice its practical truth, we must therefore reintroduce time into the theoretical representation of a practice which, being temporally structured, is intrinsically defined by its *tempo*."[18] In his study of Kabyle society, Bourdieu is critical of accounts given by Mauss and Levi-Strauss of peasant societies' practice of gift exchange. These accounts explain the practices of gift giving and receiving as predicated on formal rules of reciprocity wherein a proffered gift stimulates a reciprocal counteroffer. Bourdieu disagrees, arguing that the giving and receiving of gifts take place in and through time and space according to the agents' *habitus*—which, crucially, involves agents' notions of the possible and the impossible, the right and wrong. In his study of Kabyle society, Bourdieu notes that even highly ritualized practices are subject to innovation and manipulation by social agents.[19] Because such actions take place in and through space and time, they are inevitably ambiguous; the agents are never completely certain as to their outcomes. Thus, these performances are also *contingent* and are always performed at the risk of error, failure, and information asymmetry. It follows then that such performances are *constitutive* insofar as they create as much as iterate.

One salutary upshot of thinking through how embodiment inflects knowledge articulation involves reckoning with the vexed place of subjectivity in epistemology. Call this *somatotivity*, for the complex of embodied competences emergent at the intersection of socialization and individuality, articulated in the performances of a social practice, and instantiated in the distinct individual "style" or signature that marks every individual's particular way of performing a social practice. Human capacities (for rationality, emotions, and language) are articulated intersubjectively and transubjectively. Moreover, embodiment inscripts human knowledge within particular social collectivities riven with power and hierarchy—in the contemporary historical conjuncture, that means able-bodied/disabled, gender, sexuality, race, class, status, profession, religion, age, geographical location, political ideology, and so on.

Because humans are embodied, relational beings, human knowledge is charged with interests, values, and emotions. Human perspectives are never simply neutral but are always already vibrant with interest, anticipation, desire, fear, disgust, hate, delight, and love. Human knowledge then is interpretive insofar as it intertwines perceptions, affect, and interests. One upshot is that human knowledge is *finite* and *partial*. This is so because human capacities are limited and finite. To be a biological creature demands the acknowledgment that one is a vulnerable, afflicted, disabled, and dependent person.[20] Scientists, humanists, and artists are embodied, and as such articulate knowledge not only in "ideal" conditions of satisfaction, health, trust, joy, and hopefulness, but also in varying states of hunger, sickness, disability, fear, and anxiety. Moreover, human capacities in time atrophy and die out. Death is the inevitable horizon against which individual humans live. Additionally, by virtue of existing within space and time, human capacities can only be extended so far. Of course, humans are capable of extending their knowledges not only through cooperative activity with other humans and other nonhuman animals and creatures but also through technological instruments. Even so, there will always exist limits to how much can be known by humans, even if such limits can never be completely inscribed a priori in human practices. Finitude, it ought to be noted, is not necessarily negative. That is, it is not always to be decried or transcended. It is also positive insofar as particularity also offers plurality. Plurality is the condition of possibility for creativity; it is *constitutive* of possibility, productive differences, and innovation.

The theory of somatotivity articulated above overlaps with, even as it differs from, dominant theories articulated in the North Atlantic academy. Two particularly require greater scrutiny: Erving Goffman's dramaturgical theory and Judith Butler's performativity theory. Goffman's theory is outlined in his influential book *The Presentation of Self in Everyday Life* (1956). He argues that individuals construct the self by performing particular roles to different observers or audiences. For Goffman, the self is ultimately a product of how individuals manage the impressions they create in others and the impressions about themselves that they glean from others. The self

> does not derive from its possessor, but from the whole scene of his action, being generated by that attribute of local events which renders them interpretable by witnesses. A correctly staged and performed scene leads the audience to impute a self to the performed character, but this imputation—this self—is a product of a scene that comes off, and is not a cause of it. The self, then, as a performed character, is not an organic thing that has a specific location, whose fundamental fate is to be born, to mature, and to die; it is a dramatic effect arising diffusely from a scene that is presented, and the characteristic issue, the crucial concern, is whether it will be credited or discredited.[21]

Human communication processes, Goffman argues, are "a kind of information game—a potentially infinite cycle of concealment, discovery, false revelation, and rediscovery."[22] Impression management involves contestation, negotiation, and collusion, as individuals strive to define the situation. Goffman notes the difference between the persona that individuals enact in what he calls "front stage" settings—public or professional interactions—and "back stage" settings—situations in which individuals feel that they can "let their hair down," such as in the home or in the bedroom. Perhaps one difficulty with Goffman's theory is that his analysis is rooted in the assumptions of methodological individualism. One failing of this methodology is that it may obscure the structural forces that exert power on the individual to be oriented toward the art and craft of constant impression management. Nor does Goffman historicize "front stage" and "back stage" settings. The danger then is that his account universalizes the split between "front stage" and "back stage" contexts and fails to show how this split emerged in the crucible of liberal capitalist modernity and its obsessions with the "public" and "private" divide. Second,

Goffman does not sufficiently engage how differentials in power affect who is able to engage in impression and the forms of impression management that are enacted. For example, the very poor are almost always under surveillance and denied any resources for impression management, people with severe disabilities often are not accorded "back stage" settings into which they can retreat, and so on. Conversely, it is not for nothing that Henry James defined aristocracy as "bad manners organized"—the extremely powerful are famously boorish and utterly sociopathic, not because of anything essential about them but because they have free reign to behave as they will without consequences. Goffman's description of performance as "management" may thus be more telling here than he supposed; his theory describes a preoccupation of a very distinct group, that of the "professional managerial class" notable not only for its obsession with individual branding but also for its anxiety to mystify its class belonging.[23] Third, Goffman's account scants the biological (psychological and emotional) capacities and dispositions of being human as these are articulated with social formation. Concerned to break with the Romantic conception of the self as emergent from some "inner" core, his account nevertheless flirts with a vulgar behaviorism in not engaging sufficiently with the phenomenology of performance. Moreover, a deeper engagement with the psychic and emotional landscape of performance would have significantly complicated his rather flat portrait of impression management as a universal feature of human interaction. For some—for example, persons diagnosed with certain strains of Asperger syndrome—impression management presents multiple challenges.

Judith Butler's performativity theory draws insights from John Austin's speech act theory in constructing a poststructuralist theory of action. Her theory then proceeds to offer an account deeply influenced by Derrida's theory of language, Althusser's Lacan-inflected psychoanalytic theories of subject formation, and Foucault's theory of power. Austin, it will be recalled, brings notice to a set of linguistic utterances that "do things"—that is, that call particular relationships or activities into being.[24] Butler extends this insight in calling to attention how gender is similarly constructed. Performativity, she argues, is "the discursive mode by which ontological effects are installed."[25] The utterance "it's a girl" is far from an innocent report on an ontological state of affairs; rather, it inaugurates a process of "girling," which then proceeds apace through socialization.

Butler, however, is critical of Austin's speech act theory. She faults Austin's account for holding that speech acts always secure uptake. According to Butler, Austin's mistake lies in making the presumption that the speaker who utters a performative speech act always has the authority to make the utterance: "The subject as sovereign is presumed in the Austinian account of performativity: the figure for the one who speaks and, in speaking performs what she/he speaks, is the judge or some other representative of the law."[26] On the basis of her reading of Austin's speech act theory, Butler is critical of feminist and antiracist theorists who have advocated for the legal regulation of pornography and racist hate speech. According to Butler, these theorists are mistaken because they presume that "speech is the immediate and necessary exercise of injurious effects."[27]

Butler's critique of Austin is weakened in part by a wooden, literalistic reading of his examples. As a result, she is disposed to read his examples not as contextually specific instantiations of performatives but rather as exhausting all and every possible circumstance within which speech acts may be uttered. Nonetheless, it may be said of Austin's account that he leaves severely undertheorized the conventions that make possible the uptake of a speech act. He does not take into account how conventions are articulated through a history of power differentials, how certain conventions are "hegemonic" in the precise sense that they no longer need a recognized official in place to enforce adherence to them. In many jurisdictions, for example, a particular activity may be formally "illegal" and yet this says nothing about what governs actual relations within the jurisdiction. In other words, there may be a deeper social logic to a structural context than the formal one that is publicized.

But if Austin is dangerously close to characterizing "context" as altogether too transparent, Butler mystifies context. She is at pains to emphasize the indefinability of context. In a characteristically Derridean two-step, she moves from noting that contexts are not "static" to an outright absolutization of the fluidity of contexts.[28] She repeats the same maneuver in pointing to the possibility that pornographic and racist speech acts need not necessarily perform the injuries that they are purported to perform: "That no speech act *has* to perform injury as its effect mean that no simple elaboration of speech acts will provide a standard by which the injuries of speech might be effectively adjudicated."[29] But, of course, from the fact that hateful speech acts are not *necessarily* injurious, it simply does not follow that particular historically situated racist speech acts are *never* injurious. For a theorist that came onto the scene with strident denunciations of binarisms, it bears noting how Butler is in this instance committed to all or nothing false dilemmas.

Butler also is anxious to disavow any resonances between her account of performativity and that of theatrical performance. For Butler, theatrical performance offers a problematic metaphor for understanding action because, she claims, it relies on a conception of the self that preexists the performance of a role. Butler's performativity vehemently refuses any notion of a "subject"—which she regards as carrying with it modernist senses of an "essential," "stable" self who "originates" action. Rather Butler's poststructuralism characterizes action as akin to a cat constantly chasing after its tail. "Performativity cannot be understood outside of a process of iterability, a regularized and constrained repetition of norms. And this repetition is not performed by a subject; this repetition is what enables a subject and constitutes the temporal condition for the subject."[30] It is indubitably true that the fleshly character of the body is always already inscribed discursively. Butler however absolutizes this and thereby erases the body's biotic creatureliness—constituted by blood and bones, lymph and ligament, kidneys and cartilage—and renders it simply as an "effect" of discursive regimes. To be sure, the materiality of the body—its form as flesh and blood, capable of pain and pleasure, hunger and thirst, not infinitely malleable—is of course always saturated with sociality. But that precisely demands a recognition of the body's *temporal* and *spatial* location, its diverse but nonetheless determinate *morphology*, its irreducible *creaturely* wants and needs, and its inevitable *mortality*.

Butler's thin account of embodiedness redounds negatively in her thought about agency. Her account of performativity allows that subjects may exercise a measure of agency through repetitions with differences such as parodying gender norms and ironic speech acts. Her paradigmatic figure of agency is the drag queen. But, ultimately, her conception of agency is anchored on allegories of intersubjective encounters—thereby taking for granted the deep background of ecology, social institutions, nonhuman- and human-caused events, and social movements, as well as linguistic-phenomenological meaning—thereby failing to offer radically imaginative accounts of ecological, social, ethical, and existential transformation.

Butler's performativity theory offers bracing critiques of dominant essentialist myths about embodiment—and her ethical turn offers a more promising direction in teasing out the phenomenological dimensions of violence and resistance—but it is ultimately unhelpful to those who want to think of embodiment within the *longue durée* of ecology and the ineliminability of creatureliness, as these are entangled in sociopolitical relationships across history and time. Her work is especially unrewarding for those who desire to engender radically transformative forms of life attuned to global as well as existential flourishing.

Knowledge Is Rhetorical

How hard we find it to bear, and how we wriggle and turn in search of either transcendental guarantee or a skeptical escape.
—Hilary Putnam, *Renewing Philosophy*

I define rhetoric as the symbolic and performative articulation of social reality and meaning. Seen as such, an understanding of knowledge as rhetorical at once raises at least three vital implications. First, rhetorical study takes seriously the *form* within which knowledge warrants are articulated by. By form, I mean the constitutive elements of utterances, including embodiment, media, language, and style. This not only goes against traditional philosophy's conception of form as ancillary to knowledge articulation but also challenges traditional philosophy's desire for the transparency—that is the instrumentality—of bodies, media, and language. Second, rhetorical study demands attentiveness to the processual dimensions—that is, temporal and spatial embeddedness and movement—of knowledge articulation. This means that rhetorical study challenges any clear divide between the "context of discovery" and the "context of justification." Rather than a single-minded focus on knowledge as "product," rhetorical study invites wide-ranging engagement with the full panoply of methods of inquiry—the use of reason (justification, argumentation, logical coherence), empirical inquiry (embodied experience, experimentation, propositional accuracy, historical narrative), creative/artistic thought (literature, film, dance, etc.), and theoretical inquiry. Third, rhetorical study emphasizes the performative dimension of knowledge articulation. By performative, I primarily mean the constitutive dimension of utterances and actions such that empirical reality is not simply described but is also reorganized and transformed in the process of being mapped. These three dimensions demonstrate the contingency of knowledge articulation. Thus, to speak of the rhetoricity of knowledge articulation is also an insistence on the openness of inquiry.

Language, of course, constitutes a particularly contested dimension of rhetoricity. Conceived of as a constitutive dimension of rhetorical articulation, language ought to be seen first and foremost as *contextual.* That refers not only to the fact that symbols are arbitrarily chosen by certain collectives to hold particular meanings but also that those symbols are held in place by convention. Moreover, each word gains meaning against a tapestry of history and in relation to a chain of other terms. Thus the meaning of a particular term is intelligible only against a social background within which language users have been socialized.

Language is also contextual insofar as meanings in language are *socially polysemic.* Language is not simply and never completely determined by individual idiosyncrasies. Though humans are born with innate capacities to acquire language, specific language acquisition takes place through socialization. Even so, there is constant contestation within social collectives about the meaning of signs and symbols. Language, as formative of the deep structure of a society, is subject to constant contestation. Often, the social forces within a society that are hegemonic establish one or two languages as the official languages. Moreover, even within the deep variations within a single language, hegemonic forces often establish a particular dialect as "standard," against which every other variation compares. Within speech, particular intonations become so hegemonic that speakers of the dominant tongue regard themselves as "accent-less," while stigmatizing or identifying every other variation as "accented" or as a "dialect."[31] Mikhail Bakhtin has spoken of the *heteroglossia* of languages within a discursive field; the fact that every official language carries within it internal stratifications and differentiations.[32] Thus, no language is pure. As a result of constant interchange among speakers of various languages, all languages are *polyglossic*—that is, all languages have extensively borrowed words, phrases, syntax, and so on from other languages. Lastly, all uses of languages carry within them the signature of the individual, the ensemble of socialization, personality, idiosyncrasy, panache, and orientation to monologue, dialogue, or omnilogue.[33] Given variations in the use of language, meaning always has about it something of the amphibolous and indeterminate.

Seen in light of the contextual emergence and embodied engenderment of language, meanings come into view as emergent in a field of tension consisting in the interaction of *referential, performative,* and *expressive* dimensions. A language's *referentiality* is constituted at the nexus of embodied activity, intentionality, and contextual reference. Its *performativity* refers to the manner in which language does things, performs certain actions. And its *expressivity* refers to the manner in which language functions as a means of discharging affect.

The theory of language articulated above cuts against three theories of language that are widely prevalent in social discourse: the idea theory of reference, linguistic determinism, and Derridean deconstruction. The idea theory of reference, propagated most famously by Thomas Hobbes, argues that language references private mental events. For Hobbes, words function as "marks" for thought, enabling the person using the words to remember his/her thoughts. This theory has fueled the widespread notion that in order to determine the meaning of a word, one has to have access to the private intentions of a person in order to determine what the person means. The most prominent objection to this theory is the fact that language acquisition often involves socialization into the uses of language. Thus, language acquisition is not primarily a matter of inventing a new language. Moreover, logically there is simply no criterion of correctness for determining whether a private word has been used correctly. The theory makes the very practice of disputing the meaning of a term essentially empty, thus rendering language as a means of communication unintelligible. Indeed, even the individual who claims to have particular private words as markers of her thoughts has no way of finding out if she is using words correctly. This is because if she claims that a certain word enables her to remember sensation S, she has to devise another word to help her determine whether she has applied the word correctly—given that every event of naming is subject to error. But this in turn would demand yet another word to ensure this application is correctly adhered to and so on to infinity. This is not to mention the proliferation of words that will be needed to make her remember that S happened to her.

If the idea theory of reference tends to make unintelligible the social or shared dimensions of language, linguistic determinism inflates the power of language.[34] According to this theory, language thoroughly determines whether a person is able to experience perceptual and phenomenological events. Thus, the theory holds, if a word for a particular phenomenological state, P, exists within one society and does not exist within another society, its absence in the latter society means that people within that society are unable to experience P.[35] The theory also holds that if a society has a variety of words to describe a single object, then that must *prima facie* mean that the society has a deeper or more complex perception of the object. Thus, according to the legend widely circulated by journalistic renditions of linguistic determinism, the fact that the Inuit have a variety of words for snow indicates that they have a complex understanding of snow. One of the most widespread assumptions of linguistic determinism is a version of linguistic incommensurability, according to which various languages form discrete worlds that are wholly untranslatable. Linguistic determinism is rendered implausible by its characterization of language as a prison house. It not only fails to account for human biological capacities of perception but also fails to engage the flexibility of languages in accommodating new words, concepts, and discoveries. Language undoubtedly shapes perception, but this formation is often subtle and is by no means total. Moreover, the avatars of linguistic determinism often trumpet the power of language to render *fine* distinctions but often fail to point out that this also indicates that language may *reify* invidious distinctions.

Derrida's theory of language is concerned to emphasize the radical indeterminacy of meaning—or in the jargon that he was to become so infamous for, that language is always already catachrestic. In his article "Signature Event Context," an article that made him a *cause célèbre* in some North American humanities departments, Derrida pugnaciously attacks the notion that concepts absolutely correspond to words: Is it certain that to the word communication corresponds a concept that is unique, univocal, rigorously controllable, and transmittable: in a word, communicable? Thus in accordance with a strange figure of discourse, one must first of all ask oneself whether or not the word or signifier 'communication' communicates a determinate content, an identifiable meaning, or a describable value."[36] In a decidedly odd argumentative move, Derrida stealthily sidles from an attack on an absolutist construction of the correspondence theory of signification to affirming an equally absolutist assertion of noncorrespondence. The thrust of his argument gains power from the notion that robbed of "a unique, univocal, rigorously controllable, and transmittable" meaning, words collapse into a welter of slipping, sliding signifiers. To the response that while meanings cannot be established absolutely, they gain a certain measure of felicity from the context within which they are articulated, Derrida replies: "But are the conditions [*les réquisits*] of a context ever absolutely determinable? This is, fundamentally, the most general question that I shall endeavor to elaborate. Is there a rigorous and scientific concept of context? . . . Stating it in the most summary manner possible, I shall try to demonstrate why a context is never absolutely determinable, or rather, why its determination can never be entirely certain or saturated. This structural nonsaturation would . . . mark the theoretical inadequacy of the current concept of context." Once again, what is most notable about Derrida's techniques of arguments is his desire to construct his interlocutors as committed to the notion that contexts *absolutely* determine meaning and that those opposed to his theory are *absolutely* certain that contexts can be rigorously and scientifically fixed. But of course, the absolutisms of a correspondence theory of meaning and that of an absolute indeterminacy of meaning are both problematic. The fact that there is "no necessary correspondence" does mean that there is "necessarily no correspondence." Derrida's position is of course accompanied by a curious twist. If for him signifiers are constantly glancing off one another in an elusive differentiation and deference of meaning, they are nevertheless entrapped in an inescapable metaphysical system wherein there is no outside. Thus, the split in Derrida's rhetoric, alternating between outbursts of the revolutionary potential of the grapheme and a curiously tragic despair: "There is no sense in doing without the concepts of metaphysics in order to shake metaphysics. We have no language— no syntax and no lexicon—which is foreign to this history; we can pronounce not a single destructive proposition which has not already had to slip into the form, the logic, and the implicit postulation of precisely what it seeks to contest."[37]

The importance of rhetoric in the articulation of knowledge, then, rests on an insistence on the importance of form, that is, the mediation of embodiment, language, and style in knowledge articulation; on process, that is, the temporal and spatial embeddedness of knowledge articulation; and on performativity, that is, the manner in which discourses and actions bring new realities into being.

To be sure, dominant intellectual traditions have taken it as a central article of faith that "rhetoric" is synonymous with error and falsehood. Plato's attack against rhetoric inaugurated the genre of antirhetoric rhetoric. His is such a furious and sustained polemic that it takes on the quality of an Ahab-like obsession. In the *Apology*, he dismisses forensic rhetoric, rhetoric's claim to usefulness in courts of law. In the *Gorgias*, he launches a blistering attack against rhetoricians' claim to expertise in the political sphere. In the *Menexenus* and the *Symposium*, he mocks the rhetorical form of speech known as the epideictic (that is, ceremonial speeches of "praise and blame" then exemplified by eulogies).

Plato's specific charges against rhetoric can be roughly boiled down to four points. First, he claims that rhetoric produces belief without knowledge. In arguably his most devastating attack against rhetoric, he makes the rhetorician Gorgias admit as much. He rests his claim on the fact that rhetoric's goal is persuasion rather than truth. Rhetoric, he states in the *Gorgias*, is a mere knack because it lacks a theory of the good. It could only get things right by accident. This epistemological failing carries ethical implications as well. For Plato, insofar as rhetoric is indifferent to truth, it is also unethical. Second, and closely related to the first charge, is Plato's accusation that rhetoric is far more concerned with *form*—the devices of persuasion—and not *content*—truth itself. In several of his early dialogues, and especially the *Protagoras*, Plato mocks rhetoricians for what he claims is their small-minded fixation with proper language use and their monomaniacal bickering over abstruse subtleties. They love appearances (style and aesthetics) more than truth and make trivial things important while trivializing important things. Third, Plato charges that rhetoricians have evil motives and bad character. They use rhetoric as a tool for the manipulation of the populace. Moreover, Plato disapproves of rhetoricians for teaching people in exchange for money. Fourth, Plato charges that rhetoric did not have a subject matter. If the subject matter of weaving is the making of clothing, and music the composing of melodies, what then is the subject matter of rhetoric?[38] Plato's question is meant to undermine the rhetorician's claim to expertise on any subject. To be sure, Plato did at times concede the possibility that rhetoric could do *some* good. In the *Statesman*, he grants that rhetoric could qualify as a *techne* (an art) provided that it serve strictly as a vehicle for the transportation of philosophically generated truth.

To these charges, rhetoricians have pointed out that the historical record is far more ambiguous than the Platonic legacy has rendered it. First, as many historians of rhetoric have pointed out, the Sophists were by no means a school of thought with a singular ideology. Plato's dialogues constitute a massive caricature of the Sophists. It is scarcely possible to believe, as Brian Vickers has helpfully pointed out, that the historical Gorgias would have so readily agreed with Plato that rhetoric inculcates belief without knowledge. In Vicker's stinging words, Plato's sophistic interlocutors are little more than a "dialectician's dummy,"[39] crudely drawn, one-dimensional, monosyllabic characters that serve as useful foils for the idealized image of the philosopher. Second, Plato's dismissal of rhetorical truth rests on an implausible metaphysics that takes for granted a conception of truth as absolute and singular. He thinks that truth is not so much "discovered" *empirically* nor established through the performativity of language, but rather recalled.[40] Plato's mockery of the Sophists for their interest in the nuances of language speaks, on closer examination, to his rivals' far more sophisticated understanding of language. Plato's error lies in his conception of language as transparent, a mere vehicle for the transference of Truth. In fact, the notion of a one to one correspondence between language and reality is often confounded by the connotative and performative nature of language.[41] Even the seemingly unassailable charge that the Sophists were mercenaries, more concerned with making money than in inculcating virtue, crumbles under historical scrutiny. As Raymond Geuss has pointed out, "Plato was terrified by what he took to be the potentially subversive ('democratic') political possibilities of rhetoric: anyone who could pay the fees, regardless of their genealogy and family connections, could learn the art of speaking persuasively from professional teachers of rhetoric."[42] As to the charge that rhetoric lacks a subject matter, one could point out that such an objection rests on a category mistake. Rhetoric is the study of how embodied signs and action constitute social reality. That language and argumentation are used in a variety of subjects does not render them non-subjects. All that this could amount to is that there are a variety of rhetorical subjects, such that there are those who are experts in, say, political rhetoric and others in medical rhetoric. Lastly, there are a variety of contexts in which what is at stake is not so much the presence or absence of knowledge but rather the *will* (collective or individual) to act on that knowledge. *Pace* Plato, such a will is not an essential property that an individual has or does not have. Rather, it can be *constructed*. One of the goals of rhetorical study is to engage in the study of the techniques of motivating people to act on knowledge.

To be sure, this does not mean that fourth-century Athenian *sophoi* (rhetoricians) were right and the *philosophoi* (philosophers) wrong. That would be a too simplistic reversal. As has been pointed out, rhetoricians were not a "school of thought" and therefore were hardly in lock-step agreement about ideology and epistemology. Moreover, many of them wrongly leapt from a salutary skepticism that the reigning *doxa* constitutes absolute truth to the rather less logical claim that all truth and morality is relative.[43] Thus, my purpose in revisiting this history is not to engage in a new round of mythmaking, with the Sophists this time taking the starring role. The point rather is to shred the mythology within which epistemology has long been shrouded and to open up room for a deeper inquiry into the rhetoricity of knowledge articulation.

Knowledge Is Embedded Socially

> Perhaps what is inexpressible (what I find mysterious and am not able to express) is the background against which whatever I could express has its meaning.
> —Ludwig Wittgenstein, *Culture and Value*

All articulations of knowledge have a social dimension. Epistemology is social insofar as beliefs are constructed through *socialization* (whether in childhood or in the graduate seminar). This is true even when one's beliefs are derived negatively, that is, through oppositions to other sets of belief. Epistemology is also social insofar as certain beliefs are derived through *testimonies* (written, spoken, firsthand, secondhand, etc.). And, just as importantly, epistemology is social insofar as justifications for truth claims are *tested socially*. Given that first-person beliefs are often notoriously self-serving, it is important that third parties proffer a critique of one's knowledge claims.

A major implication of conceiving of epistemology as social is that it indicates the entanglement of knowledge articulation in relations of power. Knowledge is inflected with power in a variety of ways. One of those ways is the extent to which knowledge claims are articulated against a vast *contextual background* that can never be exhaustively spelt out. For example, certain claims rest on historical knowledges that depend crucially on several contextual exigencies and contingencies. What we know about the past, for example, often rests on information derived from those whose words were written or were thought to be important enough to be memorized and transmitted orally from generation to generation. Moreover, knowledge is inflected with power to the extent that one's *interests* often shapes one's conception of what is relevant or salient. Thus, say, one's empirical observations may be enhanced or distorted by certain experiences or social interests. For example, certain reports in the U.S. indicate that bad eyewitness identifications led to 75 percent of rape convictions that DNA evidence later proved to be wrongful. An overwhelming majority of these cases involved accusations of black men and Latinos of assaulting white women.[44] Another dimension through which power affects knowledge articulation is that particular *institutions* have greater resources and therefore greater power to set the agenda for discussions and to frame the terms of debate.

To be sure, a conception of knowledge as socially embedded thoroughly revises the dominant North Atlantic understanding of the purview of epistemology. As articulated by a philosopher such as Descartes, epistemology is conceived of as an individual activity that is interested primarily with determining true beliefs and the justifications or warrants for true beliefs. Locke, for his part, conceives of knowledge as essentially an individualistic enterprise and dismisses others views as just so many opinions.[45] One of the problematic aspects of this epistemic individualism is its contribution to the cult of the Great Man theory of epistemology (or the Argument from Genius). This romance is belied by the extensive indebtedness of claimed geniuses to other knowers.[46] Thus, social epistemology is critical of any epistemological account that begins with the individual.

Social epistemology does not repudiate the importance of truth and is just as concerned with warrants for justifying true beliefs. But perhaps what most stands out about social epistemology is that it is concerned with actually existing ways in which knowledge is articulated as opposed to idealizations of how knowledge functions.[47] Toward the end of articulating actually existing epistemic practices, then, social epistemology has pointed to the much wider range of epistemological considerations in knowledge articulation. These include parsimony, the aesthetic elegance arguments and proofs, and the consilience and coherence of knowledge claims with other well-established or powerfully compelling theories.[48] In scientific discourse, tests of theories according to principles of coherence, simplicity, plausibility, and so forth are sociologically determined. Hilary Putnam offers a striking example:

> [B]oth Einstein's General Relativity and Alfred North Whitehead's theory of gravitation (of which most people have never heard!) agreed with Special Relativity, and both predicted the familiar phenomena of the deflection of light by gravitation, the non-Newtonian character of the orbit of Mercury, the exact orbit of the Moon, and so on. Yet Einstein's theory was accepted and Whitehead's theory was rejected fifty years ago before anyone thought of an observation that would decide between the two. The judgment that scientists explicitly or implicitly made, that Whitehead's theory was too "implausible" or too "ad hoc" to be taken seriously, was clearly a value judgment. The similarity of judgments of this kind to aesthetic judgments has often been pointed out, and, indeed, Dirac was famous for saying that certain theories should be taken seriously because they were "beautiful," while others couldn't possibly be true because they were "ugly."[49]

Of course, social epistemology does not stop with simply documenting the actually existing ways in which knowledge is articulated. It also seeks to engage and critique truth claims through a radical critique of *ideological interests* and a thoroughgoing engagement with the sociology of knowledge articulation within a particular context.

The position articulated above has many affinities as well as significant differences with Alasdair MacIntyre's influential articulation of practice. MacIntyre defines practice thus:

By a "practice" I am going to mean any coherent and complex form of socially established cooperative human activity through which goods internal to that form of activity are realized in the course of trying to achieve those standards of excellence which are appropriate to, and partially definitive of, that form of activity, with the result that human powers to achieve excellence, and human conceptions of the ends and goods involved, are systematically extended.[50]

MacIntyre gives as examples of practices such activities as games (chess, football), productive activities (farming and architecture), intellectual activities (science and history), artistic pursuits (painting and music) and politics (participation in a political community). In contrast to this, he argues that certain activities do not qualify as practices (tic-tac-toe, bricklaying, and planting turnips).

MacIntyre's concept of practice rests on a key distinction he draws between what he calls "internal goods" and "external goods." He specifies the characteristics of internal goods as three-fold. First, internal goods, he argues, "cannot be had in any way but by [engaging in the practice] or some other [practice] of that specific kind." Second, internal goods "can only be identified and recognized by the experience of participating in the practice in question." He adds that those "who lack the relevant experience" of the practice "are incompetent thereby as judges of internal goods."[51] Third, the realization of internal goods "is a good for the whole community who participate in the practice." In contrast, external goods are "externally and contingently attached to" the practice "by the accidents of social circumstances." External goods, he goes on to say, are "always alternative ways for achieving such goods, and their achievement is never to be had only by engaging in some particular kind of practice." Moreover, external goods, "when achieved . . . are always some individual's property and possession."[52] MacIntyre's examples of external goods are "prestige, status, money, fame, and pleasure."

The difficulties with MacIntyre's articulation of practices begin from what he envisions they are. Notwithstanding the diversity of practices that he mentions, the bulk of his examples portray practices in the manner of games—in other words, activities with relatively clear boundaries and relatively quantifiable standards of excellence. Complex practices such as intellectual pursuits—the practice of the sciences or the practice of the arts, for example—or social practices—such as the practice of politics or economics—are of course far more difficult cases. For one, these practices are notoriously resistant to easy demarcation,[53] let alone to specifying a single standard of excellence. This is because these practices form a *deep structure*, shaped not only by a layered history but also through the interaction and contestation of different social and cultural institutions. Institutions, then, are constitutive of practices; they are part of the deep background through which agents' motives, standards of excellence, and relational orientation are formed. MacIntyre, however, seems to think that institutions are simply add-ons to antecedently pure practices. Thus he argues that while "no practices can survive for any length of time unsustained by institutions,"[54] ultimately these institutions are "characteristically and necessarily" concerned with external goods. Institutions, for MacIntyre, are at best vehicles for the advancement of practices; but his view of them as "externally oriented" renders them ultimately at odds with the pure ideals of practices. He contrasts the "ideals and creativity" of practice to the "acquisitiveness" and "competitiveness" of institutions. This allows MacIntyre to get the result he wants of practices as oriented by a single and pure teleological arc; but this is ultimately an unconvincing portrait of the embeddedness of subjects in institutions that deeply form their practices.

What follows from this is that MacIntyre considerably simplifies the motivational drives of participants to a practice. Consider, for example, his discussion of the motivational structure of practices: he is able to characterize prestige and pleasure as "external goods" by prying them apart from the desire for excellence. But this can only be done by reifying pleasure as a freestanding thing or object in competition with other motivations. Recall that part of socialization and apprenticeship for recruits to a guild or team is the sublimation of pleasure such that it is intermingled with notions of duty, honor, and excellence. In many cases, then, pleasure is *complexly emergent* from the performance of an activity or goal. Pleasure is then not simply one goal among others but rather *saturates* the desire to excel. In other words, agents participate in a practice *not* because they are only in it for the pleasure but rather because among the goods emergent in the practice is a complex matrix of pleasure, duty, loyalty, and prestige (with pain often part of the mix; Kantian moral duty is often pleasurable precisely because it is intermingled with pain). My argument here is not normative, but instead empirical. It is one thing to say that agents ought not to regard pleasure or money as the goal of practices, another to pretend that such goods are metaphysically external to practice. Why do people participate in a practice such as science? Because their motives are a mélange of self-interested, reciprocal, sometimes altruistic impulses: to discover truth, for the sake of money, for the sake of technological innovations, because of the relationships they have cultivated with fellow scientists, because of their love for play, because science gives meaning to their lives, for prestige, in order to honor past women or racial minorities who were denied similar opportunities, so as to be good role models for present generations, and so on and so forth. In other words, the reasons are many, and they often involve the entanglement of "good," "bad" and "neutral" reasons (that is, that in some contexts are good and in other contexts bad). Just because MacIntyre disapproves of a reason does not make it an external reason.

MacIntyre constructs a far too *communitarian* account of practices. It is communitarian insofar as it conceives of excellence narrowly as essentially determined by the insiders to a practice. This is problematic because of the "closed epistemology" of MacIntyerean practice. It is also problematic because MacIntyre does not sufficiently take into consideration the shared—if deeply contested and hard fought—historic and spatial field within which practices are emergent. Thus, for example, it may well be true that atheism and theism form different practices and therefore may well offer incommensurable standards for excellence. Nonetheless, for all that, participants to these different practices are embedded in a shared *ecology*, are *embodied creatures* and *encounter* one another. Whatever the differences in their practices, there are "grey zones" of contact and interaction among different practices. These "grey zones" indicate that no practices are completely closed off. Indeed, in many contexts, the clashes between different practices press upon the participants to proffer various forms of justifications and warrants in defense of their beliefs, priorities, or behavior. The upshot then is that practices overlap and clash and are rarely—if ever—neatly bounded epistemological archipelagoes. Moreover, because practices take place in time, because of their ecological embeddedness, because they are performed by embodied creatures of varying subjectivities, because of the relational disposition of these creatures not only to living participants but also to the dead and to posterity, there is an intersectionality and open-endedness to the performance of practice that defies MacIntyre's teleological narrativization of their structure.

The crux of MacIntyre's articulation of practices is the argument that it is only against the background of practices that the achievement of virtue—conceived of as the pursuit of excellence—is intelligible. He is right that Kantian and utilitarian theories proffer abstract theories that prescind from the richness of actual human epistemology and ethics; he is also right that Humean and Nietzschean theories are reductively emotivist and subjectivist. But MacIntyre's alternative does not seem to do better. What it gains by situating epistemological and ethical pursuits in a thick and textured social context, it loses in parochialism and provincialism (ultimately, MacIntyre's *After Virtue* pines for a very white, male, heterosexual, and Thomist-Christian world).[55] And if it gains in offering a psychological theory that has room for normativity in epistemology and ethics, it loses in its latent moralism.

TOWARD A NORMATIVE ARTICULATION
OF KNOWLEDGE

The sense of danger must not disappear:
The way is certainly both short and steep,
However gradual it looks from here;
Look if you like, but you will have to leap.
　　　　　　　—W. H. Auden, "Leap Before You Look"

If it is granted that knowledge is contextual, embodied, rhetorical, and social, then the emergent question is one of epistemological normativity—in other words, how ought we go about articulating knowledge? I argue that the terrain of knowledge ought to be an articulated epistemology. Below, I map three irreducibly intertwined practices of epistemological normativity: *a critical contextual rationality, a critical contextual hermeneutics,* and *a critical contextual imagination.*

Critical Contextual Rationality

> Not empiricism and yet realism in philosophy, that is the hardest thing.
>
> —Ludwig Wittgenstein,
> *Remarks on the Foundations of Mathematics*

The account of rationality that is articulated herein is necessarily expansive, emergent from an appreciation of the diversity of global forms of life and responsive to the particularity and the nonsubstitutability of various goods. Rationality thus has both an epistemic and axiological resonance.

The epistemic dimension of rationality involves an appreciation of at least three capacities: nonconceptual perceptions, conceptual perceptions, and ideational articulation. *Nonconceptual perceptions*—for example, somatic proprioception—are embodied orientations to the world constituted in response to conscious or unconscious stimuli. The rationality of nonconceptual responses are evaluated on the basis of *corporeal attunement* to the stimuli—that is, the extent to which the body *skillfully* responds to the environment it is inhabiting.

Conceptual perceptions are emergent from shared social symbols and linguistic traditions. Conceptual perceptions are not simply a priori categories that are stamped onto an external reality; rather they emerge at the intersection of sensory perception and socialization. Conceptual perceptions are rational insofar as they are responsive to the fineness of grain of the world that they purport to describe and are consilient with the linguistic web of concepts that form the social background of which they are a part.

Ideational articulation consists in the ability to infer empirical and propositional entailment, implicature, and presupposition; identify causal probability, correlations, and patterns; and realize imaginative associations. The rationality of ideational articulation is a vexed question. On the one hand, ideational articulations have to be accountable to constraints of coherence and consistency. But on the other hand, insofar as ideational articulations fully account for the embeddedness and embodiedness of persons in space and time, they have to be responsive to contingence and exigence. For precisely this double-sided dimension, ideational articulations walk the tension between logical rigor and imaginative vision, conceptual precision and creative innovation.

Rationality is therefore inextricably entangled with interpretation and imagination. Rationality is interpretive insofar as it takes seriously historical and structural embeddedness. It is thus open to diversity, difference, plurality. It is also imaginative insofar as it takes seriously the play of language and the open-endedness of time.

This account of rationality cuts in three directions: a critique of idealism, a critique of bald empiricism, and a critique of Kantian pure judgment. Idealism privileges propositions as the locus of belief. According to coherentist theories of knowledge, such as that energetically propagated by Donald Davidson, "nothing can count as a reason for holding a belief except another belief."[56] The problem with this is that coherentism provides no understanding of how our beliefs have a foothold in the objective world. It therefore lays itself open to charges of relativism. If idealism founders on the whirlpool of absolute subjectivism, bald empiricism offers few alternatives either. For the bald empiricist, empirical judgments simply present themselves to the subject from observations of the external world, irrespective of the beliefs that the observer may hold. It conceives of knowledge as a simple one-to-one correspondence between observation of an external reality and the beliefs of the observer. The result is the so-called "myth of the given," the implausible notion that empirical knowledge is acquired without any presuppositions.

Kant famously sought a *via media* between empiricism and idealism. He does so in part by scaffolding his epistemology to a distinct metaphysics—a *noumenal* world that supposedly makes space for rationality, transcendent over a phenomenal world that is exhaustively subject to causal necessity. He thereby introduces an unfortunate antinomy that has since then consumed the greater part of the oxygen circulating in North Atlantic philosophy. The metaphysics aside, he pithily sums up his epistemological insights thus: "Thoughts without content are empty, intuitions without concepts are blind. It is, therefore, just as necessary to make our concepts sensible, that is, to add an object to them in intuition, as to make our intuitions intelligible, that is, to bring them under concepts."[57] In other words, human cognitive architecture is so designed that the intuitional and conceptual elements of experience are necessarily and universally inseparable. But how exactly are intuitions and concepts synthesized? Kant argues that intuitional unity "presupposes a synthesis which does not belong to the senses,"[58] which appears to imply that intuitional constraints of sensibility are always already minimal conceptualizations. As to senses in themselves, Kant has this to say: "The senses do not err—not because they always judge rightly, but because they do not judge at all."[59] In the *Prolegomena*, Kant distinguishes between "judgments of perception," which only deliver subjective impressions, and "judgments of experience," which have objective validity.[60] Thus, by asserting the primacy of the conceptual, the Kantian synthesis would seem to lead back toward a "frictionless" idealism. His intricate architectonic of mind attributes to the faculty of judgment the objectifying role and thereby makes phenomenal properties identical to pure representational properties. The upshot is that Kant sacrifices the rough ground of the empirical world, the fineness of grain of perceptual experience, the bewildering diversity of phenomena, for the sublimity of coherence and order.

The epistemic dimensions of rationality are inextricably intertwined with the axiological. Insofar as conceptual ideation only gains intelligibility against a historical and contextual background, and insofar as the space of reason is worked out intersubjectively, political and ethical considerations are constitutive of any robust rational imaginary. This immediately means that instrumental forms of reason are questionable. Such forms of reasoning fail to engage with the value of the ends and not simply the means to the realization of certain goods. It also follows that accounts of practical rationality that construe rationality as the maximization of an agent's existing desires are mistaken not only insofar as they fail to contend with the variety of conflicting desires but also because certain desires may be ethically repugnant. Nor will prudential rationality do either if that is taken to be an avowal that an agent ought to pursue courses of action that most effectively advance his or her interests. Even putting aside vexed questions about the reconcilability of ethical considerations to interests, prudential rationality may often demand that the agent sacrifice truth for flourishing.

What makes a critical contextual rationality particularly robust is that it begins by situating agents within a rich, intersubjective social ontology. It therefore not only illuminates but also makes available for critique the deep historical and social background within which claims of rationality are made. This allows for an appreciation of the diversity and variety in what counts as rationality and yet at the same time—because rationality is taken to be a *practice*—allows for the critical scrutiny of various claims to rationality. Moreover, a critical contextual rationality makes salient the intertwinement but also irreducibility of the epistemic and axiological dimensions of ideation.

Critical Contextual Hermeneutic

> Western philosophers have always gone on the assumption that fact is something cut and dried, precise, immobile, very convenient, and ready for examination. The Chinese deny this. The Chinese believe that a fact is something crawling and alive, a little furry and cool to the touch, that crawls down the back of your neck.
> —Lin Yutang, as cited in James L. Christian, *Philosophy: An Introduction to the Art of Wondering*

Interpretation is an irreducible constituent of knowledge articulation. Interpretation is herein envisioned as an intellectual practice that enacts the arts and crafts of judgment—conceived of expansively as theoretical, methodological, and critical-contextual practices of description, explication (clarification, complication, and elucidation), understanding, analysis, explanation, translation, evaluation, and transformation.

Interpretation, then, is emergent and constitutive of context. A critical hermeneutic—conceived here as the moment when interpretation is transformed into *criticism*—begins with an understanding of context as neither undifferentiated nor transparent. What constitutes a particular context is always deeply contested. Moreover, because contexts are emergent from the intersection of historical forces and spatial movements, they are dynamic and protean.

A critical hermeneutic historicizes and maps at least four dimensions of context: emergence, performance, dissemination, and reception.[61] The *context of emergence* names the political, economic, and cultural conditions of possibility for the invention of artifacts, performances, and practices. The *context of performance* refers to the time-space in which artifacts, performances, and practices are articulated or enacted, the temporal and spatial fabric within which an association, image, story, narrative, idea, or vision takes shape on a page, a stage, a platform, a canvas, a classroom, or comes to fruition on the street. The *context of dissemination* tracks contestations over circulation, translation, and canonization of artifacts, performances, and practices. The *context of reception* is concerned with the forms in which interpreters interact with artifacts, performances, and practices. Of course, these contexts are inextricably interanimated and irreducibly entangled; they are layered, overlapping, dialectical, co-constitutive and recursive ecologies of authorship, performance, circulation, and reading.

The context of emergence, within the terms of a critical hermeneutic, is reconfigured in at least two ways. First, it is conceived of in naturalistic terms. Second, it is conceived of as entangled, that is, as dynamically brought into being through social relationships. An account of the context of emergence as naturalistic just refers to the manner in which the ontology, epistemology, and axiology of social structure ought to be seen as constituted by historical and structural events. Thus the naturalism that is made salient in this argument works within emergent and supervenient assumptions rather than reductionist logics. Such a critical hermeneutic, for that very reason, resolutely stands against the *hermeneutics of faith* and the *hermeneutics of suspicion*.

The hermeneutics of faith refers to a stance of interpretation whose imagination is constituted by beliefs and practices of obedience, love, or responsiveness to divine or supernaturalist beings. Its orientation is informed by a posture of worship toward texts deemed "holy" by the putative religious tradition of adherents.[62] The critique of the hermeneutics of faith must begin by distinguishing at least three of its major variants: *inflationary* accounts of faith, *deflationary* accounts of faith, and *sensus divinitatis* faith. Inflationary accounts of faith define faith as beliefs that lie "beyond" the limits of reason. Faith involves a kind of belief that is, in Kierkegaard's sense, "absurd." The paradigmatic example of this kind of belief is that of Abraham, a character in the Hebrew Bible, who demonstrates his faith by defying his experiential love for his child and the conventions and morals of his culture by agreeing to sacrifice his son. Fideists hold that faith is then a sort of "leap" beyond ordinary human reason. Inflationary accounts of faith fail for familiar reasons that befall divine command imperatives.

Deflationary accounts of faith are determined to argue that faith is simply the irreducible foundation of all epistemological stances. "Faith," according to this view, amounts to what is taken for granted by a community of knowers. Thus, for example, an empiricist will take it for granted that her senses are reliable—and, in that sense, the deflationary faithful would argue that the empiricist has faith in the reliability of her senses. Similarly, a rationalist will take it for granted that her reasoning faculties are intact and, in that sense, has faith in her rational capacities. A variant of the deflationary account of faith in hermeneutics is the claim that "faith" is synonymous with "trust."[63] Thus, given that "trust" is indispensable for interaction in any society, the claim goes that faith is similarly an everyday phenomenon. In that sense, hermeneuts of faith who attempt to ground their beliefs in virtue theory are arguably committed to some kind of deflationary account of faith. To these virtue hermeneuts, faith makes no more demands on us than would be required for the sustainaibility of any community.

But deflationary accounts of faith are just as unconvincing as inflationary ones. To begin with, it is still beholden to a foundationalist picture according to which the entirety of its orientation to the world rests on the will of gods or God. Second, the critical inquirer distinguishes between assumptions *of* an inquiry and faith *in* those assumptions. For the critical inquirer, such assumptions are provisional. The holding of these assumptions is contingent on the articulation of the forms of evidence adduced. In cases where there is conflicting evidence, the critical inquirer declares that she is agnostic on the question at issue, pending the gathering of decisive evidence and the articulation of the best theoretical explanation. This allows for various inquiries to be articulated, while rejecting the foundationalist *episteme* that theists consider sacrosanct. It also allows that if two or more forms of evidentially supported theories are in conflict, one need not conjure up a *deus ex machina* to plug up the holes of our ignorance. This differs from the theist who a priori decides that his belief is the right answer. Third, the critical inquirer is alert to the interaction of her assumptions with evidence from multiple forms of inquiry—empirical, rational, sociological—and alters these assumptions if decisive theoretical explanations come to light. It is doubtful if most theists allow that any new evidence can alter their beliefs about the existence or character of their god. Fourth, the assumptions held by the critical inquirer are evaluated in part on the skein of other assumptions they generate, the empirical historical record that they lay claim to, the logical implications of holding to these beliefs, and these beliefs' consilience with multiple articulations of knowledge. The credibility of hermeneutical warrants is evaluated on the basis of the strength of the presuppositional chains holding together an argument. For example, it is not simply that the theist believes that "God exists." That belief entails empirical, ethical, relational, and logical demands—ahistorical or extra-historical claims of beings that existed before the inauguration of time; empirical claims that require the acceptance of miracles and other supernatural events; sociological claims that assert that other religious groupings are globally wrong while only one "predestined people" are privy to revealed Truth; ethical demands that one offer adequate apologetics for texts of terror.[64] As against the extravagant demands of theistic assumptions, compare this with the pared down meta-ethical assumptions held by the critical inquirer. No doubt these assumptions are emergent from thick historical, rational, and sociological assumptions and will further prompt their own formidable array of propositions—but hardly as extravagant as that required by the theist.

Calvinist theology, a strand within the Christian religious tradition, posits that faith emerges from a faculty that God has implanted in humans known as the *sensus divinitatis*. This faculty is distinct from other ways of forming beliefs such as reason and perception. For the Christian philosopher Alvin Plantinga, faith is a properly basic belief, by which he means that it is the sort of belief that has immediate warrant—that is, is not derived by inference from any other belief. Plantinga argues that faith is rational because it is "undefeated"—this is the notion that faith can withstand all rational objections leveled at it. A dissenter from Plantinga's belief system will find the notion of *sensus divinitatis* troubling because of the manner in which it is so absolutely impervious to critical and empirical investigation, defeasibility, and doubt. Plantinga argues that atheism can be explained because of malformations in the *sensus divinitatis* in some people. It is of the nature of such assertoric propositions that one simply accepts them as given or finds them absurd. In any case, what is most worrisome about Plantinga's epistemology is its defensive posture toward knowledge. What counts as knowledge is what is undefeated. One would think that if there are compelling arguments on both sides of a vexed debate that otherwise cannot be settled decisively in favor of one side, this would be a reason for agnosticism. Not so for Plantinga, who thinks it sufficient that there is no knock-down definitive argument that can bring down the entirety of his views—never mind that there is probably no such knock-down argument for any sufficiently comprehensive ideology, let alone one that posits ethereal and supernatural entities as well as (*sensus divinitatis*) faculties inaccessible to any but the initiated. Plantinga's anti-evidentialist posture—cashed out in his sympathy for the thoroughly refuted theistic argument of "intelligent design"[65]—indicates how his epistemological stance offers grounds for the *rationalization* of a priori beliefs rather than engagement with critical beliefs.

The hermeneutic of faith is certainly not a preserve of theistic-minded approaches to interpretation. Worship is everywhere present in secular contexts, as is seen in the veneration of personalities (celebrities and charismatic politicians, for example), Dionysian baths of collective hysteria (sports fandom, music concerts, amusement parks), and the rites of human sacrifice that the nation-state exacts in war and in retributive punishment (the death penalty). Indeed, it has been the innovation of the modern state to develop a formidable secular priesthood in its academies, legal establishments, and social media equipped with its own elaborate hermeneutic cults. The Kantian deification of reason and the Hegelian mystification of history as the unfolding of *Geist* are transmutations of a hermeneutics of faith into an establishment secularist register. In England, a "humanistic" branch of this secular priesthood was manifested in Mathew Arnold's campaign to replace religion with a humanistic education in "the best that is known and thought"—his definition of culture. Arnold's legacy, radiating forth in the writings of T. S. Eliot, I. A. Richards and F. R. Leavis, envisioned a "Great Tradition" of literary monuments that would sluice the Philistinic unwashed in sweetness and light. If the new theories of textuality—from deconstruction to new historicism—have been notable for their insurgent campaigns to mediate the Great Tradition through Big Theory, or to add this or that villanelle to the canon, they have kept faith with the cloistral practices of pedagogy as a pact between master and acolyte.

If the hermeneutics of faith proves a dead end, a critical hermeneutic cannot however embrace what has often been declared as its polar opposite. Paul Ricoeur named this the hermeneutics of suspicion and identified Marx, Nietzsche, and Freud as its exemplary practitioners. Perhaps what is most striking about these hermeneuts of suspicion is the extent to which they proffer various *reductionist* explanatory frames. Marx, for example, proffers a far too totalistic theory of ideology as false consciousness. Nietzsche, for his part, purports to explain everyone else's base motives as a will to power. Freud also reduces the realm of phenomenological experience to an absolutistic teleology: "the aim of all life is death." These deficiencies are exacerbated by the glaring lack of a *self-reflexive critique* in the hermeneutics of suspicion, of which perhaps Nietzsche's bristling hermeneutic of contempt exemplifies.[66]

A critical hermeneutic also conceives of the contexts of emergence as entangled—that is, relationally constituted by historical and global political, economic, and cultural forces. Every interpretation bears the traces and grooves of deep histories and far-flung locales. It follows then that critical interpretation ought to be oriented by an historiography keen to the palimpsest of the *longue durée* and responsive to a global imaginary. Conversely, such a critical hermeneutic cuts against dominant hermeneutic frames that function according to the logics of possessive patrimony—the claim that a particular practice or artifact originated from the loins of a particular society and has been handed down from fathers to sons through the generations.[67] Thus, for example, the claim that certain artists—say, Shakespeare or Mozart or Flaubert—sired distinctive aesthetic artifacts that are then biologically reproduced and transmitted to future (white male) generations. Or the assumption of ownership over a distinctive practice—for example, science—as an essentially "Western" property.

Hans-Georg Gadamer offers an account of tradition that would seem to break with traditional conservativism's pious fossilization of history. In his enormously influential *Truth and Method*, Gadamer argues that "understanding is not to be thought of so much as an action of subjectivity, but as the placing of oneself within a process of tradition, in which past and present are constantly fused. This is what must be expressed in hermeneutical theory."[68] Thus, according to Gadamer, understanding takes place through the fusion of the "horizon" of the present with the horizon of the past. But Gadamer's construction of "tradition" is altogether too acquiescent to a characterization of it in ways that only the winners of history would approve. What he calls "tradition," many others know as the slaughter-bench of history at which entire peoples have perished in genocide, the remnant generations consigned to grinding and abject poverty, and their oral and written archives of learning and memory destroyed beyond retrieval. As Walter Benjamin points out, what is consecrated as "cultural heritage" are "spoils" in a "triumphal procession in which today's rulers tread over those who are sprawled underfoot": tradition, Benjamin insists, "owes its existence not only to the toil of the great geniuses, who created it, but also to the nameless drudgery of its contemporaries. There has never been a document of culture, which is not simultaneously one of barbarism."[69] This is the bloody underside to Gadamer's notion of tradition, and there is little in his pastoral vision that shows he has a sense of the radical losses, discontinuities, pluralities, and the irreducibly inassimilable trauma suffered by imperialized societies. He argues: "We always stand within tradition, and this is no objectifying process, i.e., we do not conceive of what tradition says as something other, something alien. It is always part of us, a model, or exemplar, a recognition of ourselves."[70]

It is for this reason that there are grounds to be suspicious of Gadamer's touting of "conversation" as the normative method for interacting with the past. To be sure, conversation must be included as one way among many for engaging the past; but to privilege it as the normative methodological ideal and metaphor for such engagement underscores Gadamer's conservative epistemological and political horizons. Against Gadamer, a critical hermeneutic argues that it is precisely a radicalism of vision that has any hope of doing justice to the multiple histories and contexts that constitute a "tradition." Interpretation, therefore, has to draw on multiple methods from the natural sciences to the social sciences to the humanities—from historical archeology, comparative sociology, natural and cultural anthropology, rhetorical theory and criticism, literature, philosophy—in unearthing the "chronotope" of history. It is not only Gadamer's suspicion of the natural sciences and social sciences, however, that forecloses avenues to these rich avenues of discovery. It is also his allergy to critical theory. His theory affirms a deference to the power of authority:

> That which has been sanctioned by tradition and custom has an authority that is nameless, and our finite historical being is marked by the fact that always the authority of what has been transmitted—and not only what is clearly grounded—has power over our attitudes and behavior. . . . And in fact we owe to romanticism this correction of the enlightenment, that tradition has a justification that is outside the arguments of reasons and in large measure determines our institutions and our attitudes.[71]

Gadamer rejects the notion that prejudice is necessarily negative. For him, there is a positivity to prejudice. Prejudices constitute, he argues, "fore-understandings," that is, the structures through which subjects gain a preliminary interpretation of phenomena. Even though Gadamer thinks that such prejudices are open to revision, his theory ultimately envisions such change not so much as a radical critique of social structures and power imbalances[72] but rather as a liquidation of the gap between horizons. Thus he argues that prejudices and fore-meanings speak to the fact that understanding always carries with it the "anticipation of completeness," by which he means that the subject presupposes the coherence, wholeness, and meaningfulness of what is to be understood. His conclusion: "In our understanding, which we imagine so straightforward, we find that, by following the criterion of intelligibility, the other presents himself so much in terms of our own selves that there is no longer a question of self and other."[73] Gadamer's interaction with the past would appear to be thoroughly self-validating and self-aggrandizing.

A critical hermeneutic also reconfigures the context of performance through a sustained attention to embodiment as a constitutive condition of interpretation. This has the salutary effect of significantly revising understandings of subjectivity, consciousness, and agency. Specifically, the question of subjectivity—of who can interpret, when, where, why, and how—emerges as a particularly vexing dimension of embodied interpretation. Reckoning with subjectivity involves an articulation of *interpretive habitus*, conceived of as the complex tracing of the residue of macro-historical forces and micro-biographical pressures on the formation of the interpretive knower, the centripetal and centrifugal forms of power in a field of discourse that act upon the interpreter, and the cross-pressures of dispositions, affections, revulsions, inspirations, and instrumentalities that radiate in and through the interpretive knower. A critical hermeneutic, then, begins with *radical self-reflexivity*. The Italian intellectual Antonio Gramsci writes that history deposits in subjects "an infinity of traces, without leaving an inventory." But even as he strikes a cautionary note about the devastatingly daunting task of fully coming to terms with how a particular historical era, institution, and social group inhabits its subjects, Gramsci argues that the critical project ought to begin in a ruthless confrontation with this historical inventory. It follows, then, that such a radical self-reflexivity cannot be an individualistic, introspective process—it has to be social, and it is most keenly exercised in *radical encounters* with the abjected poor, homeless, disabled, and forgotten.

A serious engagement with embodiment also expands our understanding of interpretation beyond Cartesian models that privilege the mind over the body. Moreover, it can account for the particularity of subjectivity without smuggling back the privatized, transcendental subject so central to much North Atlantic theory. Its emphasis on an embodied phenomenology, for example, differs significantly from Husserl's phenomenology. Husserl, it will be recalled, rejects the "natural attitude," what he considers to be the naïve commonsense belief that our knowledge of the external world is reliable. He argues instead for a method that he dubbed "transcendental phenomenology," through which he hopes to lay bare the very conditions of possibility for consciousness. Husserl starts from the intentionality of consciousness—the fact that the mind does not passively absorb sensations but rather is always directed toward something. In order to get a sense of the contents of consciousness, then, Husserl argues that we ought to employ a method that he calls the "phenomenological *epoche*"—the bracketing of the world in order to concentrate on mental contents that are directly experienced. Husserl's goals are ambitious: he believes that the phenomenological *epoche* leads to the discovery of the universal essences of the mind. He calls this the "eidetic reduction," because it performs a reductionist maneuver that enables the researcher to discover the universal types that are the foundation for ordinary phenomenological experiences. Husserl's method is driven by the belief that it is the only method with a pure, objective grasp of reality. Indeed, he goes as far as declaring that the phenomenological method, being apodictic, is superior to "all sciences which relate to [the] natural world."[74]

Husserl's transcendental phenomenology remains beholden to a Cartesian privileging of the mental and therefore suffers from many of its difficulties.[75] The phenomenological *epoche* reintroduces an invidious mind/body split by conceiving the mental as the locus of phenomenological experience. The unhappy consequences for a theory of interpretation are threefold. First, Husserl's mentalistic approach fails to account for the fact that it is the body that orients creatures to their being in the world. Consequently, mental phenomena take as a background the sorts of perceptions emergent from bodily embeddedness and bodily intentionality. This matters for a theory of interpretation insofar as it underscores how our socio-bodily being as particular subjects—as people who are interpellated as raced, gendered, disabled, and so on—structures much of what we see, feel, smell, respond to. Second, the person engaged in interpretation is deeply *immersed* in a context. When one is reading a book, the perceptual background that makes for interpretive activity is thick: the temperature in the room, the smells of the book, the surrounding sound, the sedimentation of memory, and the affective swirl motivating the activity. Husserl narrows his phenomenology to the mental and fails to appreciate the generative depth of social context from which the activity of interpretation is emergent. Moreover, as we become more skilled in specific activities, we develop a bodily absorption in the activity. The performance takes on a life of its own, almost seeming to render its author or creator incidental to its realization. Those attending to the practice, similarly, are "caught up" in the activity, unaware of the passing of time. In other words, interpretive activity has a "flow" to it that completely absorbs the person in its movement. The danger of Husserl's theory is its mechanistic account of interpretation—it gives a disinfected, detached account of interpretation that fails to account for its embeddedness. Third, Husserlian phenomenology reinforces the erroneous assumption that mental content is transparent whereas so-called "objective reality" (including bodily perception) is opaque. But given the social depth from which interpretation is emergent, this clearly is untenable. Fourth, Husserl's claim that the phenomenological *epoche* offers an austere, pure deliverance of absolute being renders his hermeneutic irredeemably idealist and antiscientific.

These reflections on subjectivity and consciousness are also inextricably entangled with questions about agency. A critical contextual hermeneutics defines the exigence of interpretation as gripped in the tension between *krisis* (the emergency) and *nomos* (the everyday). An interpretation charged with the exigence of crisis begins with an acknowledgment of the *irreversible cut* that every act produces. The act outstrips intentions, either good or ill; motives, be they malign or benevolent; beliefs that are clear or nebulous; and ideologies, whether systematic or incoherent. It is of little use, for example, to wax eloquently about "democracy," "human rights," or "freedom" once the machineries of war are airborne. Obliterated bodies, mass graves, and the inconsolable wail of survivors render all else obscene rationalizations. A critical hermeneutic attuned to the emergency, then, starts by acknowledging that the exigence to which it is a response is not only *constitutive* of new realities but also *forecloses* certain possibilities. Criticism awakened by crisis does not indulge the fantasy of a clean break. It begins *in media res*, a witness to maimed limbs, a gatherer of unraveled selves, a mourner of dead persons. It is only in the rubble of time, in the graveyards of space, that a critical hermeneutic cuts into the fabric of the temporal and spatial. The etymological trace of the word criticism from the ancient Greek word *krinein* is hereby particularly apt— criticism "separates, decides, divides." A criticism emergent in crisis instantiates a break—however jagged, however incomplete—against the logics of violence, an incision against the flow of inevitability.

A critical hermeneutic that inhabits crisis, then, takes itself to be witness to the afterlife and forelife of catastrophe—a poisoned ecology, a politics of plunder, an economy of pillage, a brutal imagination. In doing so, a critical hermeneutics strikes a remarkably discordant note from dominant philosophical systems and practices. For what is most recognizable in regnant systems of thought is an extraordinary attachment to a hermeneutics of redemption. Some philosophers have conjured fantastical beginnings to wipe clean the slate of catastrophe: the state of nature (Hobbes), clear and distinct perception (Descartes), the original position (Rawls). Others have manufactured fantastical endings to guarantee a triumphalist result: Plato's Myth of Er, Leibnitz's optimal cosmic calculus, Hegel's *Geist*. But if major philosophers have often disagreed as to whether redemption could be secured by looking to origins or endings, their results have been essentially the same— the triumph of people who are the spitting images of their creators.

Against this, a critical hermeneutic tarries in the ruins of catastrophe, huddles among refugees, waits in line with migrant workers, listens to the whimper of the dying. Their stories tell of irrecuperable loss, irreparable brokenness, irreconcilable desires, irredeemable damage. A hermeneutic is precisely critical insofar as it stands in solidarity with the weak, the forgotten, and the despised.

But precisely because a critical hermeneutic inhabits crisis, it refuses to lose sight of the *nomos* (the everyday). Interpretative agency involves attentiveness to the mundane, the deliberative, the slow, the dialogic, the familiar, the ordinary, the commonplace, the routine, and the prosaic. A critical hermeneutics involves the excavation of the marginal, worthless, useless, and disreputable. It is attuned to how drudgery can be the very marrow of creativity. The everyday (*nomos*) and the emergency (*krisis*) are not herein seen as two opposed realms. To live in the maw of capitalism is to live a life of precarity where the ordinary is a slow bleeding out of agency, relationships, and imagination. Thus, the task of a critical hermeneutic is to show that the "emergency situation" is the rule—thereby shattering antipolitical theodicies of normalcy, progress, and inevitability—in order, through critical social theory and practice, to bring about a deep crisis in the very ontology of global empire.

The third hermeneutic context is that of dissemination—which involves engagement with how artifacts, performances, and practices are circulated, translated, and canonized. To consider only the strand of canonization, for example, a critical hermeneutic illuminates and critiques the processes by which a social group appropriates and consecrates an artifact or practice for posterity. But it is not the purpose of a critical hermeneutic to demand the "inclusion" of a rival canon of artifacts that then stand in as "representatives" of excluded, minority identities. Such "identitarian" forms of activism remain hypnotized by the logic of canonization as purity and patrimony. Identitarianism is also mistaken in privileging *content* over institutional embeddedness. Rather, a critical hermeneutic maps out the process of generation as *structural* and the forms of transmission as appropriative and inscribed in the most mundane practices (pedagogy in schools, religious places of worship, and families; mass media form and content;

the exchange of material artifacts in the marketplace and elsewhere). Rather than take for granted the presentism of canonization and its propaganda about the impermeability and integrity of national or racial borders, a critical hermeneutic traces the trajectory of artifacts and ideas across both historical and spatial boundaries, notes that the circulation of such artifacts and ideas are never without (selective) gains and losses, is responsive to how transmission is far more about the induction of bodies into the deep structures of particular forms of literacy—whether written, visual, or oral—and interrupts processes by which selected cultural artifacts are deployed in cementing the cultural hegemony of a ruling class. As John Guillory has pointed out in the context of the U.S. debate on the literary canon debate, "one may reasonably question what necessary *cultural* relation a university-trained suburban manager or technocrat has to Plato or Homer by virtue of his or her American citizenship—no more, in fact, than an educationally disadvantaged dweller in the most impoverished urban ghetto. The suburban technocrat and the ghetto dweller on the other hand have very much more in common culturally with each other than either of them ever need have with the great writers of Western civilization."[76] Guillory notes that the process of fitting artifacts into certain categories—"scientific vs. humanistic," "technical vs. journalistic," "political vs. aesthetic," "commercial vs. artistic," "high culture vs. popular culture," "poetry vs. prose"—is far more decisive in the struggle over canonization than struggles over the specific works that get included in a canon. This categorization is the work of literacy, which is "not simply the capacity to read but . . . the *systematic regulation of reading and writing*, a complex social phenomenon corresponding to the following set of questions: Who reads? What do they read? How do they read? In what social and institutional circumstances? Who writes? In what social and institutional contexts? For whom?"[77] In the upshot, the work of a critical hermeneutical practice has to be *chronotopian*, articulated as social pedagogy.[78]

Finally, a critical hermeneutic articulates an interpretive frame for understanding the processes of reception. A critical hermeneutic engages at least three dimensions of reception. First, it articulates the horizon of reception within which authors articulate their works. This involves the study of audiences that the author imagines she is orienting the work to (whether past, present, or future audiences). Not only does this involve accounting for the author's sense of her ideal readers and, slightly differently, what authors' preferred readers[79] or inscribed readers are, but it also involves a critique of what Phil Wander has called the "third persona." If the first persona is the speaker or author, and the second persona is the implied audience in a speech act, the third persona represents audiences that are negated by a text or utterance: "'Being negated' includes not only being alienated through language—the 'it' that is the summation of all you and I are told to avoid becoming—but also being negated in history, a being whose presence, though relevant to what is said, is negated through silence."[80] Second, a critical hermeneutic empirically engages actual audience up-take of utterances, whether or not the utterances are aimed at them. Audience up-take is neither absolutely idiosyncratic and individual nor absolutely monolithic and collective. The question of how much agency audiences exercise in their response to utterances is to be engaged critically (through a critique of the power structures circulating and inhabiting audiences) and empirically (through a qualitative immersion in the phenomenology of audience reception).[81] Third, a critical hermeneutic engages the ripple of *perlocutionary force* acting on audiences in taking up utterances. There are limits to an exact mapping of perlocutionary effects, but it will include an attention to *manifest effects* (psychological and behavioral effects taken up consciously), *latent effects* (psychological and behavioral effects that seep unconsciously in the deep structure of culture), and *wildfire or snowball effects* (those effects that move like a contagion across audience populations).

Critical Contextual Imagination

Imagination! who can sing thy force?
Or who describe the swiftness of thy course?
                    —Phillis Wheatley, "On Imagination"

The imagination constitutes a third dimension of a critical contextual epistemology. The imagination, I posit, has at least three dimensions:

the *topographical or spatial dimension*, the *kairotic or temporal dimension*, and the *hermeneutic or intersubjective dimension*.[82] These dimensions, it is important to emphasize, are constitutive of the full gamut of embodied and relational capacities of human beings—including the neuropsychological, psychological, abstract, affective, ethical, and social.

The topographical imagination describes how a person's or group's inhabitation of a particular space structures their capacities, per-ceptions, inferences, judgments, and actions, and, dialectically, how they in turn constitute spatial relationships, judgments, and actions. Its neuropsychological manifestation emerges in the capacity for proprioception—that is, persons' ability to orient their bodies in space and time. More robustly, the topographic imagination describes a person or group's latent and manifest registration of their ecological background. For example, a trained driver is subliminally aware of an array of phenomena as she drives. She orients her driving according to these phenomena without necessarily being able to itemize every single phenomenon or task she is performing. Conceived as such, then, the topographic imagination need not take a conscious, rationalist form— rather, it may just as often be the "horizon" against which a person or group apprehends or interacts with objects in the foreground. Much of the insights of Gestalt psychology on the mind's capacity to articulate patterns, the background conditions that make salient or bring to the foreground the object of perception, and the capacity to fill in gaps in hitherto disconnected or fragmentary percepts are descriptive of the spatial imagination. It follows then that the topographic imagination is constitutive of epistemic capabilities. Questions such as how concepts, perceptions, and images "hang together," the relationship between and among things, and the capacity to articulate mathematical deductions, to make analytic connections, and to extrapolate metaphorical possibilities are all manifestations of the topographic imagination. There is a social dimension to the topographic imagination as well. This describes a person or group's "social imaginary," that is, the communities, institutions, and ideologies that structure a person's stance toward the world and in and by which a person orients herself in relation to others. The topographical imagination can also be exercised critically. This would occur, for example, in the capacity to articulate counterfactual thought experiments and to make radically innovative analogical connections.

As with the topographic imagination, the kairotic imagination (from the Greek, *kairos*)[83] is dialectical. It refers to how persons' embeddedness within time constitutes their capacities, judgments, and actions, and how, in turn, people constitute time in and through their relationships, judgments, and actions. As an embodied capacity, the kairotic imagination is deeply structured by dispositions inscribed in the unconscious through socialization and ideology. It can thus take both nonconceptual and conceptual forms. Its nonconceptual forms constitute kinesthetic and how-to knowledges. Its conceptual forms constitute a person or group's social memory and historical imaginary. When exercised critically, the kairotic imagination involves the capacity for utopian thought against prevailing social mythologies.

The *hermeneutic imagination* describes the complex of capacities and judgments that constitute a person's or group's distinctive sensibility, phenomenology, affect, and ideology. As with the topographical and kairotic forms of the imagination, the hermeneutic imagination is emergent from the deep structure of embodied ontology and dispositions. As such, it has been formed by conscious and unconscious affinities, affections, and revulsions inscribed in the body through socialization. When exercised critically, however, the hermeneutic imagination is the capacity to be attuned to other persons' affects—for example, through love, empathy, or desire—and the self-critical ability to view one's self from the perspective of the other.

The topographical, kairotic, and hermeneutic forms of the imagination should be seen as deeply interanimated—that is, as mutually constitutive. For example, a group's historical memory is quite often constitutive of its social imaginary and vice versa. But this does not mean that these forms of the imagination are always mutually reinforcing. At times, they can be in deep tension, as when a hermeneutic inhabitation of another's sensibility is discordant with a person's historical memory.

There are a number of implications emergent from conceiving of the imagination thus. The first is that this view emphasizes the extent to which the imagination is constituted by the ecological and social contexts of its emergence. It therefore makes salient the manner in which the imaginative faculty constrains as much as it liberates. The imagination is formed and structured by socialization, power, and ideology[84]—much of which is unconsciously absorbed. Modern theories of the imagination, however, are yet to emerge from the shadow cast by Romantic conceptions of mind. The Romantic tradition sees the imagination as generating, de novo, blindingly original and full-grown images. For the Romantics, the imagination is a tsunami pouring forth from the head of the individual genius. This Romantic account fails because it offers scant theorization of the imagination as constituted by the banalities of socialization and acculturation, but also because it fails to register the structuration of the imagination by domination, exploitation, and the will to power.

But just precisely because humans are embodied persons, it also follows that they are situated in time. Thus the imagination is not only constituted by enduring structures of constraint but is also emergent from encounters with others. It is therefore always already intersubjective. Moreover, to live in time is to be subject to the irruption of the exigent, the evental, and the sublime. The imagination, then, is as much constructed from the perduring forces of ritual, rites, and rhythms, as it is sparked from serendipitious juxtapositions, happenstance, queer mutations, and ecstatic encounters.[85] Imaginative knowledge exceeds grids of method, confounds quantifiers of frequency, scandalizes generalization. The imagination can be elusive and ineffable, as in Proust's madeleine moment when the taste of a cake offers a tantalizing hint of a memory; or it can be overwhelming and tangible, as in the intensity with which encounters with objects of love, hate, or desire renders all else irrelevant; or it can be diffuse and yet impossibly persistent, as when ennui, anxiety, or boredom cast a gloom over perception, thought, and action. Such an account of the imagination departs from Cartesian accounts of the imagination that incline us toward a picture of the imagination as a theater of the mind, consciously willed into being by an individual thinker. If the Romantic theory of the imagination fails to account for the latent fecundity

of ritual and repetition, the Cartesian account is altogether too enamored with method and control.

Moreover, any adequate account of the imagination must come to
terms with embodiedness as an irreducible ground of its emergence.
The imagination then is constituted by all the senses—visual, auditory, olfactory, gustatory, and tactile. And, insofar as these senses are
interanimated and generative, it also means that the imagination is kinesthetic, stereoscopic, and proprioceptive. The upshot is that embodiment involves reckoning with how the imagination is activated not
only through and with multiple senses but also latently (be it unconsciously or nonintentionally). For example, work in moral psychology
has demonstrated how judgments of the "moral" and the "immoral"
are often inflected by people's reactions to particular smells, tastes,
sounds, and so on. An understanding of the imagination as embodied
sees it as constituted by and, in turn, as constituting the conscious
and unconscious affinities, affections, and revulsions that structure
human judgments.

Such an embodied account of the imagination offers a decisive
critique of influential Aristotelian accounts of the imagination. Aristotle articulates the capacity of the imagination as derivative of sensory perception. In the *De Anima*, Aristotle theorizes perception as
the inscription of impressions on a wax tablet. He states: "sense is that
which is receptive of the form of sensible objects without the matter, just
as the wax receives the impression of the signet ring without the iron
or the gold."[86] Aristotle thinks that the imagination consists in the capacity to reproduce or recall these previously inscribed sensory images.
He privileges sight as the most important of the senses. Tellingly, then,
his word for the imagination is *phantasia*, a name drawn from the root
phôs, "light," and clinking within a connotative chain of terms such as
phantazō, "to show at the eye or the mind," and *phainō*, "to show in
light." As previous commentators have shown, Aristotle's account of
the imagination was extraordinarily influential. Early modern thinkers such as Locke and Hobbes often quibbled with this or other detail
of the Aristotelian account of the imagination, but they retained his
sense of the imagination as derivative of visual impressions. It is not

just that Aristotelianism's ocularcentric theory of the imagination fails to grapple with auditory, olfactory, gustatory, and tactile constituents and forms of imaginative knowledges, but it is also the case that it cannot account for the ineffable, the affective, and the kinesthetic forms of the imagination.

An embodied account of the imagination, furthermore, makes better sense of the *performativity* of the imagination. The imagination is dialectical insofar as it functions both *generatively* and *reflexively*. On the one hand, the imagination generates or projects sensory stimuli. Gestalt psychology is helpful in illuminating this dimension of the imagination. According to Gestaltism, perception not only works holistically through complex pattern cognitions and recognitions but also works generatively by filling in or filling out shapes. At the same time, however, the very stimuli projected and generated by the imagination gain a grip and hold on the person or group from which these stimuli are generated. The imagination thus is deeply constitutive of phenomenological consciousness.

Kantian accounts of the imagination prove deeply misleading in failing to account for the reflexivity of the imagination. For Kant, the imagination is a faculty that synthesizes various concepts, fills in indeterminate perceptions, and—in interaction with aesthetic phenomena—engages in a nonteleological *play* of trying out how various associations fit with our prior concepts. He makes a distinction between understanding and the imagination. Kant avers that understanding functions through the subsumption of sensory perceptions under certain determinate concepts. The imagination, in contrast, works through a form of playacting, according to which a person tries out how various associations fit with an idea, without having to decide that there is a single determinate fit. The Kantian account thus yields a severely stunted view of the imagination. Kant, by holding the imagination to coloring inside the lines of prior concepts, insists on its subordination to reason's oversight. Moreover, Kant does not register the reflexivity of the imagination, the manner in which it doubles back to constitute the affective and hermeneutic phenomenology of human subjects. Thus Kant does not only render the imagination secondary to reason, he also anticipates modernity's dismissal of it as risk-free and therefore frivolous.

Toward an Articulated Epistemology

> The results of all the schools and of all their experiments belong legitimately to us. We will not hesitate to adopt a Stoic formula on the pretext that we have previously profited from Epicurean formulas.
> —Nietzsche, *Posthumous Fragments*

A salutary upshot, then, of a critical contextual rationality, hermeneutic, and imagination is that it opens up a robust epistemology, one that involves a comprehensive immersion in the diversity, depth, and complexity of multiple methodologies and knowledges—from the theoretical and empirical natural sciences, social sciences, humanities, and the performing arts. The most robust theoretical knowledges come at the intersection of the critically rational, the critically empirical, the critically hermeneutical, and the critically imaginative. The task of knowledge articulation, therefore, is a rigorous mapping out of the continuities and discontinuities in human knowledges. One implication of this, already mentioned, is the rejection of theories that would define knowledge as foundationally based on a singular ontology or as proceeding from a single method. Another is the critique of reductionism, specifically the notion that certain research programs are reducible to others.

Consider, for example, the natural sciences, which in the contemporary zeitgeist have acquired perhaps the most dominant cultural prestige among human knowledges. Unfortunately, the "public picture" of science has come to be largely represented according to a singular science, namely, physics, and perhaps only a dated mechanistic account of physics. Actually existing sciences are diverse and multifarious and draw on a rich panoply of epistemological and methodological strategies. Just as physics is a science, so are other disciplines such as geology, archeology, ecology, and biology, which can only be studied within what practitioners call *complex systems*. Consider that an understanding of much of the sciences involves appreciating the *historical dimensions of scientific practices*. Take biology, for instance. A great deal of misunderstanding of evolutionary biology, to pick one prominent strand within the discipline, involves a failure to conceive of biological processes as *historical* phenomena, as Richard Lewontin helpfully notes.[87] Though natural selection constitutes the dominant mechanism of evolutionary processes, historical study does reveal that genetic drift constitutes another causal factor, if on a smaller scale. Another implication is that organisms—some more than others—are not simply molded by their ecological context but rather culturally adapt and, in doing so, significantly reconfigure the niches in which they live. The point, then, is that speculative just-so narratives such as sociobiology and evolutionary psychology fail not only as natural sciences, insofar as their reductive accounts of evolutionary development misconceive the nature of natural and sexual selection, but also as *historical* sciences because they scant the mediating structures of culture and power inflecting human behavior.

Given the variety and complexity of the sciences, therefore, the notion that the sciences are progressively reducible to one basic "science of everything"—the claim, for example, that psychology reduces to biology, biology to chemistry, and chemistry to physics—is mistaken. As Hilary Putnam, Jerry Fodor, and Richard Boyd have demonstrated in pathbreaking interventions in the philosophy of mind, psychological processes can be explained in naturalistic terms—that is, as constituted of physical entities—that are nevertheless irreducible to neurophysiology.[88] Similarly, in biology, Philip Kitcher demonstrated that classical genetics, which accounts for the transmission of genes by meiosis, is irreducible to molecular genetics, in which genetic transmission occurs through heterogeneous causal factors.[89]

The criteria for evaluating the robustness of scientific theories, it is then clear, are various and complex, *pace* Karl Popper's demands for the falsifiability of theory. Scholars have drawn attention to the value-ladenness of theories;[90] the imbrication and dialectic of theory and observation in scientific practice;[91] the idealization of explanatory models in accounting for causal significance;[92] the shaping of theories through considerations of consilience, congruence, and responsiveness to theoretical advances in the natural and social sciences and in the humanities; the considerations of elegance, beauty, and simplicity in judgments about the explanatory power of theories;[93] and the sociological facts of scientific practice.[94] This entails the rejection of a priori assertions of incommensurability among differing bodies of knowledge—say, the humanities and the natural sciences—even as it also demands cautious and critical articulations of continuities and discontinuities. The best scientific practices would thus be deeply informed by critical work in the humanities and the performative arts, and vice versa.[95]

Even so, this argument for an articulated epistemology does not claim that there is a seamless continuity between various bodies of knowledge. The precise point of antireductionism is the difficulty of establishing exactly how various entities and forms of valuation that are distinct are nevertheless intertwined and how precisely these entities interact. An *articulation* means precisely that: a mapping out of continuities as well as discontinuities, and an acknowledgment of the remainder, be it unaccounted for entities (dark energy, for instance) or our ignorance pending further study.

Disciplinarity, Interdisciplinarity, and the Future of Knowledge

> I am not a donkey, and I do not have a field.
> —Max Weber, as cited in *Duncan Kelly*,
> "Why Max Weber Matters"

By far the most distinctive phenomenon in higher education across the world, driven by the hegemony of North Atlantic societies, is the establishment and entrenchment of modern disciplines—that is, the taken for granted supposition that knowledges can be discretely classified into the peculiarly specific domains that they currently take. Indeed, disciplinary divisions are now seen by many academics as "natural," even "objective" divisions. This is a testament not to the truth of this supposition but rather to the success of modern technologies of socialization. For what immediately strikes a student of the history of knowledge is the relative *novelty* of disciplinary divisions. It was only in the late eighteenth century that knowledge began to take on the kind of disciplinary forms that are now recognizable to the modern subject.

To be sure, universities, in Europe and elsewhere, long before the nineteenth century did make distinctions between differing intellectual pursuits. But it is problematic to assume that there is a seamless historical continuity between, say, the subjects studied in the European medieval university and the modern Western European and North American university. To appreciate why, it is important to critique the manner in which disciplines seek to represent what they are and do to each other and to other disciplines.

Disciplines have traditionally constituted, legitimated, and reproduced themselves through the "myth of origin," the idea that disciplinary origin can be traced to particular Founding Fathers, either in ancient Greece or, in some cases, early modern Europe. Quite apart from its problematically patriarchal assumptions, this notion misreads the ancients by anachronistically reading their interests as identical with those of contemporary scholars.[96] Take, for example, one of the founding myths of analytic philosophy that its origins lie at the precise moment philosophy made itself distinct from religion, politics, economics, culture, and rhetoric. According to this reading, the *philosophoi* (philosophers) were interested in the true, the good, and the beautiful whereas the *sophoi* (rhetoricians) were interested in how to "sell" themselves and their ideas. The attractiveness of this myth for analytic philosophers is not hard to parse: it constructs analytic philosophers as solely concerned with universal truth; as above the petty and messy squabbles of politics, economics, and culture; and as epistemically and morally foundational—and therefore superior—to all other disciplines. When constrained to the use of polite language, analytic philosophers resort to the language of disciplinary specialization—it is not, they say, that they think other disciplines are inferior or illegitimate. Rather, they simply think that those other disciplines are concerned with different objects of study. For example, philosophy, rhetoric, sociology, literature, and what have you have clearly demarcated spheres of research: sociologists are interested in social structures, rhetoricians are interested in the arts of persuasion, and philosophers are interested in truth.

Whatever the merits of these arguments as a description of contemporary disciplinary practices, it is thoroughly and comprehensively anachronistic if it is thought to describe ancient Greek schools of thought. What divided the *sophoi* (rhetoricians) and the *philosophoi* (philosophers) was not fundamentally different objects of interest but rather a substantive disagreement about the nature of wisdom. In other words, the activity of the ancients ought to be characterized for what it is: a genuine disagreement about the hard problems of truth, ethics, politics, and aesthetics. Moreover, it is misleading even as a description of early modern European inquiry. Consider that many of the early modern philosophers now deified as the embodiment of "pure" philosophers were in their own time known as much for their activity in a variety of different fields. Hume was a "man of letters," as anxious to be considered an historian and *literateur* as a philosopher. The actually existing Kant, as opposed to the one now taught in the contemporary university, developed courses in anthropology and geography and is responsible for introducing these courses into the German universities. As Emmanuel Eze has pointed out, "Kant offered 72 courses in 'Anthropology' and/or 'Physical Geography,' more than in logic (52 courses), metaphysics (49 times), moral philosophy (28), and theoretical physics (20 times)."[97] Moreover, the materials Kant assembled in his "Anthropology" and "Physical Geography" courses were used in his lectures in ethics and metaphysics.[98]

The historical, sociological, and rhetorical reasons for the legitimation and naturalization of disciplines as coherent systems are complex and entangled and defy any easy narrativization. But such an account would have to grapple with the alienation of labor wrought by capitalism; the articulation of discourses of white supremacy, patriarchy, class and status hierarchies, and heteronormativity as "commonsense," taken-for-granted ideologies; and the ascendance and establishment of the natural sciences as privileged producers of knowledge.

Capitalism's alienation of labor has, of course, been promoted as a natural outgrowth of economic growth and thus as an inevitable demand for the efficiencies of dividing labor. Such an account is, however, woefully partial. As historical entities, disciplines are not coherent analytical definitions or concepts;[99] that is, they did not develop as a result of thoughtful deliberation on the precise dimensions that would make for efficient discoveries of knowledge. In historicizing disciplines, we begin to see their emergence and contours as contingent, accidental features reified by political power. Their inner workings are a concatenation of different practices, often feverishly at odds with other parts.

If capitalist alienation is one salient element in the emergence of disciplinary ideology, it is inextricably intertwined with discourses of white supremacy, patriarchy, and heteronormativity. The fabrication of the "West" as a civilizational bloc gave these discourses a genealogical pedigree. Under the color of this dubious historiographical category, the intellectual traditions of societies that were constructed as nonwhite were stigmatized as "religious," "mythical," and "irrational." Immanuel Kant, for example, drew from Hume's *Observations on the Feeling of the Beautiful and Sublime* the notion that blacks naturally and inherently lacked capacities for rational and moral achievement. When Kant articulated what he referred to as the "essence of humanity," that which endowed the person with dignity as a member of the "Kingdom of Ends," he meant a person like himself: white, European, and male.

Major contemporary philosophers have zealously extended this racist legacy precisely through the willful blinders of disciplinarity. As the African philosopher Emmanuel Eze demonstrated, the failure to read Kant's *Critiques* as integrally linked to his engagement with anthropology and geography enables contemporary philosophers to avoid coming to terms with the white supremacist assumptions rife in the discipline. Thus, disciplinarity has ratified a deeply ideological account of Kant's oeuvre, "attributable to the overwhelming desire to see Kant as a "pure" philosopher, preoccupied only with "pure" culture and color-blind philosophical themes."[100]

Disciplinarity has thus served to underwrite current sociological exclusions and epistemic injustices. A refusal to engage the breadth of interests within a discipline can be used as a proxy for preventing a thorough engagement with a variety of topics. One can simply rule that certain topics that interest feminists or critical race scholars or Africans are not "philosophy" and thus shut down the possibility of pursuing certain lines of research. Analytic philosophers in the United States ruthlessly police their membership by confronting nonwhite people with the question: "How is this philosophy?"[101]

But the story of disciplinarity would not be complete without accounting for the ascendance of the natural sciences and their accumulation of cultural capital in the world at large. This has tended to push many disciplines toward mimicking the methods of the sciences or, equally perniciously, has led many to believe not only that each discipline has a single legitimate method but also that certain disciplines are reducible to other disciplines. The cultural capital of the sciences was, however, established on a narrow and deeply reductionistic picture of the sciences. According to this picture, "physics"—and moreover, a very mechanistic concept of physics—was the paradigmatic science.

Most of the fissures within the social sciences and humanities were fought over attempts to remake these disciplines to conform to this narrow, reductionist, and scientistic picture of scholarship. Within the social sciences, a variety of disciplines sought to achieve scientific credentials through a methodological emphasis on quantitative data-gathering. Of those disciplines, perhaps no other has labored to achieve the semblance of scientificity with as much vigor as economics. But this has been only a matter of degree. If actually existing politics has never quite lived up to be the way political scientists wanted it to be— sanitized, predictable, technical—many in the political science discipline have nevertheless clung to an image of themselves as the "scientists" that their titles advertise them to be. Communication studies, which had started as a discipline that conceived of itself as carrying on the traditions of the ancient Greek Sophists, made a social scientific turn with the propaganda studies of the mid-twentieth century. Even history, long thought to be deeply humanistic, experienced a sharp social scientific turn.

It should be clear that this present study does not hold that the turn to "science" was bad. A distinction should be made between, on the one hand, a careful drawing upon of scientific methods, including a deep immersion in mathematical models, and, on the other hand, *scientism*—which is the positivistic dogma of naïve realism. Scientism is conceived herein as the uncritical belief not only that the quantitative trumps or renders subsidiary all other forms of evidence but also that such quantitative pieces of evidence are self-evident, that is, are not dependent on the arts of interpretation. It is this uncritical embrace of scientism that has been, on the whole, problematic. Scientism in the social sciences and the humanities has meant that complexity has been sacrificed at the altar of simplistic model building and monocausal statistical significance. Speaking in the wake of the worst recession in the United States since the Great Depression, economist Paul Krugman argued that the economic crisis had devastated the disciplinary *doxa* of his discipline, which, till then, had been vociferously insistent that it was a science. States Krugman:

> Until the Great Depression, most economists clung to a vision of capitalism as a perfect or nearly perfect system. That vision wasn't sustainable in the face of mass unemployment, but as memories of the Depression faded, economists fell back in love with the old, idealized vision of an economy in which rational individuals interact in perfect markets, this time gussied up with fancy equations. The renewed romance with the idealized market was, to be sure, partly a response to shifting political winds, partly a response to financial incentives. But while sabbaticals at the Hoover Institution and job opportunities on Wall Street are nothing to sneeze at, the central cause of the profession's failure was the desire for an all-encompassing, intellectually elegant approach that also gave economists a chance to show off their mathematical prowess.[102]

Thus, in the name of scientificity and quantification, economists have pretended that sellers and buyers were rational and driven by enlightened self-interest, that the "market" could perfectly determine proper prices when left to its devices,[103] and that therefore the economy that was most efficient was that which was not regulated. For all that these assumptions proved devastatingly misleading, they remain the cultic credo of orthodox economists.

The upshot of coming to terms with these historical factors is that it brings into question the supposed "naturalness" of disciplinary divisions. We ought to historicize disciplines, seeing them as having emerged historically. We ought to be sensitive to the contingent, accidental features that determined their contours and the conceptual joints by which they map the world. Seen as such, a number of implications present themselves.

First, a critique of disciplinarity will take seriously the fact that all forms of study are complexly entangled in power relations. The belief in "pure" knowledge is a fantasy. All disciplines hand out credentials and endorse certain people as authorities, knowers, experts, teachers, and professionals. Note also that these forms of credentialization are endowed on embodied persons. And where we have bodies, we have *culture, interests, affinities, attachments.* What this means is that power differences in the wider society are all too often reproduced at the disciplinary level—even when these power differences are justified through redescriptions and rationalizations.

Such power differences are sublimated in the language of professionalism, rigor, objectivity, merit, reputational rankings, and pedigree. Thus, the coherence of any specific discipline is significantly constituted by the fact that one faction has the upper hand in determining the rankings, job opportunities, grant funding, and access to journal publishing within the discipline. Perhaps one of the most insidious ways in which disciplines mask power hierarchies is through the transmutation of embodied nonverbal forms of communication, methodological moves, and linguistic style into principled objections to other ways of knowing. Analytic philosophy's rhetorical repertoire, for example, consists in its ideology of innate "smartness," its fetishism of clarity, its adversarial style, its reliance on intuitions, and its machinery of thought experiments.

A corollary to this point is that it brings into crisis the rhetoric of professionalism. It still requires emphasizing that knowledge is not only articulated within the walls of the university. Perhaps another way to put this is that it is important to distinguish between the study and understanding of a body of knowledge and the discipline within which some—but not all—of the study is carried out. It is by no means a foregone conclusion that the best work in epistemology or metaphysics or ethics will be carried out in the discipline of "philosophy." Perhaps one of the greatest triumphs of modern socialization is the assumption that philosophers, psychologists, rhetoricians, critics, and intellectuals are just those credentialed by universities.[104]

Second, if the ideology of disciplinarity ratifies a form of expertise that is used to exclude outsiders, it is just as important to bear in mind that it also imposes a false continuity and uniformity *within* disciplines. The notion that there is some metaphysical bond tying Plato, Aquinas, Descartes, Kant, and Nietzsche to Paulin Hountondji, Kristie Dotson, Raymond Geuss, and Sally Haslanger beggars belief.[105] An examination of the tenuous uniformity and unity claimed by disciplines can be seen in a close reading of the presuppositions of practitioners within a discipline, presuppositions that indicate just how vastly different and incompatible are their visions of the purposes and boundaries of the discipline. Early and high modern thinkers, for example, are distinguished by their attempts to radically transform philosophy. Kant posits that *first philosophy*, the foundation upon which the medieval university sought to ground its learning, could no longer be thought of as first. Before launching any philosophy, it was important, Kant thought, to establish a critical account of the very possibility of such a philosophy. Hegel rejects this Kantian goal, arguing that such an ambition was akin to "trying to learn to swim before one enters the water." I think an argument can be made that, against both Kant and Hegel, Nietzsche discovered that there was no reason to try to construct, out of whole cloth, a new critical philosophy, for ancient societies already had traditions and individuals critical of "First Philosophy." Nietzsche, who delivered lectures in the history of Greek rhetoric, argues, provocatively as he was wont to do, that "every advance in epistemological and moral knowledge has reinstated the sophists."[106] Nietzsche even hails the sophists as his "co-workers and precursors."[107]

Thus, disciplinarity is responsible for significantly narrowing the range of thought within a particular domain of intellectual practice. In building up a myth of Great Disciplinary Fathers, disciplines succeed in diminishing the horizons of current practitioners by making them labor under the shadow of a few Masters. They thwart detailed engagements and debates not only across differing areas of study but also by preventing internal diversity *within* disciplines. Wayne Booth recounts an all too unfortunate common occurrence in his book *The Rhetoric of Rhetoric*:

> In 1960, I was at a post-lecture reception in Oxford. Chatting over drinks with a don, I asked him what subject he taught. "Chiefly eighteenth-century literature. What is your field?" "Basically it's rhetoric, though I'm officially in 'English.' I'm trying to complete a book that will be called *The Rhetoric of Fiction*." "Rhetoric!" He scowled, turned his back, and strode away.[108]

The contemporary configurations that disciplinarity has taken under neoliberal capitalism are such that it systematically forecloses paradigm-shattering, ambitious scholarship. Sweeping, wide-ranging examinations of macro-structures have been edged out in favor of micro-trends, analytic word-parsing, and recycled "folk" prejudice. The conditions—not universal and not by any means typical, but nonetheless present—that made possible W. E. B. Du Bois in sociology, Karl Polanyi in economics, C. L. R. James in history, Kenneth Burke in rhetoric, and Sylvia Wynter in cultural studies have atrophied to the cute trivialities of Steven D. Levitt's *Freakonomics*, the puerile thought-experiments in Jeff McMahan's *The Ethics of Killing*, and the warmed-over banalities of Jonathan Haidt's *The Righteous Mind*.

This point should emphatically not be read as a desire to resurrect a Great Man theory of scholarship. And neither is it a nostalgic hankering after epochs that never were. Rather, it is precisely a *sociological* critique of the undeniable narrowing of the intellectual imagination by the microphysics and biopolitics of neoliberal capitalism—specifically, the cultic worship of pedigree through pseudoscientific "reputation" rankings; the clipping of ambition to read and write across disciplines; the almost complete death of writerly style; the pressure against qualitative interpretations of epochal and global phenomena; the enforcement of quietism in the guise of theoretical, methodological, and empirical modesty; the policing of thought through tribal citation patterns; and the fetish of Big Data.

To some, of course, a critique of disciplinarity will sound quaint. Within the postmodern humanities, for example, the critique of disciplinarity is now taken for granted because of the circulation of a high theory canon that cuts across several humanities fields. Even in areas beyond that of the postmodern humanities, interdisciplinarity is now a buzzword of administrative-speak, bandied about whenever the carrot or stick of grants is invoked. But consider that one of the deepest problems with the postmodern humanities—a problem that it disavows because of its eclecticism—is a persistent inability to understand power as embedded institutionally. Citation of Jacques Rancière and Alain Badiou may sound very interdisciplinary, but hiring is still done at the level of the department, and decision making still conducted at the level of the disciplinary associations (the AHA, the MLA, the APA, the NCA). Also, consider that while most professors will consider themselves interdisciplinary, what this actually amounts to is that they read certain canonical theorists in other fields—usually, white male authorities—which they then translate into their idiom. For example, while many analytic philosophers, to take a rather common example, congratulate themselves in their close association with the sciences (particularly psychology), they are proudly ignorant about other fields and theoretical discourses in the humanities (such as, say, critical race theory) which they deem unimportant. But perhaps the most significant point is that interdisciplinarity offers no attempt at a radical reimagining of scholarship. At best it means collaborating with peers in other disciplines while keeping one's fundamental assumptions intact.

A robust critique of disciplinarity, therefore, ought to go beyond a lukewarm endorsement of interdisciplinarity and proffer a radical reimagination of the social structures and practices from which knowledge and aesthetics are emergent.

Intellectual Practice, Social Ontology, and the Good Life

> In philosophy where one begins generally makes a difference to the
> outcome of one's enquiries.
> —Alasdair MacIntyre, *Dependent Rational Animals*

In this chapter, I have endeavored to offer an intellectual ontology
of knowledge articulation. The overriding stakes for the importance
of such a project consists in understanding the intellectual life as constitutive of the good life. I say so for at least three reasons. The first
is to demonstrate that knowledge articulation is embedded in political, economic, and cultural structures—that is, that knowledge is a
social practice. In other words, knowledge is not merely propositional
but rather is an embodied, relational, and institutional practice. And
precisely because knowledge is embodied, relational, and institutional
practice, it must be reckoned with as a vital constituent of any adequate account of a broader social ontology. This is not only because
knowledge articulation is the site in and through which a society argues and contests theories and intuitions of legitimation, justification,
and value (that is, it is the locus for working out power and ideology),
but it is also because it is through institutions and practices of knowledge articulation that a society imagines its visions of the possible and
the futural.

There is a second reason why I argue that an adequate intellectual ontology is constitutive of the good life. This is the fact that if
knowledge is understood as an embodied, social practice, then it follows that it is most robustly realized when it is understood as a way of
life. To be sure, this runs against the grain of dominant understandings of knowledge production that hold that knowledge is reducible to
justified, true beliefs or propositions. Understood as such, contemporary accounts of knowledge—exemplified by reigning epistemological theories—proffer thin, lukewarm accounts of the intellectual life
as a serial accumulation of facts. This chapter, in mapping out an

intellectual ontology, intimates that alternative practice, one drawn to the emergence of intellectuals rather than simply knowers, is possible.

Finally, I argue, it is vital that an adequate account of an intellectual ontology be seen as a prerequisite for working out a normative theory of knowledge. This is because normative theories of knowledge that do not account for the contextual conditions of knowledge articulation invariably proffer idealized—and therefore misleading—understandings of knowledge. For example, Platonic and Cartesian theories of knowledge that characterize knowledge articulation in acontextual, disembodied, antirhetorical terms advance misleading notions of knowledge as absolutist, universalist, and unmediated. This chapter argues, instead, for normative theories that proceed from embedding knowledge articulation in a layered social ontology.

In the chapter that follows, I want to put flesh to the argument articulated in this chapter by considering different embodiments of the intellectual in the contemporary context. If, as I have argued, knowledge articulation is emergent as well as constitutive of particular intellectual ontologies, this raises the question of what sort of intellectual performances constitute the contemporary institutional and geopolitical landscape. In the following chapter, I aim to suggest a few answers to that very question.

CHAPTER 2

Embodied Knowledge

Intellectual Practices as Ways of Life

Difficulty of philosophy, not the intellectual difficulty of the
sciences, but the difficulty of a change of attitude. Work on philosophy is . . . actually more of a kind of work on oneself. On one's own
conception. On how one sees things. (And what one demands of
them.)
——Ludwig Wittgenstein, "Philosophy: Sections 86–93 (pp. 405–35)
of the So-Called 'Big Typescript' (Catalog Number 213)"

This chapter endeavors to articulate the various ways of inhabiting or
embodying the intellectual way of life. I do not intend, nor is it possible, to provide an exhaustive account of all the figurations of the intellectual. Rather, drawing primarily from North Atlantic and African
institutional and social practices, I suggest a few of the dominant performances of the intellectual as a form of life. The intellectual forms of
life articulated below, moreover, are properly seen as complexes—that
is, embodied dispositions, rhetorical repertoires, critical *habitus*—
rather than as neat, self-contained, and mutually exclusive categories.
Thus, they not only overlap considerably but are best seen as *performances* that can be taken up and embodied by the same person depending on the social forces operating within an institutional context

and the imaginative capabilities available to that person. I will articulate three major embodiments of knowledge: masters, mediators, and critics.

SOCIAL EMBODIMENTS OF KNOWLEDGE

Masters

> ...the secret of authority: never to disappoint. Authority has
> no other end than this: it dies or it disappoints. It is not in the
> least undermined by what others must avoid: its own despotism,
> injustice, inconsistency. On the contrary, it would be disappointing
> to observe how it arrived at its pronouncements.
> —Walter Benjamin, "Karl Kraus"

Mastery articulates an orientation toward knowledge that positions the embodied knower as possessing "total" or "comprehensive" knowledge. Other weaker versions of this claim articulate it in two ways. One version conceives of mastery as an engagement and a wrestling with what it means to grasp knowledge as a totality. Another states it as the disposition or capacities that orient one toward knowing all that it is important to know. The embodiment of knowledge as mastery has historically taken at least four forms: the transcendental master, the gnostic master, the cosmopolitan master, and the philosophic sage.

The Transcendental Master

> The free intellect will see as God might see, without a here and
> now, without hopes and fears, without the trammels of customary
> beliefs and traditional prejudices, calmly, dispassionately, in the
> sole and exclusive desire of knowledge—knowledge as impersonal,
> as purely contemplative, as it is possible for man to attain. Hence
> also the free intellect will value more the abstract and universal
> knowledge into which the accidents of private history do not enter,
> than the knowledge brought by the senses, and dependent, as such

knowledge must be, upon an exclusive and personal point of view
and a body whose sense-organs distort as much as they reveal.
—Bertrand Russell, *The Problems of Philosophy*

Transcendental mastery constructs the knower as poised on an Archimedean standpoint from which he or she possesses a commandingly sweeping view of the landscape of knowledge. The transcendentalist master is pictured as, ideally, disembodied; as pure or sheer Knowledge free of the particularities of perspective, finitude, and history; and as absolute Truth, incapable of error, doubt, or uncertainty. The transcendental master has, not *a* view, but *the* view from everywhere.

Historically, the dominant embodiment of the transcendental master is that of the theologian, priest, spiritual medium, and the *magister*. Even the "secular" transcendental master's aura is usually parasitic on religious motifs. At its normative best, the transcendental knower dazzles with sheer breadth and range in assimilating materials and subjects across specialties and guilds. The attractiveness of the epistemological theory of transcendent knowledge comes from its representational account of knowledge. It promises to lead the knower to a strategic vista, offering a wide-angled sweep of field that situates all subjects in their proper place. In the early modern period, the European *magister* sought to be a living library, a walking concordance, and a speaking thesaurus. Moreover, it is not simply that the transcendental knower possesses a treasury of seemingly limitless knowledge. At its normative best, the transcendental knower's astringent, unyielding will to know all that can be known is remorselessly sacrificial. The tradition of transcendental knowledge conceives of transcendence as mastery over not only other knowers and objects of knowledge but also the body. The transcendental master practices *askesis*, an intense program of sacrifice and renunciation that extirpates desire.[1] Indeed, many transcendental masters practice the ascetic way of life.

The ancient Egyptians articulated a conception of knowledge as transcendental mastery. At least three factors make Egyptian mastery distinctive, factors that, as we shall see below, continued to resonate in many other traditions of knowledge. First, it positioned the knowledge of the priests and the scribes as transcendent and universal. In Egyptian society, the priestly caste claimed to commune with Thoth, the divinity of wisdom and scribe of the gods. Second, for the ancient Egyptian scribes, knowledge entailed the mastery of how to live. According to Jan Assmann, what is striking about the instructions in Middle Kingdom Egyptian wisdom texts is that they "claim a general validity; they refer not to specific skills or 'tricks of the trade' but to the totality of social existence—a codification of social competence, rather than a simple prescription."[2] Egyptian knowledge was conceived of as an entry into a way of life, a practice, rather than simply the acquisition of a set of propositions. One would think that there would be a tension between the claims of universality and the initiation into a specific way of life. But these tensions were powerfully mediated by ideology: initiates believed that Egyptian education marked an inauguration into a governmental machinery that was conceived of as the center of the world. As Assmann points out, Egyptian education was the furthest thing from vulgar "political indoctrination from above." It was an education that was addressed not simply to myrmidons of the state but at the power strata of the Egyptian state: the kings and the royal elite. Some Egyptian texts speak of the work of learning as possible only for those with leisure in their hands. Its justificatory discourse was that of refinement and cultivation, and the structure of feeling within which its students experienced it was that it served as a "medium of self-illumination." It marked an induction into a specialized class within the fearsome apparatus of the Egyptian state, an induction that inculcated a very specific, very fine-grained *habitus* of mastery:

> [Egyptian] knowledge—and this is a point of cardinal importance— was not a form of specialized expertise that ensured the correct performance of administrative or religious duties. Rather, it was knowledge of the fundamental normative and formative attitudes of Egyptian culture, the acquisition of which made an apprentice scribe into an educated, well-brought-up, right-thinking Egyptian. To know these texts by heart (the Egyptian expression means literally "giving them into one's heart") was to be in possession of the basic cultural

attitudes, interpretative patterns, and value systems that constitute an "invisible religion."[3]

The third distinctive factor was that Egyptian wisdom was primarily inculcated through apprenticeship and discipleship:

> "School" in the ancient Egyptian sense was something very different from what comes to mind when we use the term today. There were no professional teachers; literacy and numeracy were acquired by apprenticeship at the centers of written culture, the major administrative offices and the temple scriptoria. Beginners received instruction in small groups; more advanced learners became assistants to high-ranking officials or priests. There were no teaching manuals. The ability to write was acquired through learning texts by rote and re-writing them from memory, pericope by pericope.[4]

Discipleship was thoroughly patriarchal insofar as schooling was characterized as a genealogical bequest, from father to son:

> The texts codifying these norms are called instructions and invariably feature a father teaching his son. The instruction is both initiatory and testamentary in character. The aged father draws together the sum of his experience and passes it on to the son. Both father and son stand at the threshold of social and vocational existence, but while the father is about to depart, the son is about to enter.[5]

It is hard to dispute the fact that the Egyptian model of knowledge as wisdom bears a weighty legacy. But the geographic regions that it most influenced as well as the precise dimensions of its influence have been matters of heated debate in the United States. Martin Bernal, drawing from decades of unrecognized and unheralded work by African and African-American scholars, has sought to show how an "ancient model" of history and memory that looked to Egypt as the template of learning and wisdom was overturned by a "new model" that declared ancient Greece as the *fons et origo* of "Western civilization."[6]

Mary Lefkowitz furiously launched a counterattack dismissing Bernal as a fraud.[7] There is no doubt that Bernal convincingly and thoroughly makes a case for the fabrication of the notion of "Western" civilization. Fueled by a variety of motives—nationalistic and imperialistic ambitions that were entangled with Egyptophobia and Judeo-phobia—the Philhellenic movement constructed an "Aryan myth" that crafted Germany as the racial heir of the ancient Greeks.[8] Where Bernal goes wrong, as the distinguished Egyptologist Jan Assmann points out, is that he takes the "old model" as fact when it too was fueled by a variety of political goals. In any case, the search for origins is deeply misplaced. Add to this that both Afrocentric Egyptophiles and "Western Civ" mythologists tend to characterize influence rather simplistically. According to these two antagonistic schools, influence simply amounts to a linear transfer of an idea or practice into another culture. Needless to say, this theory of reception and circulation mistakenly makes subjectivities one-dimensional and flattens power differences. As Edward Said has pointed out, the movement of ideas, theories, and practices "necessarily involves processes of representation and institutionalization different from those at the point of origin."[9] The conditions within which every idea or practice is received is a fraught and freighted space: when the idea is taken up, it is always transformed in some way and it often meets some form of resistance. Another dimension of the complicated forms of reception is highlighted by Assmann. He wishes to bring to attention what he calls "normative inversion," the phenomenon by which a culture abominates practices of its cultural other while appropriating and encrypting practices reviled by the enemy culture. For example, Judaic monotheism emerged, Assmann suggests, by appropriating a figure that the Egyptians loathed, the Pharaoh Akhenaten, who had attempted to destroy polytheism in Egypt.

Whatever the precise forms that Egyptian influence took, it can scarcely be doubted that a certain image of Egypt loomed large in the ancient Greek imagination. To the Greek Pythagoras, the philosopher is a "lover of wisdom," the one who contemplates the First Being—defined by Pythagoras as the number and proportion constituting the nature of all things—the one in possession of "knowledge of things beautiful, first, divine, pure, and eternal."[10] Pythagoras was here articulating a commonplace known to many of his Greek listeners. The word *theoros* initially referred to the messenger sent to consult an oracle, and *theoria* the term that city-states used to designate their ambassadors to the sacral festivals of neighboring city-states. Given that these sacral festivals occurred in the context of sports and games, *theoros* came to mean "spectator at games"; *theoria*, the observation of a spectator at these games.[11] Isokrates, the Athenian orator[12] who believed that Pythagoras brought *philosophia* [philosophy] to the Greeks from Egypt, lauds the Egyptian caste system, which, according to him, "produced the *aner theoretikos* (contemplative man), who used his superior wisdom for the good of the state. The division of labor allowed a 'leisure,' *schole*, 'which allowed for *schole*, 'learning.'"[13]

Roughly stated, Plato, Isokrates's rival, went further in developing a theory of knowledge based on the Egyptian caste system.[14] Plato distinguishes between *episteme* (true knowledge), which he considers to be absolute, universal truth, and *doxa* (opinion), which he believes to be merely concerned with particulars. *Episteme*, he argued, consisted of either *noesis*, pure reason that apprehends the Ideal Form qua Ideal Form, or *dianoia*, which refers to the cognition of pure mathematical entities. *Doxa*, on the other hand, he divides into *pistis*, belief or conviction about perceptible or empirical objects, and *eikasia*, cognitions about images or likenesses of perceptible or empirical objects. According to Plato, whereas *episteme*, in the form of *noesis*, proceeds from *archai* (originals; first principles), *doxa* on the other hand merely traffics in appearances. It is only in seeing the Idea or Form in itself that one comes to the state of knowledge (*gnosis*).[15] Based on this typology, Plato made a case for an ideal republic ruled by Guardians, those who possess *sophia* (wisdom or philosophical knowledge). In his own time, Plato was harshly critical of the sophists, rhetoricians who he claimed purveyed mere *doxa* without regard for moral virtue.[16]

Aristotle, Plato's pupil, elaborated on and often subtly transformed his teacher's model. Though it would not be possible to exhaustively document every permutation in Aristotle's complex account of knowledge, at least three deserve notice: *Sophia, praxis,* and *poesis*. Aristotle believed that the highest form of knowledge was philosophical wisdom (*sophia*).[17] He characterized *sophia* as universal and exact or precise knowledge; the type of knowledge that was of the greatest difficulty to master, by virtue of being the furthest from the senses; and was, moreover, the clearest, given that it lent itself to the greatest intelligibility of things.[18] For Aristotle, *sophia* was not properly speaking even "human," since the *nous*—through which *sophia* was reached—entered human beings from outside the body and thus was a participation in the divine.[19] Aristotle further distinguished two components of *sophia*: knowledge about the nature of first principles—*nous*—and the knowledge of logically establishing these first principles—*episteme*.[20] He defined *episteme* as knowledge of the syllogistic form required for the establishment of first principles (*archai*) or causes (*aitiai*). Aristotle goes on, in the *Nicomachean Ethics*, to speak on virtue (*arête*). He distinguishes between two intellectual virtues. The first is theoretical wisdom (*sophia*), which is concerned with "unchanging realities" and, he says, consists of knowledge of "the highest good in all of nature." The second is practical wisdom (*phronesis*), which is deliberation aimed at acting well in particular circumstances.

Praxis is another major activity that Aristotle highlights. Praxis referred to political activity, activities that Aristotle considered to be uncertain, particular, and contingent, lacking in the precision, universality, and eternity of *sophia*.[21] Thus, for Aristotle, *praxis* required *phronesis*—practical reasoning in the contingent, uncertain situations faced by the citizen of the *polis*. Lastly, *poesis* referred to purposeful action geared toward the production or making of a thing. Unlike praxis, which according to Aristotle did not produce an "object" and thus simply involved *doing, poesis* was aimed at a particular end (*telos*)—the making of a particular product.[22] *Poesis*, according to Aris-totle, required *techne* (art). Aristotle conceives of *techne* as a "trained ability of rationally producing," that is, the art of how to make particular things as is required in specialized crafts such as building houses. In the *Rhetoric*, Aristotle makes note of two forms of *techne* that do not have a subject of their own but rather are methods that can be applied to a wide variety of subjects: rhetoric and dialectic.

As Lobkowicz has shown, Aristotle's distinctions were highly specific to particular people within the Athenian city-state. He was unconcerned with *nomos*, the hard labor, toil, distress, suffering, and sickness that he considered as characteristic of the lives led by the *polloi kai phortikotatoi*, the multitude and the most vulgar.[23] Aristotle dismissed such lives as unworthy of attention because they were pursued merely "for the sake of the necessities of life."[24] He was referring, here, to slaves, fully half the inhabitants of his city-state, who carried out all the hard manual labor in the *polis*, and foreigners, who were more often than not artisans, merchants, and retailers. Both these groups were not considered citizens in Aristotle's city-state; foreigners were able to secure their legal status as free persons only by paying a special tax. Thus, when Aristotle opposed *episteme* to *praxis*, he was addressing only the citizens of the Athenian city-state, the *charientes*— the men of refinement. For according to Aristotle and the city-state elite, only these people were "truly human," since they were by nature in possession of *logos*, reason as demonstrated by a person's ability to engage in articulate speech.[25] And just as there were some who were naturally refined, so Aristotle believed that others are *phusei douloi*, natural slaves, "ensouled tools" much like "domestic animals."[26] Similarly, foreigners—branded "barbarians" because of their "bar . . . bar . . . bar . . ." speech patterns[27]—were dismissed by Aristotle as having the same nature as slaves. Only the military and deliberative classes were "truly men," that is, had "full humanity." They were thus specially fitted for citizenship because they occupy the realm of freedom—this meant, above all, that they were free from the necessities of life and from menial occupations. Aristotle well recognized that this freedom stemmed directly from the enslavement and menial work performed by others: he argued, in a telling passage, against the granting of citizenship to artisans, even though during his time Greek-born artisans were already citizens, for this would mean "that the 'citizens virtue'—that is, his being capable of participating in the government—would not belong to every citizen; only those released from the *erga anagkaia*, from necessary and menial occupations, have the leisure required for governing."[28] Nor did Aristotle deem the gender category of "women" as epistemologically reliable. As far as he was concerned, women were imperfect or deformed versions of men, "more prone to despondency and less hopeful than the man, more void of shame, more false of speech, more deceptive."[29]

It is in this context that the special place claimed by Pythagoras and Aristotle for *philosophoi* should be understood. Taking their departure from the hallowed place accorded to political activity by the Athenian city-state elite, they argued that the benefits of political activities not only were found in philosophical contemplation as well, but were found there in far superior forms:

> For example, contemplation had to be described as less tiring and therefore more "continuous" than politics: no one could be expected to till the ground as intensively and incessantly as he discussed and argued at the Assembly; but contemplation could be carried on even more continuously. Or again, contemplation was an activity least similar to and least involved with activities related to the necessities of life: while certainly both the philosopher and the political man required the necessities of life, the philosopher, unlike the politician, did not need other men and therefore was the least dependent of all— the man most sufficient in himself (*antarkestatos*). Or again, politics presupposed leisure from the procurement of the necessities of life. Already Plato had said that a business is not disposed to wait until the businessmen is at leisure. Aristotle had no difficulty in convincing his hearers that political business was at least as unleisured as menial occupations. In any case, contemplation certainly required a greater leisure than politics.[30]

For Pythagoras, the philosopher is the "truly free man": "he is free of the unrest and the agitation of those who yearn for money or fame. In a similar way the philosopher is removed from the agitation and transitory character which life has for ordinary man: he contemplates the divine order and takes part in its eternity, thus somehow succeeding in transcending what the Greeks experienced as man's most distinctive character, his 'mortality.'"[31]

In modern African intellectual circles, one of the most prominent transcendental masters is the theologian and philosopher John S. Mbiti. Mbiti's *African Religions and Philosophy* (1969) is an astonishing achievement, the conclusion of a herculean study of the different varieties of religious traditions across the entirety of the African continent.

In this book, Mbiti seeks to free African traditional religions from European colonial condescension as "heathenish" or "savage" religions. But he does so by portraying pre-Christian and pre-colonial African traditional religions as *Praeparatio Evangelica*, that is, as worldviews that were always already seeded by the Christian God to prepare the way for the missionizing of the continent to the one true religion—Christianity.[32] Mbiti's implausible theory was subjected to multiple critiques. But as befitting his cultivation of the transcendental master, he often did not deign to respond to criticism. One of his fiercest critics, the Kenyan philosopher Odera Oruka, who launched several devastating critiques of Mbiti's arguments, never got so much as the satisfaction of an acknowledgment.[33]

But if transcendental mastery promises remarkable gains in knowledge, it also likely yields spectacular error and ethically disastrous intellectual dispositions. Perhaps one of the most pernicious aspects of transcendental mastery is its consecration of the notion of the knower as "chosen" (religion) or as genius (philosophy and art). It willfully ignores the social basis that undergirds the formation of the master and the bodies upon which the master trundles over in pursuit of disembodiment. The social theorist Pierre Bourdieu has done more than anybody else to strip away the illusion upon which this myth has been constructed:

> *Khâgne* [the preparatory training for the entrance examinations for the *grandes écoles*] was the site where French-style intellectual ambition in its most elevated, that is to say, philosophical, form was exhibited. The total intellectual, the model of which had just been invented and imposed by Sartre, was called for by a curriculum which offered a vast range of disciplines—philosophy, literature, history, ancient and modern languages—and which, through its training in the dissertation *de omni re scibili* (as Durkheim put it), the keystone of the whole edifice, encouraged a self-confidence often verging on the unself-consciousness of triumphant ignorance. Belief in the omnipotence of rhetorical invention could only be encouraged by crafted, theatricalized exhibitions of philosophical improvisation.[34]

Bourdieu pithily captures the self-reinforcing nature of this system: "One became a 'philosopher' because one had been consecrated and one consecrated oneself by securing the prestigious identity of 'philosopher.' The choice of philosophy was thus a manifestation of status-based assurance which reinforced that status-based assurance (or arrogance)."[35] Transcendental mastery derives its institutional power through the generation of two types of intellectual figures: the disciple and the ignorant. Disciples and converts make up the retinue of conscripted surrogates through which the master's teachings are disseminated and through which the legend is constructed. The ignorant are often constructed in animalistic imagery and are always represented in quantities or large numbers—thus, for example, "the ignorant herd," "flock," "masses," "crowd," and the "mob." The ignorant function both as a warning to the disciple not to become one of "them" and as a mission for evangelizing and conversion. The upshot, then, is that the aura that the transcendental master enjoys is institutional; stripped of these, his charisma shrivels to an oddly bathetic shadow, as is amusingly and strikingly illustrated by George Eliot's oddly pitiable Casaubon and his promised (re)search for a mythological key.

The Gnostic Master

> The secret gives one a position of exception; it operates as a
> purely socially determined attraction. It is basically independent
> of the context it guards but, of course, is increasingly effective
> in the measure in which the exclusive possession of it is vast and
> significant. . . . From secrecy, which shades all that is profound
> and significant, grows the typical error according to which
> everything mysterious is something important and essential.
> Before the unknown, man's natural impulse to idealize and his
> natural fearfulness cooperate toward the same goal: to intensify the
> unknown through imagination, and to pay attention to it with an
> emphasis that is not usually accorded to patent reality.
> —Georg Simmel, "The Secret and the Secret Society"

Gnostic mastery references a knower's claim to the possession of *gnosis* or secret knowledge. Whereas *gnosis* has a long history as one of the most potent weapons deployed by the transcendental *magister*, claims to *gnosis* subtly differ from the warrants marshaled by transcendental masters. The transcendental master asserts a claim over *all* knowledges, whereas the gnostic master lays claim *only* to particular, esoteric forms of knowledge, which he or she claims as the "essence" or the "real" knowledge. The transcendental master often grants that other knowers have knowledge—though in his view their knowledge remains partial and limited in contrast to his own synoptic view—whereas the gnostic master is often in the business of delegitimizing other knowledges as false, irrelevant, frivolous. The religious versions of *gnosis* tend to hold that it is some form of "revelation" vouchsafed only to the master. In their secular forms, *gnosis* is often claimed as based on the master's possession of capacities and powers to unlock linguistic, theoretical, or experiential codes that no one else can make available.

From the early modern period within the North Atlantic tradition, claims to *gnosis* have often been marked by a notable double-headedness. On the one hand, many scholars in this tradition have laid claim, albeit in different idioms, to being privy to "secret" or "special" knowledge that no one else is privy to. But on the other hand, this has also often been accompanied by the claim that the knowledge they possess is "self-evident," "commonsensical," and "universal." Descartes, for example, lays claim to "clear and distinct" knowledge even as he frames his narrative in classically *gnostic* forms. His claims to the instauration of a new basis for knowledge come to him in a dream revelation that he receives "in a state of divine exaltation, inspiration, or possession."[36] He conveys the apocalyptic momentousness of his project by invoking the purification, the purging necessary before the instauration: "As regards all the opinions which up to this time I had embraced, I thought I could not do better than endeavor once and for all to sweep them completely away, so that they might later on be replaced, either by others which were better, or by the same, when I had made them conform to the uniformity of a rational scheme."[37] As Michael Keefer reports, citing Descartes' first biographer Adrien Baillet, this involved going through excruciating pain: "He had no less to suffer than if it had been a matter of stripping away his very self."[38] Descartes has three dreams in which, among other things, he is assailed by the ghosts of his demonic body, driven into a church by an evil demon, and eventually discovers a poem that he interprets as heralding the joining of "Philosophy and Wisdom."[39] The double-movement between claims to openness and claims to *gnosis* would be repeated during the Scottish Enlightenment. No one was more bullish than the Scottish *literati* in the invocation of "commonsense." Even so, as George C. Caffentzis has pointed out, an often overlooked aspect of David Hume's social theory is his emphasis on "secrecy" and "invisibility" as a potent tactic for the transmission of the Scottish Enlightenment.[40] And so the same with Hegel, who talked of a "still and secret" revolution of human ideas and attitudes while at the same time proclaiming that "there is no longer anything secret in God."[41]

It is arguable, nevertheless, that no one quite performed the role of the gnostic master as Heidegger.[42] In his book *Being and Time*, Heidegger argued that philosophy should be the "torch bearer" of the sciences insofar as it was only philosophy that was an "ontological science," or a "science of being."[43] In other words, while the other sciences merely presupposed the being of the class of entities studied, it was philosophy that studied Being as such. Heidegger argued that the sciences were based on a cluster of "regional ontologies" that failed to really penetrate into "fundamental ontology." In *Being and Time*, he issued forth a call for a "deconstruction" (*Destruktion*) of the history of ontology so as to discover the "fundamental ontology" that had underpinned and given shape to all knowledge in the history of the "West." Heidegger conceives of his philosophical task as "unveiling" this concealed truth.

For all of Heidegger's belief that he was single-handedly correcting the trajectory of knowledge that had been in place for millennia, he indulges one of the most dominant *mythoi* of North Atlantic philosophical discourse—to wit, the conviction that philosophy is the "queen of the sciences," at whose heel all other knowledges lie prostrate. It is redundant to spell out the self-serving interests subtending the belief: if philosophy is the "queen of the sciences," the *gnostic* master is the sovereign of all knowledges. As political turmoil roiled Germany in the wake of the Nazi power grab, Heidegger got an opportunity to enact his vision for radical university reform. In his inaugural Rectoral address as the *Fuhrer-Rektor* of Freiburg University, Heidegger outlined his plans for the reshaping of university departmental divisions and the subordination of the university to the Nazi political program. It was not to be. His manifesto for a "conservative revolution"[44] was shattered—at least politically—by the emergence of new configurations of power in the wake of World War II.[45]

North Atlantic postmodern *gnostics* added an interesting twist to the idea of *gnosis*. On the one hand, postmodern theorists stridently attacked and repudiated the concept of *gnosis*. Many postmodern theorists claimed to shift their emphasis to "surfaces" and "depthlessness." This was part of a broader movement that included an attack on the Marxist hermeneutic of depth. For Jacques Lacan, any claim to causal factors spoke to a futile desire for a phantasmic unity. For Derrida, not even Lacan is untainted by the metaphysics of essentialism. Even to claim that there such a thing as an economy of desire, a trajectory within which it circulates, means that one is subject to the fantasy of truth as "adequation."[46] But if the postmodern masters repudiated *gnosis*, this did not mean that *gnosis* repudiated them. For one, their dismissals were couched in a baroque idiom that only initiates were thought to be capable of grasping. Derrida's dazzling pirouette is instructive. Having scoffed at all attempts at the interpretation of meaning as covert essentialist appeals to objective truth, he then reasserts a fideistic, tragic account of truth—which, for all its agonizing, portrays truth in strikingly monolithic terms: "Paraphrasing Freud, speaking of the present/absent penis (but it is the same thing), we must recognize in truth 'the normal prototype of the fetish.' How can we do without it?"[47]

Gnosis has had just as vexed a history in Africa as it has had in other polities. The most prominent account of gnosis has been advanced by the Congolese philosopher and philologist, V. Y. Mudimbe. For Mudimbe, such was the comprehensive colonization of African practices and mentalities by the "West" that one can no longer speak of actually existing African philosophies. Those discourses that circulate as "African knowledges" are no more than mimetic reflections of European "philosophies of conquest."[48]

The fact of the matter is that, until now, Western interpreters as well as African analysts have been using categories and conceptual sys-tems which depend on a Western epistemological order. Even in the most explicitly "Afrocentric" descriptions, models of analysis explicitly or implicitly, knowingly or unknowingly, refer to the same order. Does this mean that African *Weltanschauungen* and African traditional sys-tems of thought are unthinkable and cannot be made explicit within the framework of their own rationality? My own claim is that thus far the ways in which they have been evaluated and the means used to explain them relate to theories whose constraints, rules, and systems of operations suppose a non-African epistemological locus.[49]

In a sequel to *The Invention of Africa*, Mudimbe vigorously elabo-rated on his views in a book entitled *The Idea of Africa*: "Yet the fact is there: African discourses have been silenced radically or, in most cases, converted by conquering Western discourses."[50] Mudimbe char-acterizes African knowledges as *gnosis*, a secret wisdom that always already eludes Western representation. But the premise with which Mudimbe engages his study—the idea of a monolithic "West" that sup-posedly extends from Herodotus onward—is deeply flawed. It pre-supposes a static notion of context and it concedes, rather than chal-lenges, spurious claims to the *ownership* of certain knowledges—science or the humanities—by the dominant ruling classes in the G8 economies. Moreover, Mudimbe's epistemological assumptions are problematic. He characterizes *gnostic* knowledges as indigenous conceptual sys-tems, but by doing so radically presupposes a deeply idealistic, even divinized, ethereal, and mystical account of knowledge. It remains unclear why Mudimbe thinks *gnostic* knowledge is more significant than ordinary empirical knowledges, or why artistic and performative knowledges emergent from Africa are any less "real" than *gnosis*. Mu-dimbe seems to straddle the contradictory forces of anti-modernism and postmodern *gnosis*. His *The Idea of Africa* echoes with a Heideg-gerian threnody for Africa's lost Being. At the same time, like Derrida, he writes in a style befitting the gnostic master. His prose is unremit-tingly obscure and impenetrably muddy.

Where Mudimbe is satisfied with existential gestures of despair,[51] Andrew Apter has endeavored to make a case for forms of *gnostic* mastery in African contexts. Apter argues that Yoruba cosmology and ritual is a revolutionary form of critical practice. Yoruba ritual, he claims, has deep symbolic and material dimensions. These rituals generate revisionary modes of consciousness and enable participants to challenge authority structures:

> The most basic opposition in Yoruba cosmology is between official, public discourse about the world and "deep knowledge" [*imo jinle*]: that which is hidden, and powerful, and protected. It is more a pragmatic than semantic opposition, since it marks restricted access to powerful truths while stipulating nothing about their content. Those who have deep knowledge—priests [*aworo*] and priestesses [*olorisa*], diviners [*babalawo*] and herbalists [*onisegun*]—are initiated into the secrets [*awo*] of their work and are trained for years in esoteric techniques. They can detect witches, cure infertility, recall the past, influence the future, and empower chiefs and kings. They have protected the community from imminent disasters by converting into concrete community gains the dangerous potentials of missionaries and colonial administrators; in recent times, the threats from party politicians and military regimes are just as real, and communities look to those with deep knowledge for the same kind of protection.[52]

Apter articulates two levels at which *gnosis* is enacted. The surface or public level occurs in festivals of deities. In these festivals, *gnostic* knowledges are legitimated, interpreted and made intelligible:

> Bodies personal and social receive the powers of *orisa* to cure infertility, thwart witchcraft, guarantee abundant harvests and commercial success, and reinvest the king with *ase*—the power to rule effectively and issue commands over others. Modeled on the logic of social exchange, the *orisa* is fed with sacrifices, glorified with praise [*oriki*], and invoked in the bush, where its dangerous powers are enlisted and embodied by priestesses, contained in calabashes and bottles that are

balanced on their heads, and carried through the town to the palace and central shrines where they are "cooled" and "delivered" on behalf of the king and his subjects.[53]

But it is beneath this surface level at which a critical practice unfolds:

> The work of ritual is one of passage: from the bush into the town, from the old year to the new, from a polluted to a purified condition. In the liminal moments of this passage—crossing thresholds, bringing the deities into the town, and investing the king's body with the *orisa*'s power—the authoritative taxonomies of the natural and social world are erased and reconfigured. It is here, in the forbidden discourses of deep cosmological knowledge (which allow a free play of signifiers and celebrate the arbitrariness of the sign) that priestesses become kings (wearing royal icons and addressed as "*Kabiyesi*," "Your Highness"), unleash their witchcraft, and negate the king with rival historical memories that dismember his sovereignty into multiple dynastic claims. Only after such contact with the *orisa*, the king, thus empowered, is "re-membered" with official history. In brief, the king—indeed the whole body politic—is ritually deconstructed and selectively reconstructed; hegemony is thereby unmade and remade. The point I wish to emphasize is that the status quo is revised and, when conditions are right, even radically transformed.[54]

If Apter is manifestly right in arguing that Yoruba ritual is as much a critical practice as those that are currently dominant across the world—for example, the ritual practices that are currently enacted in North American universities—such a comparison also offers reasons why, nonetheless, it falls short of a *radical* critical practice. Yoruba ritual may lead to significant changes in who holds power, but it remains committed to arbitrary institutional hierarchies. Power is still held by a coterie, and where it allows for challenging official discourses, this is vitiated by its rhetoric of "protectionism," "paternalism," "purity," and "sacrifice." Its epistemological practices—insofar as they conceive of knowledge in essentially religious and mystical terms—only further mystifies that institutional power.

The Cosmopolitan Master

> Whoever hasn't yet arrived at the clear realization that there might
> be a greatness existing entirely outside his own sphere and for
> which he might have absolutely no feeling; whoever hasn't at least
> felt obscure intimations concerning the approximate location of
> this greatness in the geography of the human spirit: that person
> either has no genius in his own sphere, or else he hasn't been
> educated yet to the niveau of the classic.
> —Friedrich Schlegel, *Critical Fragments*

Cosmopolitan mastery constructs the embodied knower as possessing
multiple cultural perspectives. It is powered primarily by a moral commitment to a humanistic value system. It sees as its *telos* the promotion of human comity. Toward that end, the cosmopolitan master sees
world travel as a virtue insofar as it allows him or her to appreciate diverse ways of living. This value system supports congeries of tightly-
woven epistemological virtues: curiosity, open-mindedness, unpreju-
diced observation. The cosmopolitan sees himself as having mastered,
and therefore transcended, the entanglements of locality, nation, or
way of life.

Most self-described cosmopolitans look to the ancient Greek
Cynics as their intellectual forebears.[55] These claims notwithstanding,
however, the institutional and structural formation of the cosmopolitan is likely emergent from processes of embourgeoisement that took
place from the Italian Renaissance down through to the Prussian Enlightenment. This period witnessed the emergence of a mercantile and
professional class invested in the trafficking of commodities across the
world—including the commodification of humans as slaves. It is this
global market that gave rise to a self-conscious strata of scholars and
intellectuals dedicated to offering comparative assessments across cultures, "races," and nations. The initial articulation of the "bourgeois"
in the early modern period received its meaning from the "estates"
or "orders" from which it notionally contrasted itself.[56] Looking up-
ward, it distanced itself from the *aristocratic* and the *feudal* in one direction and the *clergy* and the *religious* in the other direction. Looking

horizontally, it contrasted itself with the *bohemian* and *artistic*. Looking downward, it opposed the *radical* and the *revolutionary*. Against these groups, it leveled both moral and epistemological critiques. It not only opposed the aristocracy because its privileges accrued from assertions of bloodlines and nature rather than capital and work, but also opposed its investment in nonutilitarian values of martial honor. Instead of honor, the bourgeoisie put forward respectability and reputation, both of which were tied (if not always explicitly) to a person's credit-rating. Against the clergy, it charged that the privileges it claimed to derive from a transcendent metaphysical were illegitimate. The bourgeois were also hostile to the clergy's proclamations of values that outstripped the "canons of quotidian rationality."[57] Raymond Geuss succinctly summarizes the bourgeois *habitus*:

> an Order like the bourgeoisie, which is devoted to peaceful, systematically organized commerce, requires a world that is stable, "disenchanted," secure, unchanging in its basic structure, surveyable and analyzable, and about which it is possible to make reliable predictions. In contast to the mercurial temperament of the aristocrat who wagers all on the outcome of a single battle or a throw of the dice, and to the otherworldly faith of the clergy, the bourgeois is sober, orderly, moderate, calculating, utilitarian, but has a characteristically distorted temporal horizon, being oriented toward the acquisition of objects of solid value in the short- and medium-term future, but relatively unconcerned with the distant past, the fleeting moment, or an eschatological world-to-come. In strong contrast to the official ideology of the clerical establishment, the bourgeois is actively and intensely engaged in this-worldly transactions in a manner which in practice *at the very least* shows no fundamental disgust at these activities, taking them as if participation in them did not require special justification. The characteristically bourgeois attitude toward this world and its objects is deeply *affirmative*.[58]

If bourgeois opposition to the aristocracy and the clergy was directed at entrenched estates that were relatively well defined, its opposition to the bohemian and the radical was far murkier, less a matter of principle and clear-cut propositions than a matter of olfactory, en-zymatic reactions. The bourgeoisie find bohemians distasteful because they give off the whiff of "disrespectability" (and, perhaps, far worse, seem indifferent to the reputational economy prized by the bourgeoi-sie). The bohemian's abandonment to immediate gratification, their Dionysian revelry, and their aesthetics of display, appearance, and per-formance are offensive to the bourgeoisie's commitment to profes-sional propriety, civil exchange, and family-appropriate fun.

As to the radical, the part that they play in the bourgeois imagina-tion is even more vexed than that of the bohemian. On the one hand the bourgeois is committed to criticism of aristocratic and clerical privi-lege. On the other hand, once their preferred system gained hegemony, the bourgeois came to think of its basic structure as fundamentally sound. All that remained was continual negotiation over procedural matters and debates over whether this or that individual right deserved inclusion in the penumbra of state-recognized statutes. For the bour-geois then criticism is properly directed at reforms of the system:

> the whole idea of putting "critique" or "criticism" of a restricted kind into the center of human attention was itself an integral part of the bourgeois project. A feudal lord or a high cleric did not "criticize": the lord originally used his fist or sword, or, later, appealed to "tradition" or to the inborn tact and judgment of the gentleman, who knew what was required in every situation without necessarily being able even to say beforehand what that was; the cleric appealed to faith, the consen-sus of the Church Fathers, or the decision of the Pope. Commitment to "criticism" (of a further undefined sort) was therefore not in itself in any sense a commitment to leave the comfortable world which the bourgeoisie had made for itself. "Criticism," after all, was the watch-word and main tool of that arch-bourgeois figure, the Encyclopedist.[59]

Geuss concludes that bourgeois thought is marked by two char-acteristics: first, "a commitment to the existence of a clear, well-grounded, secure or certain, instrumentally useful kind of knowl-edge"; and, second, "a basic commitment to a positive solution to the problem of theodicy . . . , i.e., commitment to the view that it is possible to demonstrate discursively that the world as a whole is rational, good, and basically comformable to human interests, needs, aspirations, so that we should 'warmly embrace' and affirm it."[60]

No African philosopher, for good and ill, has so effortlessly cultivated the figure of the cosmopolitan master than Kwame Anthony Appiah. At his best, there are few living philosophers who can speak to as many constituencies with such fluency in their own languages as Appiah is able to. His discursive style is engaging, perhaps as befits an avid promoter of "conversation" across differences, and he charms even when discoursing on the recondite and the recherché. In his book *In My Father's House* (1992) Appiah is concerned to articulate a pan-African identity that is not based on a mythical racial foundation. Instead, he argues for a cosmopolitan notion of identity based on rational solving of Africa's problems. By rational problem-solving, he is referring to the abandonment in Africa of a belief in the "ontology of invisible things," by which he means beliefs in spirits, for what he takes to be a belief in science. Appiah believes that the absence of a scientific conception of reality in Africa can be attributed to the lack of literacy on the continent. Noting the progress of literacy rates on the continent, Appiah urges what he calls the new "generations of literate African intellectuals" to examine and analyze African traditions and produce "new, unpredictable, fusions" of knowledge.[61]

Even in this early book, many of the limitations that have attended much of Appiah's intellectual work are fully apparent. There are, to begin with, Appiah's Whiggish historiographical assumptions that posit literacy as a sleek vehicle towards the sunlit uplands of scientific and moral progress. He patronizingly urges African intellectuals to be tutored in the ways of the modern world: "we [Africans] have the great advantage of having before us the European and American—and the Asian and Latin American—experiments with modernity to ponder as we make our choices."[62] The implication is, of course, that other continents are modern while Africa remains "traditional." But what is most telling about Appiah's book is his conception of the political as essentially consisting of technical problems, as a matter for suitably educated technocrats to puzzle over and solve. Thus, there is little engagement with the historical gravity within which particular problems emerge and are contested, little understanding of the fact that many of the deep conflicts in Africa are powered by radically different *interests*, far more than by a lack of education or a simple matter of conceptual confusions.

As Timothy Brennan has argued, for one to really get a grasp of cosmopolitanism, it is imperative to move beyond the formal list of positive cognitive values it espouses. Rather, "one's judgment of cosmopolitanism's value or desirability . . . is affected by whose cosmopolitanism or patriotism one is talking about—whose definitions of prejudice, knowledge, or open-mindedness one is referring to."[63] Appiah's list of prejudices turn out to be a rather predictable list of what one would expect of a bourgeois cosmopolitan living in the United States in the twenty-first century. He thinks Judaism makes Zionism a plausible and realistic candidate "for a common and non-racial focus [of] nationalism," but thinks this cannot be made "plausible in the case of pan-Africanism."[64] What is problematic about this is *not* Appiah's case against the strains of racialism that did exist in certain streams of the pan-African movement, but Appiah's remarkable, taken-for-granted moral deference to Zionist settler-colonialism and his erasure of Palestinians.[65] His critique of pan-Africanism, moreover, is highly selective and distorted. Appiah's critique myopically focuses on selected individual thinkers and fails to engage with Pan-Africanism as a historical and institutional movement. In doing so, Appiah does not account for many trajectories within Pan-Africanism that self-consciously repudiated racialism. As Archie Mafeje points out, in a brilliant coruscation of revisionist attempts to tar Pan-Africanism as racist *tout court,* the history of Pan-Africanism involved deep forms of solidarity across race, including the establishment of non-racial institutions of learning such as the respected Council for the Development of Social Science Research in Africa (CODESRIA). States Mafeje:

> It is, therefore, surprising that all of a sudden a long-standing member of CODESRIA, Mahmoud Romdhane, finds it necessary to make apologies for being a "non-black African." Is he afflicted by social amnesia or has he been infected by a new virus in CODESRIA? If so, it is well to remind him not only did he become a *bona fide* member

of CODESRIA but that the issues he is raising had long been resolved before his time. If he did not know, CODESRIA was founded by North Africans led by Samir Amin as a Pan-Africanist organisation. The sub-Saharan Africans took the latter at face-value and embraced CODES-RIA with both hands and became its backbone. Although latter-day reactionaries tried to introduce "race" in the organisation by making references to strange notions such as "Arabophone," in CODESRIA circles North Africans were referred to as such. This was consistent with the division of Africa into four sub-regions—West, North, East, and Southern Africa for purposes of representation. Not only this, if Romdhan's memory is failing him, it is well to remember that the North Africans played a very prominent role in the formation of the OAU [Organisation of African Unity]. Such figures as Gamal Abdel Nasser and Ahmed Ben Bella became shining symbols of the Pan-Africanist movement and to this day nobody in his/her right sense could question their Africanity. In passing it is also worth noting that during the Congo crisis in 1960 that led to Lumumba's assassination, his sons were immediately given permanent custody by an Egyptian family, "black" as they might have been. Wherefore, pathetic and tendentious responses from old colleagues such as Romdhane, who should know better, are to be regretted. In contrast, novices such as Achille Mbembe who believe that "Pan-Africanism defines the native and the citizen by identifying them with black people" are to be forgiven for they know not.[66]

The Philosophic Sage

> My propositions serve as elucidations in the following way: anyone who understands me eventually recognizes them as nonsensical, when he has used them—as steps—to climb up beyond them. (He must, so to speak, throw away the ladder after he climbed up to it.) He must transcend these propositions, and then he will see the world aright.
>
> —Ludwig Wittgenstein, *Tractatus Logico-Philosophicus*

If transcendental and cosmopolitan mastery are intent on the mastery of knowledge, philosophic sagaciousness is the project of seeking an epistemology of the loss of mastery. It describes epistemological practices that are keyed to responsive living and thinking with and through limits and limitations. Limits and limitations of what? Of epistemological practices that aim at a once and for all mastery—for example, that claim to have identified the essence of a concept, meaning, or practice that transcends history and context; that claim to transcend embodiment; that disavow perspective-taking and, with that, any notion of social differences. A key beginning to such epistemological ways of living and knowing is a critique of both modern and postmodern approaches to limits. The modernist Kantian project is aimed at identifying a priori limits, that is, those that are universal and necessary. But to begin by arguing a priori that there exist certain specific limits to an activity or concept or language is to already demarcate what the precise boundaries of the limits are. In that sense, Kant's delineation of limits is itself a certain kind of attempt at (bad faith) mastery. The postmodern Foucaultian project, on the other hand, seeks to transgress the limits deemed universal and necessary by Kant:

> if the Kantian question was that of knowing what limits knowledge has to renounce transgressing, it seems to me that the critical question today has to be turned back into a positive one: in what is given to us as universal, necessary, obligatory, what place is occupied by whatever is singular, contingent, and the product of arbitrary constraints? The point, in brief, is to transform the critique conduced in the form of necessary limitation into a practical critique that takes the form of possible transgression.[67]

But Foucault's project of transgression still works within the terms set by Kant. And to that extent, it remains deeply beholden to mastery.

Against these two projects, philosophic sagacity conceives of its goal as a responsiveness to the epistemology of limits—precisely as a practice, rather than as a project that *pictures* or *represents* those limits. There is therefore something profoundly paradoxical about sagacious mastery. It results in a double movement: on the one hand, it makes epistemic demands that the knower *masters* a certain body of knowledge—language, methods, arguments, propositions, and so on.

But on the other hand, having used the ladder to climb to a certain epistemic height, it insists that the knower resolutely kicks the ladder, throws it away. The metaphor of the ladder is of course drawn from Wittgenstein, who models the practice of sagacious mastery. Wittgenstein indicates the extent to which we are enthralled by a certain picture of knowledge. But in coming to a realization of our thralldom, it is not that we are then to transgress the picture à la Foucault, but rather to realize that "what lies on the other side of the limit will be simply nonsense."[68] The precise sense of what it means to master an epistemic practice or climb to an epistemic height is itself radically put in question.[69]

I would argue that it is this practice of philosophic sagacity that is embodied in the work of the Kenyan philosopher Odera Oruka. Oruka is widely recognized as the founder of the sage philosopher project, a program in philosophical research aimed at identifying embodiments of wisdom in communities across the African continent. He explained his motivations thus:

> In this concern one of our major aims was to help substantiate or disprove the well-known claim that real philosophical thought had no place in traditional Africa. Implied in this claim is that any existence of philosophy in modern Africa is due wholly to the introduction of the Western thought and culture to Africa. If we could find sages [that exhibit second-order philosophic thought] in traditional Africa then this fact should amount to a proof for the invalidity of the claim in question.[70]

There is no doubt that Oruka started his project in the grip of a picture theory that asserted the existence of an essential Platonic-ideal of the "philosopher": "A person who makes a wise statement can be challenged to justify it. He can also be requested to apply it in practice. If the person has a philosophic frame of mind, he will no doubt be able to offer some rational answer to the challenge. If he lacks this gift, he is likely to offer an unimpressive answer or even refuse to give an answer."[71] I have previously proffered a comprehensive critique of the falsities that attend Oruka's transcendental picture of philosophy.[72]

Nonetheless, I am persuaded by students of the sage philosophy project who argue that while Oruka initially articulated an unyielding conception of the philosopher as Platonic genius, his notion about what constituted philosophy—and philosophers—changed with his engagement of actually existing sage philosophers. F. Ochieng-Odhiambo for example has argued that Oruka's thought evolved from an uncompromising hostility to ethnophilosophy, where his favored term for describing his project was "philosophic sagacity," to a much more accommodating stance, where he preferred using the term "sage philosophy" to describe his project.[73]

Oruka's account of sagacious mastery involves at least three acknowledgments—acknowledgments because they run athwart the transcendental picture that transfixed him as he set out on his sage philosophy project. The first is Oruka's acknowledgment of the *temporal* in the articulation of philosophy; specifically, how the temporal inflects the veritistic value of knowledge. According to Gail Presbey, Oruka's work is significantly marked by an interest in the futural—described as a sense of what the future will be like given major structural stratifications, behavioral dispositions, and the ethical stances we ought to take in light of our knowledge of future states.[74] But precisely because the future is open to possibility rather than brute necessity, Oruka conceives of knowledge in this realm as contingent. As Presbey puts it, Oruka "did not consider himself a soothsayer or even a scientific know-it-all. He humbly stated that, despite his membership in World Futures Studies Federation, 'we can only guess but we cannot rightly claim to know' what the future centuries hold."[75]

The second acknowledgment is Oruka's articulation of the *diversity of epistemological practices*. Against the notion that only propositional knowledge counts, he states: "There is a tendency to treat a Greek sage such as Heraclitus as a philosopher but to deny the label to an African sage such as Mbuya Akoko. The African sage is seen as a mere peasant storyteller. Philosophy may indeed employ stories, poetry or oracles. Indeed, Heraclitus, the dialectician, and Parmenides, the founder of abstract logic in the West, expressed their philosophies using oracular epigram, epic poem and storytelling."[76] Oruka often indicated a disposition that was not so much multidisciplinary as critical of demarcations of knowledge. Multidisciplinarity, after all, leaves the disciplines just as they are, only with a greater exchange of correspondence between colleagues, while Oruka's critical posture radically questions the very basis of these distinctions:

> The normative role [of the sagacious philosopher] is very important. Indeed it is this normative aspect of philosophy which differentiates what I would call the sage proper from the mere philosopher. The mere philosopher, one could call him a scientist of the mere thought in a broad sense, he looks for thought, he looks for principles that guide nature, for principles that guide society, he looks for knowledge. The mere philosopher looks for pure knowledge and tries to express knowledge, but the sage cares about knowledge, and he adds to knowledge morality, the moral spirit. He aims at the ethical betterment of the community that he lives in. So, to me, the sage has these two policies: he has the science, the knowledge, plus ethical obligation for himself, for the community and for the world.[77]

The third acknowledgment has to do with the undercurrent of *naturalized affect* that runs through Oruka's work. By naturalized affect, I mean to contrast it with supernatural or religious affect at the heart of the North Atlantic philosophical tradition. Of those forms of supernatural affect, "wonder" stands out as a particularly valorized affect. An oft-told tale in North Atlantic philosophy is Socrates's declaration that "wonder is the feeling of a philosopher, and philosophy begins in wonder."[78] There is nothing of course that is wrong in principle or essentially with the affect wonder. However, in the context within which it is often pedagogically invoked, it is constructed as rapt attention to the ineffable and the mysterious. If philosophers have portrayed wonder as a response to the ineffable, they have often conceived of themselves as particularly attuned to it, much more than those less sensitive to it. The Christian philosopher Teri Merrick claims wonder as no less than a Christian or "spiritual virtue." Merrick's definition of wonder is telling: "Because I will defend wonder as both a pious and indiscriminant welcoming of the unexpected, it is important to retain the Cartesian notion of wonder as a response to an object prior to or independent of any definitive judgment as to its utility, value or worth."[79] For

Martha Nussbaum, wonder "responds to the pull of the object" and is an important ingredient in other emotions such as grief, "in which one sees the beauty of the lost person as a kind of radiance standing at a very great distance from us," and the development of love and compassion in children.[80] For the philosopher Luce Irigaray, wonder is the proper response to the other.[81] What is problematic about these constructions of wonder is not simply their essentializing of wonder but the enshroudment of it in religious awe. In Merrick's case, this is straightforwardly thought to be a prostration before a deity. But even Nussbaum and Irigaray's highly moralized account of wonder should arouse suspicion. To conceive of the other with wonder appears awfully close to exoticization rather than understanding. Moreover, these accounts of wonder conceive of it as preceding knowledge, thus implying that once we know, one loses a sense of wonder.

Against this, the forms of affect that run through Oruka's African sage philosophy project are naturalized. He registers discovery with not wonder—as if we are witness to the miraculous—but rather by registering its *strangeness* or *eccentricity*. The ethical correlate in Oruka's epistemology is *critique* (of, not least, himself), *appreciation* (of intellectual communities, interlocutors, and critics) and *humility* (for example, at how little is known and is yet to be discovered). Oruka has an eye for the *aesthetic* in epistemology, as seen in some of his most moving prose. Moreover, his scholarship seems *radically hopeful*, perhaps because of Oruka's futural stance and openness to chance, luck, and the agency of others. All of these *naturalized affects* run through various aspects of Oruka's work, but a statement he makes in an interview with the philosophical anthropologist Kai Kresse strikingly illustrates the Oruka *habitus*:

> We take, e.g. the text of one given sage, folk sage or philosophic sage, then we subject that to analysis, to investigation and examination, and so they contribute to positions of our own debate. We have been doing this, and e.g. this year I gave a course at one college near Nairobi which was simply called "Sage Philosophy, the Roots of African Philosophy and Religion." There we subjected a number of texts of these sages to critique and analysis between me and the students. It was becoming

very interesting because e.g one discussion we had was on the issue of wisdom. And there was a sage who had given a definition of what he sees as wisdom, who is wise and who is not wise. When we were discussing this concept of Stephen Kithanje, it was clear that we were not able to go beyond what he had been able to define, what he had projected forward. He was so deep in his thought that we had to confess that although we had read all those books from Western thinkers and so on, we had not yet met a thinker who has anything better to give than that philosophic sage on the question of what is wisdom.[82]

Mediators

Conceptions of limit, measure, equilibrium, which ought to
determine the conduct of life are, in the West, restricted to a servile
function in the vocabulary of technics. We are only geometricians
of matter; the Greeks were, first of all, geometricians in their
apprenticeship to virtue.
                —Simone Weil, *The Iliad, or the Poem of Force*

Mediation articulates an orientation toward knowledge that puts an emphasis on the techniques, methods, performances, or the *how-to* of knowledge acquisition or inhabitation. Below, I articulate three embodiments of mediation: the professional, the bricoleur, and the artisan.

The Professional

Nowadays, there are philosophy professors, but no philosophers.
                —Thoreau, *Walden*

The professional is a capitalist creature, shaped in part from premodern guilds but reworked into one of the most durable identities of the modern era. The institutional form established by professionalism is the *career*, usually a life-long social service performed by mostly middle-class individuals. The career is often taken up after intensive education and training. Such is the success by which professionalism inhabits the bodily practices of the middle class that it comes to be seen as more than simply an institutional artifact. Burton Bledstein puts it well:

> The middle-class person in America owns an acquired skill or culti-vated talent by means of which to provide a service. And he does not view his "ability" as a commodity, an external resource, like the means of production or manual labor. His "ability" is a human capacity—an internal resource—as unlimited in its potential expansion and its powers to enrich him financially and spiritually as the enlarging vol-ume of his own intelligence, imagination, aspirations, and acquisitive-ness. "A salesman is got to dream, boy. It comes with the territory": the requiem for Willy Loman caught the spirit of men desperate to establish their own importance and respectability.[83]

Professionalism is intimately linked to technicism, which involves a mass of tangled ideologies that construe education as a neutral tech-nology for the transmission of skills and fetishizes the possession of technological skills. Another distinctive dimension of professionalism is its focus on the division of labor. In its academic forms, this is the ar-ticulation of knowledge as disciplinarity, that is, the notion that knowl-edges belong to discrete domains or disciplines, each of which offers a different perspective on a larger whole.[84] Professionalism derives its identity by contrasting itself with a host of intellectual figures: the tran-scendental master, the amateur, and the aesthete. Against transcenden-tal mastery, it not only posits its local expertise but also claims that its epistemological humility marks it out as more trustworthy than the generalist ways of the master. But this claimed epistemological mod-esty is tossed out when the professional confronts the amateur, who is dismissed as uncredentialed, a dilettante and a hobbyist. Against the aesthete, the professional asserts the sanctity of quantification and cal-culability as the only legitimate methods of assessment.

In Africa, few philosophers have fought as vigorously for the estab-lishment of philosophy as a distinct discipline as Paulin Hountondji. Below, I will closely map the contours of Hountondji's thought as it offers a particularly fruitful starting point from which to understand the topography of African disciplinarity. Born in Abidjan in 1942 and educated in Paris at the École Normale Supérieure in the mid-1960s at the height of Althusser's influence, few figures have been as lionized and influential in the African intellectual landscape as Paulin Hountondji. Not entirely paradoxically, however, there is also probably no philosopher who has been as much reviled within African philosophical discourse. This is largely traceable to Hountondji's confrontation with a school of thought that he derisively dubbed "ethnophilosophy." Ethnophilosophers like Placide Tempels and Alexis Kagame had asserted that African philosophy, insofar as it existed, consisted in communally shared, anonymous (because collective) *beliefs*. Hountondji charged that ethnophilosophy reiterated Eurocentric caricatures of Africans as members of a herd-like mob, devoid of the capacity to think as independent individuals. His critics in turn shot back that Hountondji was a Western stooge, even a Trojan horse for a second, postcolonial *mission civilisatrice* in the African continent.

Hountondji carved out a place in the field of African philosophy largely on the strength of his major work, *African Philosophy: Myth and Reality* (1976).[85] Twenty years later he published an intellectual memoir translated as *The Struggle for Meaning: Reflections on Philosophy, Culture and Democracy in Africa* (1997).[86] The term "intellectual memoir" may be misleading. Its original French subtitle, *Un itinéraire africain* [An African Journey], offers a better description of it as an attempt to retrace and explain his intellectual development.[87] After an initial discussion of his own intellectual inheritance and influences (notably Husserl and Althusser), much of the book consists of Hountondji's attempt to defend his work from the veritable cottage industry that sprang up in response to his critique of ethnophilosophy.

Hountondji affirms four main ideas concerning the definition and role of philosophy, all of which are intended to establish the domain in which an African philosophy might be articulated, while excluding "ethnophilosophy" as an impostor (if not as a contradiction in terms). First, in his book *African Philosophy*, Hountondji defines African philosophy as a "set of texts, specifically the set of texts written by Africans and described as philosophical by their authors themselves."[88] Though the definition at first sight comes across as disarmingly straightforward, it in fact rests on a number of assumptions diametrically opposed to the school of thought that Hountondji dismissed as "ethnophilosophy." Like other critics, Hountondji traces the origins of ethnophilosophy to the work of the Belgian missionary Placide Tempels (1906–1977). In his book *Bantu Philosophy* (1945) Tempels argues that Africans conceive of reality as a hierarchy of interacting forces. According to Tempels, this view of reality is held by all Africans and is attributable to the natural disposition of the African mind. The Rwandese philosopher Alexis Kagame (1912–1981) attempted to extend and refine Tempels's theory, notably in his books *La Philosophie bantu-rwandaise de l'être* (1956) and *La Philosophie bantu comparée* (1976). Kagame, unlike Tempels, argued that African philosophy emerged from a shared cultural essence rather than an African nature. This shared culture consisted in African traditions, customs, and language.

It is these notions that Hountondji's definition of philosophy as a "set of texts" seeks to challenge. The emergence of philosophy, Hountondji holds, is dependent on a dialectical or critical method that can only take place with literacy and written or "archival" transmission. According to Hountondji,

> oral tradition favors the consolidation of known into dogmatic, intangible systems, whereas archival transmission promotes better the possibility of a critique of knowledge between individuals and from one generation to another. Oral tradition is dominated by the fear of forgetting, of lapses of memory, since memory is here left to its own resources, bereft of external or material support. . . . Written tradition, on the contrary, providing a material support, liberates the memory, and permits it to forget its acquisitions, provisionally to reject or question them because it knows that it can at any moment recapture them if need be.[89]

Philosophy existed in the West, Hountondji asserts, because "the history of the West is not directly cumulative but *critical*: it moves forward not through a mere plurality of knowledge, . . . but through the periodical questioning of established knowledge, each questioning being a crisis."[90] Ethnophilosophy, Hountondji contends, errs in naming as philosophy forms of thinking that are merely implicit and unwritten. For Hountondji, genuine philosophy renders legible and meaningful bits of knowledge into a *text* of knowledge. Hountondji's insistence on written texts as philosophy partly hinges on his belief that texts offer some form of evidence against which duelling interpretations may be compared to determine the correct one. "The discourse of ethnophilosophers," he argues,

> be they European or African, offers us the baffling spectacle of an imaginary interpretation with no textual support, of a genuinely "free" interpretation, inebriated and entirely at the mercy of the interpreter, a dizzy and unconscious freedom which takes itself to be translating a text which does not actually exist and which is therefore unaware of its creativity. By this action the interpreter disqualifies himself from reaching any truth whatsoever, since truth requires that freedom be limited, that it bow to an order that is not purely imaginary and that it be aware both of this order and of its own margin of creativity.[91]

In his intellectual memoir, Hountondji elaborates on a second reason why he opposes ethnophilosophy's claim to being genuine philosophy. Insofar as ethnophilosophy attributes to Africans an implicit philosophy, Hountondji condemns it for making a category mistake. "If we pose that it is absurd to speak of unconscious algebra, geometry, linguistics, etc., and if we accept that no science can exist historically without an explicit discourse, then by the same token we must regard the very idea of an unconscious philosophy as absurd."[92] Ethnophilosophy is a rank failure because of its obliviousness to the difference between first order and second order forms of knowing. Africans, Hountondji holds, did and do possess—as do all humans—the capacity for abstract thought. Husserl had shown that there exists a universal architectonic of consciousness. By alleging that the African's thinking was "communal," ethnophilosophers were undermining the most basic condition of possibility for the existence of philosophy, namely, the universality of individual human consciousness.

Third, Hountondji contends that philosophy designates, in its role as clarifier of scientific concepts, the privileged method for the discovery of truth. Husserl's method of the transcendental *epoché*, the brack-

eting of the world and the natural attitude, deeply influences Hountondji and inspires his general disdain for empiricism. For Hountondji,
empiricism is mere "psychologism."⁹³ He states in *African Philosophy*
that he remains attached "to a certain idea of philosophy which, since
Plato, demands that it be *episteme* rather than *doxa*, science rather
than opinion; to Husserl, who identifies in a very technical manner
some of the intellectual devices and methods that allow philosophy to
become 'a rigorous science'; to Descartes' cogito; and to all the doctrines that value intellectual responsibility and demand that each affirmation be sustained by a proof or a rational justification."⁹⁴ One reason why Hountondji regards ethnophilosophy as something other than
philosophy is because he thinks its empiricist methods reduce it to a
form of anthropology. Moreover, Hountondji's adoption of the *epoché*
as a methodology also strongly influences his own intellectual *habitus*.
It is at least partly what drives his remarkable capacity for relentless
argumentation, his readiness to methodically follow a train of thought,
concept, or argument down to the furthest reaches of its claims.

Fourth, Hountondji argues that, by making explicit the unarticu-
lated, philosophy made possible the emergence of science. Hountondji
follows Louis Althusser in conceiving of philosophical knowledge as
signifying a *rupture* or break that founds a new science by a violent
repudiation of subjectivism, myth, and *doxa*. The history of philosophy, he states, "does not move forward by continuous evolution but
by leaps and bounds, by successive revolutions, and consequently follows not a linear path but what one might call a dialectical one—in
other words, that its profile is not continuous but discontinuous."⁹⁵ If
this signifies epistemological progress, it is no less a moral one as well.
Philosophy is possible in literate cultures, he avers, because literacy
"liberates the memory." He continues: "Such is the real function of
(empirical) writing. It leaves the task of conservation to matter (books,
documents, archives, etc.) and liberates the mind to make innovations that may shake established ideas and even overthrow them completely."⁹⁶ In his memoir, Hountondji hails his critique of ethnophilosophy as marking nothing less than an "intellectual liberation."⁹⁷
Drawing on Husserl and Althusser, he argued for a conception of philosophy as *Wissenschaftslehre*, "a theory of science necessarily called

upon by the very movement of science as realization, or at least the condition of realization of this need for integral intelligibility that permeates science."[98] Through this method, Hountondji claims, ontology could then be clarified as knowledge of a universal essence or foundation upon which all subsequent sciences can then be built: "Therefore, there is an order of things, an objective articulation of being, a universal legality that regulates the sphere of truth. Scientific discourse must account for this preexisting order."[99] The ultimate goal of philosophy is nothing less than a Platonic "duty to truth and the desire for apodictic certainty."[100]

Hountondji lays out the implications of these critiques in stark terms. "We [Africans] must relearn how to think," he states.[101] Ethnophilosophers, he argues, "have not seen that African philosophy, like African science or African culture in general, is before us, not behind us, and must be created today by decisive action." To get it started requires that the African admit that African philosophy "is yet to come."[102]

In *African Philosophy*, Hountondji is prone to dismiss those he disagrees with as engaged in a discourse other than philosophy. But he does so only on the strength of his definition of philosophy as a "set of texts." In doing so he simply begs the question. The lack of a textual basis for ethnophilosophy condemns it as nonphilosophical in advance. "Unfortunately, in the case of African 'philosophy' there are no sources; or at least, if they exist, they are not philosophical texts or discourses. Kagame's 'institutionalized records,' or those which Tempels had earlier subjected to 'ethnophilosophical' treatment, are wholly distinct from philosophy. They are in no way comparable with the sources which for an interpreter of, say, Hegelianism, or dialectical materialism, or Freudian theory, or even Confucianism are extant in the explicit texts of Hegel, Marx, Freud, or Confucius, in their discursive development as permanently available products of language."[103] What Hountondji does not acknowledge here is that the status of what counts as "philosophy" and "philosophical discourse" is exactly what is being debated. It's not enough to define rival discourses as not-philosophy and declare the argument won. Nor is it enough to treat the field of philosophy, oriented by a neo-Althusserian emphasis on revolutionary breaks, in terms that effectively reduce its structuring principles to a heroic clash between the ideas of Great Men.

The first thing that Hountondji fails to account for is the historical determinations that structure his own philosophical thought. In *African Philosophy*, he points to the historical conjuncture of racialist supremacy and African nationalism as the impetus for the favorable reception of ethnophilosophy. What he does not do, however, is subject his own philosophy to the same contextual critique. In his intellectual memoir, when he engages the influences on him, he offers a litany of Great Men (notably Immanuel Kant, Edmund Husserl, and Louis Althusser) as his forebears, and he offers his text-based definition of philosophy as superior to other definitions because he sees it as simply referencing the "philosophical intention of the authors, not . . . the degree of its effective realization, which cannot be assessed."[104] It is a short step from here to the bald assertion that philosophy is what the writer says it is.

And yet Hountondji's work bears ample testimony of the contextual determinations that structure the presuppositions of his beliefs. There is, to begin with, a set of broadly "modernist" assumptions that he takes for granted—modernism is here defined as a historical conjuncture marked by the struggle for self-definition of the "professional" classes, the rationalization and bureaucratization of the life world (including processes of standardization, routinization, and surveillance), and the emergence of a "global" public sphere through the emergence of mass media technologies.[105] Modernization was of course highly variegated, and the response to processes of industrialization, mass commodification, professionalization, and standardization were highly differentiated from field to field (thus, what is often termed "modernist" art and literature tended to be antimodernizing in their thrust).

Hountondji's work is best understood in light of this historical conjuncture. Consider his portrayal of philosophy as primarily a value-free method, which goes hand in hand with his suspicion of "engaged" subjectivity. Hountondji finds "seductive" Husserl's argument for a science that foregrounds an "ethics of effacement."[106] In such a science the subject abandons itself to truth, "neutralizes itself, to be nothing more than a pure spectatorial gaze."[107] The "neutrality" Hountondji invokes in his critique of ethnophilosophy's cultural relativisms is based in the presumption that reason is not reducible to the accumulation of sensory impressions or the accumulation of cultural habits. His emphasis on the necessary and universal (a priori) conditions of cognition and experience, however, opens the door to a frictionless idealism.

Hountondji's own writing bears traces of the intellectual and ideological imprint of the Cartesian style on the modern French university. He lavishes praise on his teacher Georges Canguilhem for the "beauty of his writings—rigorous analyses, an austere style, and conceptual rigor."[108] It is a style that brilliantly shimmers in Hountondji's own prose: a pithy, impacted form of expression that is seemingly effortless in its translucence. It's a style that resonates with that ethos of objectivity so prized in our "professional" era. But precisely because it works so hard at performing its transparency, there is at the same time an antipathy in Hountondji's work to this very performance. It is no wonder, then, that Hountondji himself is contemptuous of rhetoric, dismissing his opponents as "rhetoricians" and contrasting his own logic to their "rhetoric."[109] The paradox then is that for all of his contempt for "rhetoric," Hountondji's rhetorical style is in tune with modernity's ideology of clarity and transparency as signature strategies of distinction.[110]

It is in the light of his professionalism and technicism therefore, that one ought to understand Hountondji's fetishism of writing and literacy. Hountondji regards literacy as essentially a neutral medium for the acquisition and engagement of knowledge. He claims that his definition of philosophy is intended to be neutral: "I wanted to take note of the fact of [African philosophical] writings, outside of any assessment of value judgment."[111] It is not a particularly convincing argument, for his definition is structured around a series of oppositions favorable to his own position: philosophy versus ethnophilosophy, skeptical written philosophy versus spontaneous oral thought, and explicit written texts versus implicit oral utterances. Hountondji assumes that written texts are explicit, articulated philosophies by virtue of the fact that they are . . . *written.* But what is written, of course, is often as implicit as what is spoken. That is, written texts are utterances that are explicit about some things, implicit about others, and necessarily rest on certain assumptions. It is therefore important to try to reconstruct how Hountondji is blind to the diverse forms of written texts and reduces them to a single manifestation—texts that explicitly argue a case, generally in the form of a *book*. For Hountondji, in effect, the only philosophy is written, and the only philosophical writing worthy of the name is presented as a book. This idea of the book as a stand-in for all written texts is itself embedded within a very particular representation of the medium as inseparable from another activity, namely, reading. It is not just that books are assumed to automatically possess explicit or critical *traits*; this can only be assumed because they confer particular *skills*. Reading is metonymic of technique, and contributes to a modernizing technicism. However unconvincing the series of leaps required to enable Hountondji's conflation of the written with the philosophical, it dovetails with the modern state's bureaucratic function of cataloguing, measuring, recording, and, not least, accrediting.

African professional philosophers such as Hountondji, while severely critical of the ethnophilosophers and their epigones, have not therefore entirely rejected the Western/African binary. But their binary has been made at another register, that of culture, specifically, that Western culture is characterized by "literacy" while African culture is characterized by "orality." This claim emerges from a now well-established orthodoxy in the European-American academy. As Ruth Finnegan has demonstrated, there are widespread claims that "literacy" is "responsible for just about all the 'goods' of modern Western civilization."[112] Harvey Graff draws attention to the breathtakingly "daunting number of cognitive, affective, behavioral, and attitudinal effects" made on behalf of literacy:

> These characteristics usually include attitudes ranging from empathy, innovativeness, achievement-orientation, "cosmopoliteness," information-and-media awareness, national identification, technological acceptance, rationality, and commitment to democracy, to opportunism, linearity of thought and behavior, or urban residence. Literacy is sometimes conceived of as a skill, but more often as symbolic or representative of attitudes and mentalities. On other levels, literacy

"threshholds" are seen as requirements for economic development, "take-offs," "modernization," political development and stability, standards of living, fertility control and so on.[113]

According to Finnegan, the miracle of literacy is said to have birthed "rationality, abstract thought, sophisticated literary expression, individual self-consciousness, . . . the growth of science."[114] A literacy enthusiast, Roy Harris, argues confidently that "the writing revolution was not merely of political and economic significance. The autonomous text was naturally suited to become the basis not only of law but of education and literature."[115] Walter Ong goes further, arguing that writing fundamentally restructured the mental architecture of the brain.[116]

But the difficulties with the "Great Divide"[117] theory of literacy are simply overwhelming, even despite the potent ethnocentrism that has been the major reason for its popularity. Critiques against it can be boiled down to three objections. First, it cannot account for the fact that there *were* precolonial cultures in Africa that have long writing traditions.[118] One would want to know how the "mental architecture" of, say, Ethiopians differs from the mental architecture of, say, Kenyans. The point, then, is that such sweeping units of analysis such as the "Western" versus the "African" are ahistorical. It flattens the spectacular diversity of African and, yes, "Western" societies into a one-dimensional caricature. What goes by the name of the "West" is a small subset of countries and, moreover, refers to the elite echelons of those societies.

Second, it cannot be stated enough that reading, writing, and speaking take place in a context. In other words, to reiterate John Guillory's trenchant point, literacy is not simply the capacity to read in a vacuum. Rather, literacy is "the *systematic regulation of reading and writing*, a complex social phenomenon corresponding to the following set of questions: Who reads? What do they read? How do they read? In what social and institutional circumstances? Who writes? In what social and institutional contexts? For whom?"[119] Assertions on the supposed effects of literacy have generally posited a technologically determinist, monocausal analysis. Often couched in hyperbolic rhapsodies on the wonders of literacy, these accounts assume that writing is a *sin-*

gular technology producing the *same* results. Eric Havelock enthuses about the "thunder-clap in human history" that marked the advent of writing, "an intrusion into culture, with results that proved irreversible."[120] Ong asserts that "more than any other single invention, writing has transformed human consciousness."[121] What are elided in these accounts are examinations of the relation of writing to other forms of communication, investigation of the institutional structures mediating the teaching, functions, and understanding of writing, and accounts of human agency—including contestation—in determining the role of writing in a particular society.

Conversely, proponents of the Great Literacy Divide have generally been content to extrapolate the effects of orality as the mirror opposite of their suppositions on the effects of writing. Thus, there is often little engagement with research on the effects of orality.[122] The operative assumption of these theorists is that orality is a "natural," "unproblematical" phenomenon. Ong, for example, in drawing a sharp distinction between the effects of writing and orality defines literate people as "beings whose thought processes do not grow out of simple natural powers but out of these powers as structured, directly or indirectly, by the technology of writing."[123] But what the Great Divide theorists fail to account for is that there no such thing as reading and speaking *simpliciter.* Language is far from a uniform phenomenon, as the existence of deeply textured tonal languages richly attest. Human speech is a *technology* in itself, one moreover articulated in differentiated, complex, contradictory matrices of social conventions, rules, taboos, etiquette, and performances.[124] Finnegan's studies indicate the necessity for taking into account local idioms and intricate speech codes within speech. In her ethnographic study of the Sierra Leonean social formation, the Limba, she demonstrates how a people dismissed in the Great Divide literature as "non-literate" are constantly engaged in complex interpretive engagements with language, including abstract, reflective thought and discourse.[125] Proponents of the Great Divide such as Walter Ong are oblivious to the range of mediated formations operating within most societies. In other words, there are ways of communication other than through reading and writing—art forms (sculptures, paintings, images), performances (dances, theater), complex nonverbal and nondiscursive forms of communication, and so on. Closely related to this point is the fact that a significant amount of theorizations on the literacy/orality divide rely on Weberian "ideal types" as a method of assigning cultures to one or the other category. These ideal types are then posited as a grid for slotting in various cultural traits. But, as Ruth Finnegan has argued, this gesture is willfully blind to the fact that most social formations have in practice been characterized by combinations of media (oral, imagistic, and, at times, written media).[126]

To be sure, there have been empirical studies on the effects of orality in societies designated by subscribers to the "Great Divide" theory as "oral cultures." But these studies are often theoretically and methodically suspect and empirically selective. Some of the most influential work in support of the Great Divide thesis are vulnerable to these charges. For example, Jack Goody, in his influential book *The Domestication of the Savage Mind*, argues, "Writing puts a distance between man and his verbal acts. He can now examine what he says in a more objective manner." Thus, he continues, "the shift from the science of the concrete to that of the abstract . . . cannot be understood except in terms of basic changes in the nature of human communication."[127] Goody is, however, only able to make this claim by assuming a theory of language as a transparent mirror, through which his disembodied universal "Man" gazes at an acontextual, ahistorical Reality. In actually existing societies, one has to take account of not just the institutional-contextual residue of linguistic utterances, but also to the fact that linguistic utterances resonate and refract with connotations and ideologies. The theoretical limitations of Great Divide theories are compounded by methodical shortcomings. For example, Alexander Luria's 1930s study argued famously that nonliterate people in Uzbekistan and Kirghizia were deficient in theoretical and logical thinking.[128] Luria's monocausal, determinist narrative ignores the different experiences of the people interviewed (i.e., the extent to which some of the people interviewed and considered literate were engaged in collective forms of farming as opposed to others that were not). Scribner and Cole's (1981) study *The Psychology of Literacy* among the Vai of West Africa, for example, shows the folly of relying on such monocausal factors. In their comparison of so-called cognitive skills among the literate Vai and the nonliterate Vai, they show how a host of factors play into these cognitive skills.[129] Marshall McLuhan further popularized technological determinism.[130] Yet another problem with these studies is their empirical impoverishment and selectivity. The studied indifference of proponents of the Great Divide to such findings is particularly significant in light of some of their indifference to their own findings. Thus, for example, Milman Parry and Albert Lord who were categorical that oral and written techniques are "contradictory and mutually exclusive" not only fail to offer evidence for this but end up contradicting themselves when it emerges that some of the poets they described as "traditional" and nonliterate were literate, and most of them indirectly in touch with those engaged in writing.[131]

The upshot then, and my third and final point, is that the Great Divide myth simply reaffirms the civilized/primitive binary in another register. By making "literacy" (read narrowly as reading) coterminous with Western, it certifies the attribution of Western ownership to rationality, democracy, wealth, morals, *humanity*. Roger Abrahams rightly critiques the "naïve mechanistic evolutionism" of the Great Divide theories: "The radical discontinuity argument is commonly made for ideological rather than scientific reasons. Oral people are either regarded as backward and uncivilized, or at least underdeveloped—the position out of which the literacy campaigns for developing countries have developed—or they are innocent prelapsarians who have not yet entered into the alienating process of capitalistic production and exchange."[132]

To return then to Hountondji. The Great Divide that he posits between literacy and orality is riddled with problematic and discredited assumptions. Hountondji's advocacy of the Great Divide is however only one strand of a tangled modernist ideology that he subscribes to. Hountondji's claims of transparent objectivity notwithstanding, it is clear that his critique springs from a deep vein of *moral* disapproval of ethnophilosophy. If there is one word that echoes throughout his *African Philosophy*, it is the word "courage." African philosophy, he states, "may today be going through its first decisive mutation, the outcome of which depends on us [Africans] alone, on the courage and lucidity we show in bringing it to its conclusion."[133] For Hountondji, ethnophilosophy was symptomatic of a kind of dogmatic sleep of consciousness that his compatriots ought to be awakened from. As he elaborates in his intellectual memoir, "What I refused deep down was a philosophy in the third person (that) consisted in lazily taking refuge behind group thought, in abstaining from taking a personal position and from giving one's opinion on the problems to which, in its own way, this thought of the ancestors was a response. In place of this lazy recourse to group thought, I appealed for the intellectual responsibility of the thinker, of each thinker."[134]

Hountondji's anger at ethnophilosophy for what he calls its extraversion—its orientation toward "the West" and its desire to prove that Africa was equal to Europe—thus, after all, springs from a sensibility he shared with the ethnophilosophers: the quest for recognition. He dismisses the ethnophilosophical consciousness as motivated by a "desire to show off," which "grows increasingly hollow until it is completely alienated in a restless craving for the most cursory glance from the [Western] Other."[135] Ethnophilosophy is thus faulted for its cringing desire for approval from the West. In the interstices of Hountondji's rhetoric, then, seeps not only anger but also *shame*. He thought that ethnophilosophy, despite its flourishes about restoring African pride, heralded another era of African abasement: "The same subservience, the same wretchedness, the same tragic abandonment of thinking by ourselves and for ourselves: slavery."[136] Hountondji's broader polemical stance betrays the burden of this shame. His country Benin, he argued in 1972, "was characterized politically by the loss of all meaningful sovereignty, by its international mendacity, servility in its relations with great or middle level powers, its inability to keep to its internal and external financial commitments, and its 'creepy-crawliness' and obsequiousness."[137]

In the upshot, Hountondji's rejection of ethnophilosophy's attribution of African philosophy to a collectivistic *mentalité* is as much prompted by moral scruples as it is an epistemological critique. Philosophical truth is only truth insofar as one can attribute it to individual agency. As he puts it, philosophy is produced "when every thinker, every author, engages in total responsibility: I know that I am responsible for what I say, for the theories I put forward. I am 'responsible' for them in the literal sense of the word, because I must always be prepared to 'answer' for them; I must be ready to justify them, to attest to their validity."[138] It is here that his notions of what it means to be an intellectual can be plumbed all the way down to Immanuel Kant. Kant, it will be recalled, defined Enlightenment in forceful terms: "Enlightenment is man's emergence from his self-imposed immaturity. Immaturity is the inability to use one's understanding without guidance from another. . . . Laziness and cowardice are the reasons why so great a proportion of men, long after nature has released them from alien guidance, nonetheless gladly remain in lifelong immaturity, and why it is so easy for others to establish themselves as their guardians."[139]

Though Hountondji's language of modernism is suffused with moral, even moralistic sentiment, it is deeply invested in the disavowal of values. Thus he strains to couch his claims in the idiom of disciplinarity—an idiom, one has to remember, that is embedded in modernity's interpellation of certain classes and functions as "professionals." Hountondji's definition of African philosophy takes for granted the disciplinary divisions that are the norm in the modern university. He argues, for example, that "scientific method demands that a sociological document is interpreted first in terms of sociology, a botanical text (written or oral) first in terms of botany, histories first in terms of historiography, etc. Well then, the same scientific rigor should prevent us from arbitrarily projecting a *philosophical discourse* on to producers of language which expressly offers themselves as something other than philosophy. In effecting this projection, Kagame—and Tempels before him, along with those African ethnophilosophers who followed suit . . . committed what Aristotle called . . . a *metabasis eis allo genos*, i.e., a confusion of categories."[140]

The modernist intellectual stance that Hountondji cultivates, to use Michel Foucault's characterization, is that of the *specific* rather than the *universal* intellectual. To Foucault, the universal intellectual— for example, Jean-Paul Sartre—should be and has been replaced by the specific intellectual, exemplified by the American physicist Robert Oppenheimer. The universal intellectual is the "master of truth and justice," "the consciousness/conscience of us all." The specific intellectual, on the other hand, works "within specific sectors, at the precise points where their own conditions of life or work situate them (housing, the hospital, the asylum, the laboratory, the university, family, and sexual relations)."[141] But one drawback to this stance is that its commitment to specialization remains resolutely conservative. Of all the ironies of African philosophy—conceived as a discipline—one of its central ironies is the fearsome manner in which African professional philosophers have policed the borders of disciplinarity. No doubt these professional philosophers are right in condemning ethnophilosophy for its patronizing assembly of various African proverbs and fables and labeling these African knowledge. But in the name of fighting ethnophilosophy, African professional philosophers have made it their task to reentrench the naturalization of the arbitrary borders of knowledge imposed by nineteenth-century European universities. It is a singular failure of the imagination. One wonders what the history of knowledge in Africa would have been if African philosophers had embarked on a reimagining of the relationships between and among various bodies of knowledge: university knowledge (in the forms of *episteme, techne,* or *gnosis*), political knowledges (in the forms of *bie, metis,* or *praxis*), knowledges within the interstices of civil society (in the forms of *doxa, mythos,* or *kerdos*), local knowledges (*nomos*), and worldly or universal knowledges (*kosmopoliteia*).[142]

Consider, if you will, some of these knowledges, starting with university knowledge. Hountondji embraces what Pierre Bourdieu in another context termed "logicism"—an attempt to found science on general a priori rules, but that in its idealism and romanticization of scientific practice falls into an idle scholasticism.[143] The *episteme* versus *techne* divide may wrongly give the impression that different methodologies are a priori mutually exclusive or conflictual.[144] Even worse, in its claim that one method is superior to another it leads to a pernicious and ultimately destructive "arms race" for disciplinary cultural capital. Such struggles for cultural capital are not only provincial but ultimately undermine the autonomy of intellectual practice insofar as they prevent the kind of constitutive practices—for example, radical critiques of the way that disciplines carve up knowledge—necessary for establishing a contextual (and therefore deeper) *rigor.*

Universities are, of course, not the sole spaces for the articulation of knowledge. Hountondji's critique of ethnophilosophy tends to conflate its "spontaneous philosophy" with *doxa* and *mythos*. He thereby loses an opportunity for a more finely grained critique of not only the different strains of *doxa* and *mythos* but also the extent to which power relations are constitutive of what is legitimized as *episteme* and what is ruled out as *doxa* and *mythos*. As Steven Feierman has shown in his brilliant ethnographic study in the Shambaai, peasant intellectuals articulated a complex discourse that demonstrated a far more thoroughgoing elaboration of democratic theory and practice than the official discourse.[145] To be sure, the field of *doxa*, no less than that of *episteme*, ought not be romanticized. What are often described as "civil societies" in Africa are quite often not so much shoots of "grassroots community" activism but rather appendages of U.S. State Department policy and fundamentalist evangelical churches' paternalism.[146] The same critique would apply to *mythos*. Hountondji's secularist commitments must stand, alongside that of the Kenyan philosopher Odera Oruka, as one of the finest legacies to African philosophy and intellectual theory. Apart from ethnophilosophy's dissemination of the canard that Africans think as a herd, one of its most pernicious legacies was to legitimize the notion that African people are generally in the sway of religious or supernaturalist thought, indeed, that in their animism they are unable to make any distinction between the natural and the supernatural. The Kenyan theologian John Mbiti would carry on with this ethnophilosophical myth: "African people do not know how to exist without religion," he claims; "religion is their whole system of being."[147] Hountondji did more than anyone, in the field of philosophy, to expose such myths for what they were. And yet, here again, it is necessary to make distinctions. It is obvious, for example, that Hountondji's thought is bereft of any sustained engagement with African art, literature, music, film, and architecture. Such an engagement might have offered him a far more subtle, more complex understanding of the different varieties of *mythos*, and perhaps even tempered his graphocentrism.[148]

Hountondji's eidetic bracketing serves not only to valorize the primacy of philosophy, it also functions as a firewall between philosophy and politics. For Hountondji, this was not an entirely abstract discussion. His philosophy was worked out not only within an African philosophical discourse marked by feverish contention among rival schools of thought that had deep ideological divergences, but also within the constraints of living in repressive states that demanded fealty to the ruling ideology. In his intellectual memoir, Hountondji recounts his experience of teaching in universities in Zaire (now the Democratic Republic of Congo) at the height of the dictatorship of Mobutu. On return to his own country, Benin (formerly Dahomey), he witnessed the seizure of power by a Stalinist junta. These experiences had a lasting effect on Hountondji's view of both politics and philosophy. The fierce debates within African philosophical circles in the 1970s are best understood in light of the convulsions that were occurring in African states and intraphilosophical debates about the identity of philosophy vis-à-vis other disciplines and the (political, economic, cultural) world. Some schools (the ethnophilosophers, for example), advocated for a reactivation of a "traditional" African *Weltanschauung*. The major proponents of this school included Alexis Kagame and William Abraham. Other schools, which included major political figures such as Kwame Nkrumah and Julius Nyerere, made intellectual work and politics virtually identical. Hountondji led a charge that sought to pry apart and keep separate politics and intellectual work.[149] Hountondji took on the rival schools of thought with brio. In his memoir, he states that one of his main purposes in the 1970s was to "put politics in its right place."[150] For Hountondji, the materialist thesis, as exemplified by Lenin's *Materialism and Empirio-Criticism*, was mistaken because of the different registers in which politics and philosophy operated. He states that "the uncontested authority of the Russian revolutionary [Lenin], a midwife of history, and henceforth, indispensable in the area of political theory and practice, did not necessarily give him comparable authority in the quite different field of speculative thought."[151] If the place of politics was "unity of action," the place of thought was "free and responsible thought."[152] To that end, and against Lenin's denunciation of idealism as reactionary, Hountondji celebrates "the intellectual daring of Descartes who, in his quest for apodictic certainty, readily accepted the risk of madness and, through the argument of the dream, provisionally rejected all belief in the existence of bodies including his own."[153] Hountondji prefers Althusser's early conception of philosophy as the "theory of science, or the theory of the theoretical science" to his later characterization of philosophy as "class struggle in the realm of theory." Oriented by its scientific vocation, "philosophy does not merge with ideology any more than algebra or linguistics do."[154] He levels the same sort of critique at Kwame Nkrumah's book *Consciencism*.[155] Hountondji objects to Nkrumah's notion that politics presupposed a philosophy. He finds Nkrumah's claim that idealism favors oligarchy while materialism favors egalitarianism to be "arbitrary": "Our political choices stand on their own feet. If they need justification, it must be political justification, belonging to the same level of discourse and not to what is the completely different (*ex hypothesi*) level of metaphysical speculation."[156]

In the context within which he offered his critique, at a time when regimes such as the one he had to contend with in Benin imposed "ideological correctness" tests on intellectuals, Hountondji's intervention was intellectually bold and bracing. The dogmatism of the Stalinist regime in Benin was such that it prevented an appreciation of the depth of Marx's own texts, let alone those vilified as "bourgeois." As Hountondji put it, "there is a danger that the time may soon come when, in the name of Marxism, we will be forbidden to read Marx."[157] Nonetheless, in much the same manner as he does when he reifies disciplinary categories, Hountondji consistently takes for granted the categories within which his analyses proceed. In other words, he fails to offer an account of the *relationship* of philosophy to politics, including all the political oppositions that he establishes. If the problem with Stalinism is its vulgar reduction of theory to politics, therefore, the problem with Hountondji's idealism is that he assumes that politics is in and of itself "vulgar" by definition. After Kant and Husserl, Hountondji acknowledges a transcendental subject, the universal "I think" of scientific consciousness; after Althusser, however, he dismisses the *political* subject as nothing more than an effect of structure, an obedience "interpellated" by ideology. The account of politics it paints is monolithic, given that ideology is conceived of as singular and, ultimately, disabling of agency.[158] It is, in other words, a mechanistic and instrumental conception of politics.[159] To be sure, Hountondji is rightly suspicious of reductive accounts of intellectual work as politics by other means, and was right to dismiss Stalinist suggestions that his Parisian *agrégation* proved he was an ally of the imperialist enemy. By taking his Stalinist opponents as representatives of philosophical materialism, however, he fails to engage a much richer and more complex Marxist corpus. As Raymond Williams argues, the notion of determination bears at least two senses: "There is, on the one hand, from its theological inheritance, the notion of an external cause which totally predicts or prefigures, indeed totally controls a subsequent activity. But there is also, from the experience of social practice, a notion of determination as setting limits, exerting pressures."[160]

The upshot is that Hountondji's own philosophical theory cuts deeply against his professed desires. Hountondji is right to want to seek autonomy for intellectual practice. And yet such autonomy cannot be secured through individualism and methodological fetishization. Engagement with history should be a dimension of any inquiry. Moreover, the autonomy of an intellectual field must begin from a radically self-reflexive critique of the *institutional deep structure* that is the condition of possibility of specialized knowledge. As an articulation of an intellectual *habitus*, Hountondji's enlightened modernism represents perhaps one of the most attractive and influential intellectual characteristics and styles in the African context. Considered alongside most prominent alternatives, the *transcendental mastery* of a Mbiti, the *Whiggish cosmopolitanism* of an Appiah, the postmodern eclecticism of a Mbembe, Hountondji's intellectual power and brilliance is without compare. And yet thanks to his uncritical belief in several fetishes of the modern intellectual—rigor, objectivity, compartmentalization, specialization—Hountondji loses an opportunity to reexamine how the documents of civilization he has rightly championed are nonetheless also documents of barbarism.

The bricoleur

Although Omar Khayyam may have claimed that the results of his studies were that he "evermore came out by the same door as in I

went," he neglected to notice that he was facing a different direction
when he came out.

—Ronald Huntington, as cited in James L. Christian, *Philosophy:*
An Introduction to the Art of Wondering

Claude Levi-Strauss articulates the figure of the *bricoleur* as an embodiment of knowledge articulation in what he deems "primitive
societies." He posits three characteristics of the *bricoleur.* The first is
the negative contrast between the *bricoleur* and the engineer: whereas
the engineer defines in advance and with finality all the materials and
pieces with which he or she is going to work, the *bricoleur* seizes what
is at hand in the making of a project. Second, the *bricoleur* collects
material resources even in the absence of a clear sense of what their
final uses will be. *Bricolage* involves the use of materials in ways that
defy their original purposes to serve ends that are often articulated
midstream, spontaneously. Third, the *bricoleur* is embedded in the
environment and draws from the detritus and debris scattered across
landscape. The *bricoleur* thus makes use of the environment without
scarring it.[161] Levi-Strauss's notion of the *bricolage* triggered fruitful engagements with the notion in ways that sought to overcome his
ethnocentric assumptions. Postmodern theorists sought to refashion
the notion of *bricolage* to transcend the limitations of modern disciplinarity. For these theorists, *bricolage* is a form of radical interdisciplinary research that draws on a variety of theoretical perspectives in
engaging a problematic. For the postmodern theorist, his "tools" are
canonical theories that are used in the interpretation of texts.

The notion of *bricolage* offers fruitful engagements and critiques
of the technicism and professionalism of modernity. Nonetheless, it
has its limitations, particularly in the form that they have taken in
postmodern theoretical appropriations. The first is the worrying absence of a reckoning with the residual historical gravity of the theoretical tools that the *bricoleur* would seek to turn to his uses. In other
words, avatars of *bricolage* often speak as if tools are neutral and can
simply be turned around to fit the *bricoleur*'s purposes.[162] Denzin and
Lincoln, for example, argue that the postmodern scholar ought to put

to use "hermeneutics, structuralism, semiotics, phenomenology, cultural studies, and feminism" to the purposes of better interpretation, criticism, and deconstruction.[163] The eclecticism is telling of a failure to reckon with the historicity and specificity of philosophical schools. Deplaned from the frictionless stratosphere of abstraction and confronted with the interests they represent and the bodies they inhabit, these diverse theories turn out to be in *conflict*. The upshot is that postmodern *bricolage* draws on the worst aspects of structuralism—its economy of the formal equivalence of positions in a structural field—with the worst aspects of liberal individualism—its voluntarism and abstract theory of agency. What is often championed as interdisciplinarity by postmodern humanists is almost wholly a text-based eclecticism; the obligatory Derrida citation here, a Deleuze allusion there, and the odd Lacan riff to top it off. There is no engagement with what interdisciplinarity would look like institutionally, not least within the institution that the theorist is embedded. There is also obliviousness to the resonance between theoreticist eclecticism and the frenetic choice offerings at the bazaar of late capitalism, the shopping mall.

The Artisan

> "I did nothing today."—What? Did you not live? That is not only
> the most fundamental but the most illustrious of your occupations.
> —Montaigne, *Essays*, III, 13, "Of Experience"

Three characteristics are particularly distinctive of artisanship. First, the institutional basis for artisanship is the *constellation*. The constellation stands in contrast to two social formations: the community and the corporation. The community functions according to the logic of identity and similarity, whereas the corporation functions according to the logic of production (that is, the completion of discrete tasks toward the end of coming up with some unit or item). The community's orientation toward knowledge is *transmission*; the corporation's orientation toward knowledge is *production*; and the constellation's orientation toward knowledge is *articulation*. The constellation is oriented by a self-conscious engagement in making possible pluralistic, relational, and creative ways of life. The community often stands ready to crush individual initiative and distinctive signatures of living that do not conform; the corporation, on the other hand, imposes a public-private divide in the life of the individual that often leads to alienation. Against these two formations, the constellation seeks to find ways of navigating the tension between things held in common and proffering contexts for creative self-making.

Second, and this is closely connected to the first point, if the constellation is oriented to a way of life, that does not mean it is diffuse. This is because constellations are oriented by *praxes*—the creation or care of artifacts and resources; the articulation of knowledge for its own sake; experiments in self-making. Thus, for example, this would be the care for spaces such as public parks, or the making of artifacts such as baskets, or the building of infrastructure such as bridges for shared use, all within a context that values social relationships for their own sake. Third, there is a self-critical engagement between democratic access and participation, which seeks to draw in and involve all people whatever their diverse beliefs and behaviors, and the valuing of performative skill. These tensions are engaged for the most part through *apprenticeship* and through sustained critique of discipleship and mastery.

A glimpse of an actually existing form of artisanship can be gleaned from Pamela Akinyi Wadende's ethnography of a constellation of Luo women in Western Kenya.[164] The daily practice of the women revolved around *chwuech*—the making of artifacts such as pottery, basketry, and *muono* (a form of indigenous architecture). The women called themselves *Bang' Jomariek,* "After the Wise Ones." The women explained that they came up with the name because "when they compared themselves to similar groups, they considered themselves a little sluggish in attaining the kind of fruitful organization they currently had."[165] The name speaks to an ironic, self-critical sensibility within the *Bang' Jomariek* group. The constellation organized itself by appropriating a traditional form of spatial organization known as the *kit dak.* The *kit dak* lays out space in such a way that common areas of interaction and collective participation are nested within enclaves for individual withdrawal.[166] This allows, Wadende argues, for relationships of "engagement and distance."[167] In the course of her study, Wadende finds that the women's participation in *chwuech* cannot be reducible to the utilitarian. For the members of *Bang' Jomariek*, *chwuech* involves an immersion in deep social relationships and often constitutes a radical transformation of the self.

Critics

> Not only in their answers but in their very questions there was a mystification.
> —Karl Marx and Frederick Engels, *The German Ideology*

Social critique articulates an orientation toward knowledge aimed at transforming the society within which the intellectual is embedded. Below, I map out four embodiments of the social critic: the pedagogue; the prophet; the insurgent; the polemicist; and the aesthete.

The Pedagogue

> What place shall the philosopher occupy within the city? That of a sculptor of men.
> —Simplicius, *Commentary on the Manual of Epictetus*

The pedagogue is emergent from established institutions of learning and opinion-making within a society. The embodiments of the pedagogue take widely differing forms in various societies: the *griot* (prominent in many West African societies); the *mallam* or *karamoko* or *shaykh* (in Islamic societies); the wandering holy men and the Catholic friar (prominent in early modern Europe); the curator and the docent (modern Europe); and the professor or teacher (now a global phenomenon). The pedagogue performs many roles, often simultaneously. The West African *griot*, for example, functions as a historian, a public speaker, a journalist, a scholar, a musician, and even an entertainer. The North Atlantic docent is a museum host, a historian, an entertainer, and a guard (preventing eager tourists from touching the art on display).

The pedagogue often finds herself ambivalent about her institutional location. On the one hand, the pedagogue is ensconced in her society's established institutions and thus, largely, serves as a representative of her institution and even of her society. Partly because the pedagogue performs services for her institution, both out of self-interest and for its own sake, the pedagogue is deeply committed to conservation of what she deems the best of the cultural treasures in her society. But partly because the pedagogue is located within institutions of critical discourse, partly because the multiple perspectives the pedagogue is privy to from her students, peers, and from the public, and partly for its own sake, the pedagogue is also deeply committed to innovation and critique. For this and many reasons, the pedagogue's rhetoric is deeply *epideictic*—that is, balanced on a thin wedge between doxological rhetorics of praise and prophetic rhetorics of blame.

At her best, the pedagogue displays what Edward Said in a different context described as a "relentless erudition, scouring alternative sources, exhuming buried documents, reviving forgotten (or abandoned) histories."[168] Unlike the prophet and the polemicist, the pedagogue is scrupulous about detail and exacting about complexity. The pedagogue works within a larger historical canvass than the prophet or polemicist and thus has the perspective of the *longue durée*. These virtues are pregnant with potential vices. At his worst, the pedagogue can be deeply reactionary, keen on the preservation of existing hierarchies under the banner of the "best that has been thought and said." Pedagogic institutions lie at the intersection of various publics, but are for all of that prone to their own insularities and *idées fixes*. Moreover, precisely because the pedagogue is trained in the arts of rhetoric, argumentation, and performances, they are far more prone to the pathologies of self-serving attributional biases than other publics.

It is arguable that fewer places rivaled Timbuktu as a center of learning in the medieval world. Established because of its strategic location as a center for commerce, Timbuktu grew into one of the most vibrant centers of learning and scholarship in the ancient world. According to John Hunwick, "Timbuktu's most celebrated scholar, Ahmad Baba (1564–1627) claimed that his library contained 1,600 volumes, and that it was the smallest library of any of his family."[169] Ahmad Baba wrote the following about his *shaykh* (teaching master), worth quoting because it offers a striking illustration of the *habitus* of the celebrated *shaykhs* of Timbuktu:

> Our *shaykh* and our [source of] blessing, the jurist, and accomplished scholar, a pious and ascetic man of God, who was among the finest of God's righteous servants and practising scholars. He was a man given by nature to goodness and benign intent, guileless, and naturally disposed to goodness, believing in people to such an extent that all men were virtually equal in his sight, so well did he think of them and absolve them of wrongdoing. Moreover, he was constantly attending to people's needs, even at cost to himself, becoming distressed at their misfortunes, mediating their disputes, and giving counsel. Add to this his love of learning, and his devotion to teaching—in which pursuit he spent his days—his close association (*ßu ‚ba*) with men of learning, and his own utter humility, his lending of his most rare and precious books in all fields without asking for them back again, no matter what discipline they were in. Thus it was that he lost a [large] portion of his books—may God shower His beneficence upon him for that! Sometimes a student would come to his door asking for a book, and he would give it to him without even knowing who the student was. In this matter he was truly astonishing, doing this for the sake of God Most High, despite his love for books and [his zeal in] acquiring them, whether by purchase or copying. One day I came to him asking for books on grammar, and he hunted through his library and brought me everything he could find on the subject.[170]

The Prophet

> Epochs are in accord with themselves only if the crowd comes into these radiant confessionals which are the theaters or the arenas, and as much as possible, . . . to listen to its own confessions of cowardice and sacrifice, of hate and passion. . . . For there is no theater which is not prophecy. Not this false divination which gives names and dates, but true prophecy, that which reveals to men these surprising truths: that the living must live, that the living must die, that autumn must follow summer, spring follow winter,

that there are four elements, that there is happiness, that there are innumerable miseries, that life is a reality, that it is a dream, that man lives in peace, that man lives on blood; in short, those things they will never know.

—Jean Giraudoux, as cited in Stanley Cavell,
Must We Mean What We Say?

Prophecy as an institution was a phenomenon that was widely practiced across several polities and societies in Africa, the ancient Near East, and many other parts of the world.[171] Prophets have often been liminal characters, on the one hand conversant with the deep structures of the society within which they are emergent, and on the other hand relative outsiders to the dominant institutions of their societies. In other words, they have often taken positions at a relative distance from the dominant institutions of their society.

This thus raises the question of whence the authority of the prophet has sprung, given their liminality. Historically, there have been at least three institutional streams within which prophecy has thrived: religious institutions, political institutions, and aesthetic or artistic institutions. In the ancient Near East, dating from the eighth to the sixth century BCE, arguably the most distinctive and intense prophetic institution was that which existed among the Hebrews. This was a thoroughly religious stream of prophecy. The Hebrew word for prophecy is *nabi*, which means "one who is called." The prophet was called by God to deliver a message and claimed that their power derived from "revelation." According to Abraham Heschel, "the prophets see the world from the point of view of God, as transcendent not immanent truth." Such a transcendent truth, Heschel adds, just *is*: "There are no proofs for the existence of the God of Abraham. There are only witnesses." And not always willing witnesses—often, prophets delivered their oracles against their will. The truth revealed by God was absolute. It was an absolutism of belief and temperament, not of detail and evidence.[172]

Not all traditions have articulated prophecy within religious institutions. In East Africa, for example, there exist prophetic institutions that self-consciously distanced themselves from religious revelation as the basis of truth-telling. As Gail Presbey notes, drawing on the work of anthropologists on the prophetic traditions in East Africa, certain strains of the East African prophetic tradition articulated their judgments by drawing on publically accessible forms of knowledge and by pointing to collective forms of social participation and agency. She quotes Chaungo Barasa, a Kenyan sage philosopher, who argues that prophetic truth—unlike the revelatory truths claimed by religious figures—aimed at "insight and foresight."[173]

A third form of institutional prophecy is emergent from artistic or aesthetic movements. The artistic prophet's vision explodes in the utopian impulses of art forms and performances. The poet and prophet William Blake proffers a powerful definition of the artistic prophet: "Every honest man is a prophet. He utters his opinion both of private and public matters thus: 'If you go on so, the result is so.' He never says: 'such a thing shall happen, let you do what you will.' A prophet is a Seer, not an Arbitrary Dictator."[174] Blake thinks it is the prophet's task to smash the "mind-forged manacles" of industrial society.

The prophet conceives of truth as primary. The language and tone of the prophet is charged with urgency and is heedless of calculation and strategy. The prophet conceives of time as *kairos*, "the interpenetration, almost simultaneity of past, present, future."[175] For the prophet, the temporal crackles with *crisis* and thus demands decision making.[176] And yet because of such a conception of time, there is always a deep temporal tension in religious prophecy between the "now" and the "eternal." In artistic prophecy, there is a deep tension between the "now" and the "utopian." For that reason, the prophet's speech is relentlessly millennial, apocalyptic in diagnosing the ills of the body politic, utopian in its invocation of a future restoration.[177] The prophet, Heschel reports, "makes no concession to man's capacity. Exhibiting little understanding for human weaknesses, he seems unable to extenuate the culpability of man."[178] The prophet is ruthless in stripping foes of every shred of respectability in part because the prophet sees civility as a fig-leaf to cover up the moral depravities of oppression and injustice. The abolitionist Frederick Douglass is categorical: "If there is no struggle there is no progress. Those who profess to favor freedom and yet deprecate agitation, are men who want crops without plowing up the ground, they want rain without thunder and lightning.

They want the ocean without the awful roar of its many waters."[179] For William Blake, "The road of excess leads to the palace of wisdom."[180] For Theodor Adorno, "All thinking is exaggeration, in so far as every thought that is one at all goes beyond its confirmation by the given facts."[181]

There is a very close connection between the prophetic form and its content. Both religious and aesthetic forms of prophecy are performative, demonstrative, and theatrical. The Hebrew prophet Isaiah walked around naked and barefoot for three years to prophesy the future enslavement and humiliation of the Egyptians and the Ethiopians. Jeremiah staggered about with a wooden yoke on his neck to advise submission to the Babylonians. Nietzsche speculates that the prophet is particularly attuned to suffering, hence the enactment of the prophetic critique through embodied performances:

> You have no feeling for the fact that prophetic human beings are afflicted with a great deal of suffering; you merely suppose that they have been granted a beautiful "gift," and you would even like to have it yourself. But I shall express myself in a parable. How much many animals suffer from the electricity in the air and the clouds! We see how some species have a prophetic faculty regarding the weather: monkeys, for example (as may be observed even in Europe, and not only in zoos—namely, on Gibraltar). But we pay no heed that it is their *pains* that make them prophets. When a strong positive electrical charge, under the influence of an approaching cloud that is as yet far from visible, suddenly turns into negative electricity and a change of the weather is impending, these animals behave as if an enemy were drawing near and prepare for defense or escape; most often they try to hide: They do not understand bad weather as a kind of weather but as an enemy whose hand they already *feel*.[182]

Prophets have thus often sought to make their case by sheer example, by embodied action. And yet such performances defy dismissal or ridicule, for the prophet awes with implacable principle and electric charisma. The prophetic biography is "a kind of legend," compelling in its sheer presence.

Prophets have often engaged in a thoroughgoing critique of the society from which they emerge. Such a thoroughgoing critique has by no means only taken egalitarian forms. Certain strains of prophecy have been radical—in the sense of an acute critique of the oppressive structures of society—but other strains have been reactionary, intent on shoring up the power and privilege of a beleaguered ruling class. Conservative prophets conceptualize the "roots" of a society as a return to its "origins," and thus demand the turning back of the clock to a time when the few ruled over the many.[183] Radical prophets, on the other hand, do not conceive of a society as an organism and thus are critical of the idea that society has "roots." Rather, radical prophets are interested in a critique of the *structures undergirding* social relations in the society. Conservative and radical prophetic traditions have sharply diverged on moral boundaries. Conservative strains have tended to be exclusivist, focused on their local, national, and religious in-group. Conservative prophets conceive of themselves as tasked with a special mission and their exhortations ring with calls for purity and separation. The metaphors that they invoke to excoriate others are metaphors against contamination, promiscuity, infidelity. Radical prophetic traditions, in contrast, have tended to be universalistic, refusing the narrow loyalties of tribe and nation and embracing the outsider, the different, the weak.

The Insurgent

> While you here do snoring lie,
> Open-eyed conspiracy
> His time doth take.
>
> —William Shakespeare, *The Tempest*

Insurgent knowledges are the forms of know-how articulated in fugitive, irreverent, and unofficial spaces as a means of survival against hegemonic or totalitarian forces. There are as many types of insurgents as there are different societies. They include the trickster, the *femme fatale*, the outlaw, and the fool.[184] The insurgent uses for her defense, in the famous words of James Joyce, "silence, exile, and cunning." I would translate Joyce's pithy statement into four kinds of knowledges: *metis*, or cunning intelligence; *pronoia*, or strategic intelligence; *gnosis*, or silent/secret intelligence; and *ekstasis* (think of ecstasy in its original sense of *ek-stasis*, a standing outside oneself, a shattering *un-doing* of one's mastery, in equal parts pleasurable and painful). *Metis* involves forms of trickery, subterfuge, and deception deployed by weak, vulnerable, or oppressed groups. This is the kind of knowledge that North Atlantic blacks had to resort to as they sought a way of living through slavery, colonialism, totalitarianism, and mandatory capitalism. The escaped slave Harriet Jacobs referred to this form of knowledge as the "weapons of the weak": "Who can blame slaves for being cunning? They are constantly compelled to resort to it. It is the only weapon of the weak and oppressed against the strength of their tyrants."[185] Insurgent *pronoia* refers primarily to the kinds of *strategic knowledges* of how to exercise one's agency against powerful enemies intent on manipulating the weak or crippling their agency through fear or despair. Another way of thinking of insurgent *pronoia* is that it refers to theories of how to conspire in fighting back against sovereign power. Insurgent gnosis refers to "secret knowledges" that circulate among the oppressed as "news," "information," "memory," and useful knowledges. They include encrypted memories of traumatic events that official histories cannot or will not record; relationships and heroes that are unacknowledged by establishment historians; rumors and gossip that are censored by the official media; medicinal knowledges and so-called "old-wives tales" on such matters as midwifery and herbal medicines; and "conspiracy theories" detailing the nefarious acts of the ruling class. Insurgent *ekstasis* refers to social articulations of affect, often expressively enacted in ways that are frowned upon by the hegemonic society or, at times, concealed or hidden from official festivals and "public" events. Insurgent *ekstasis* can be "spontaneous" acts such as riots and "mob" events, but they can also be "organized" demonstrations such as pride parades, carnivals, and even lynch mobs.

Perhaps one of the most striking narratives of the deployment of insurgent knowledges—the articulation of insurgent *metis* and *pronoia*—is witnessed in the anthropology of E. E. Evans-Pritchard among the Nuer. Evans-Pritchard traveled to Nuerland in the wake of punishing imperial raids that the British had been carrying out to subjugate the Nuer. Given that Evans-Pritchard's research was itself funded by the British, there is reason to think that his research findings were sought for their intelligence value on the Nuer resistance. Evans-Pritchard met with a chilly reception from the Nuer.[186] He goes on to recount his experience in trying to get the Nuer to open up to him:

> Nuer are expert at sabotaging an inquiry and until one has resided with them for some weeks they steadfastly stultify all efforts to elicit the simplest facts and to elucidate the most innocent practices. . . . The following specimen of Nuer methods is the commencement of a conversation on the Nyanding river, on a subject which admits of some obscurity but, with willingness to co-operate, can soon be elucidated.
>
> I: Who are you?
> **Cuol:** A man.
> I: What is your name?
> **Cuol:** Do you want to know my name?
> I: Yes.
> **Cuol:** You want to know my name?
> I: Yes, you have come to visit me in my tent and I would like to know who you are.
> **Cuol:** All right. I am Cuol. What is your name?
> I: My name is Pritchard.
> **Cuol:** What is your father's name?
> I: My father's name is also Pritchard.
> **Cuol:** No, that cannot be true. You cannot have the same name as your father.
> I: It is the name of my lineage. What is the name of your lineage?
> **Cuol:** Do you want to know the name of my lineage?
> I: Yes.
> **Cuol:** What will you do with it if I tell you? Will you take it to your country?
> I: I don't want to do anything with it. I just want to know it since I am living at your camp.
> **Cuol:** Oh well, we are Lou.

> **I:** I did not ask you the name of your tribe. I know that. I am ask-
> ing you the name of your lineage.
> **Cuol:** Why do you want to know the name of my lineage?
> **I:** I don't want to know it.
> **Cuol:** Then why do you ask me for it? Give me some tobacco.
> I defy the most patient ethnologist to make headway against this kind
> of opposition. One is just driven crazy by it. Indeed, after a few weeks
> of associating solely with Nuer one displays, if the pun be allowed, the
> most evident symptoms of "Nuerosis."[187]

It is important to keep in mind two critical points. The first is that insurgent knowledges are resonant with, even entwined with, but not *reducible to* or *identical with*, the hegemonic knowledges to which they bear a family resemblance. That is, even though insurgent *gnosis* bears striking similarities to *gnostic* mastery, and insurgent *pronoia* resembles hegemonic *techne*, these knowledges remain qualitatively different. For one, whereas gnostic mastery alludes to mystical or divine kinds of insight, insurgent *gnosis* is emergent from material and institutional interpretations of what one needs to survive a particular situation. Moreover, insurgent *gnosis* differs from gnostic mastery in the fact that insurgent *gnosis* is deployed by the less powerful, whereas gnostic mastery is the knowledge that accrues to the powerful. For the most part (though as I point out below, not in all cases), insurgent knowledges are deployed for the ends of survival and in the hopes of emancipation. Hegemonic knowledges, in contrast, are often (though not always) used in the interests of the aggrandizement of power and for the purposes of subjugating others. But perhaps the most striking difference between *gnostic* mastery and insurgent *gnosis* is that insurgent *gnosis* constitutes a critique of *gnostic* mastery. This critique challenges the notion that knowledge is always to be found through "insider access." Rather, insurgent gnosis points out that knowledge is often right in the open and it is simply because the powerful have an ideological interest in not acknowledging what is manifest that they render the poor invisible. The insurgent critique of *gnosis* is thus in a sense a critique of hermeneutics of suspicion that ignore the manifest content and go rummaging for the latent. In many cases, the manifest content is the ideological cover-up.

But—and here is the second important point to keep in mind—if insurgent knowledges are not reducible to hegemonic knowledges, it is not the case that insurgent knowledges are straightforwardly "good" or "better" than hegemonic knowledges. The knowledges of the weak are not immune from the misinformation deployed by hegemonic forces. Moreover, the oppressed are not one-dimensional. Among the oppressed are men and women, able-bodied and disabled, heterosexual, transgender, gays, lesbians, intersexual. Thus, even among the oppressed, insurgent knowledges can be deployed to the end of subjugating those lower down on the rung of oppression rather than challenging the power structure. This is the manifest case with the insurgent knowledges that too often circulate among oppressed groups. If rumors, gossip, and so-called "old-wives tales" often speak to the deep knowledges that circulate among the oppressed in ways that subvert and by-pass official channels of propaganda, it is also the case that significant strains of these knowledges can sometimes be false or, in certain cases, represent misinformation injected into the secret pathways of the oppressed by the powerful. The point, then, is that the oppressed may at times accurately diagnose the fact that secret and overwhelming material forces are at work in destroying their livelihoods and unraveling their lives, material and institutional forces that are unacknowledged in the wider hegemonic society. But this does not mean that they always offer accurate interpretations of how these material pressures should be mobilized against. In other words, in certain cases, the insurgent gnosis may be a powerful and insightful hermeneutic of suspicion (*insurgent gnosis*), but it may also be deeply mistaken and ineffectual in offering a hermeneutic of agency (*insurgent pronoia*).

For example, Comaroff and Comaroff have unveiled an "occult economy" operating in what they describe as post-revolutionary economies, according to them starkly exemplified by South Africa.[188] This occult economy consists of the "deployment of magical means for material ends," and is manifested in "ritual murders," epidemics of witchcraft and the killing of suspect witches, and moral panics about the piracy of body parts. These events, that are inscribed by generational and gender subjectivities, emerge from the contradictions of "millennial capitalism and the culture of neoliberalism":[189]

> On the one hand is a perception, authenticated by glimpses of the vast wealth that passes through most postcolonial societies and into the hands of a few of their citizens: that the mysterious mechanisms of the market hold the key to hitherto unimaginable riches; to capital amassed by the ever more rapid, often immaterial flow of value across time and space, and into the intersecting sites where the local meets the global. On the other hand is the dawning sense of chill desperation attendant on being left out of the promise of prosperity, of the *telos* of liberation. In South Africa, after all, the end of apartheid held out the prospect that everyone would be set free to speculate and accumulate, to consume, and to indulge repressed desires. But, for many, the millennial moment has passed without palpable payback.[190]

Comaroff and Comaroff's argument point to the consequences of the contradictions engendered by the occult economy:

> That these not-quite-fathomable mechanisms—precisely because they are inscrutable, occult—have become the object of jealousy and envy and evil dealings; that arcane forces are intervening in the production of value, diverting its flow for selfish purposes. This, in turn, underlies the essential paradox of occult economies, the fact that they operate on two inimical fronts at once. The first is the constant pursuit of new, magical means for otherwise unattainable ends. The second is the effort to eradicate people held to enrich themselves by those very means; through the illegitimate appropriation, that is, not just of the bodies and things of others, but also of the forces of production and reproduction themselves.[191]

If it is important not to romanticize insurgent knowledges as always already emancipatory, it is just as important to indicate how official epistemologies lack the wherewithal to come to terms with insurgent knowledges. Take, once again, the kind of knowledges emergent from occult economies as insightfully mapped by the Comaroffs. If the poor cannot always put a name to global capitalism's ravages, they can accurately discern that mysterious and arcane forces are behind their impoverishment and the destruction of their livelihoods. To these arguments, however, positivists and rationalists are inclined to respond that such accounts are "spooky superstitions." Surging, wildfire festivals of revolution and carnival testify to subaltern agency and determination to carve out autonomous spaces of delight and celebration. To these cascading fires of embodied solidarity, however, conservatives and liberals look askance, declaring them "irrational," "savage," "vulgar." The global underclasses are aware that more than just coincidence is at work in the polluting of their environments. To such concerns, ever so serious policy makers lecture the global South to let go of their "paranoia." When the poor detail the array of forces massed against them and to their sense that it would take a revolution to effectively respond to the terrifying nightmare of American empire, conservatives respond with bromides about "personal responsibility" while liberals counsel an end to "empty utopianism."

I would go further. It is not simply that dominant epistemologies have proved too feeble in engaging adequately with insurgent knowledges. Rather, they ought to be seen as entangled—if complexly so—in broader efforts to delegitimize and discredit fugitive knowledges. This is strikingly illustrated by the virtually concerted chorus—from modernists to postmodernists, Republicans[192] to Liberals—in delegitimizing attempts to understand the workings of the global ruling class. According to these theories, to map out the concerted trade-offs that the G8 powerhouses perform on behalf of their interests and against the interests of poor countries is to indulge in so much "conspiracy theory" and "paranoia." One would expect that these efforts at delegitimation would be particularly powerful in the conservative social sciences—economics, political science—but they have been as equally powerful within the so-called "radical humanities." Take Baudrillard's virulently anti-essentialist argument for example. He diagnoses the current age as a "passage to a space whose curvature is no longer that of the real, nor of truth, [an] age of simulation [that] begins with a liquidation of all referentials—worse: by their artificial resurrection in systems of signs, a more ductile material than meaning, in that it lends itself to all systems of equivalence, all binary oppositions and all combinatory algebra."[193] For Baudrillard, therefore, "the age of simulation" does not merely reverse the binary oppositions between truth and falsehood, dissimulation and simulation, sign and meaning, surface and depth, presence and absence, but, rather, heralds the triumph of "simulacra and simulacrum" and the end of ideology. The perverse consequence is that Baudrillard cannot conceive of interests that serve the rich and starve the poor; he refuses to acknowledge wars where bodies are maimed and people killed.

The Polemicist

> Not ideas, but interests—material and ideal—directly govern men's conduct. Yet very frequently the "world images" that have been created by "ideas" have, like switchmen, determined the tracks along which action has been pushed by the dynamic of interest.
> —Max Weber, *From Max Weber: Essays in Sociology*

If, as it is said, the public relations agent is the organic intellectual of late capitalism, then the polemicist is the organic intellectual of partisan causes. Like the prophet, the polemicist appears as if born for a crisis. Unlike the prophet, the polemicist is something of a professional provocateur. He or she takes active pleasure not so much in the results of activism, in the accomplishment of goals, as in the exhilaration of seeing the battle joined and the enemy vanquished. At her best, the polemicist is a steely realist and will have none of the transcendentalist's "objectivity" or the pedagogue's "neither-norism." He or she recognizes that people have deep differences of opinion and interests, and that these differences cannot be smoothed over by platitudinous calls for "dialogue" and "conversation." The polemicist, moreover, recognizes that not all beliefs and behavior deserve respectful hearing and painstaking debate. She accepts the manifest fact that many beliefs are absurd, that people do not debate in good faith, that it is in the self-interest of many to brazenly lie and cheat and steal, and that the conclusion to most disputes is that someone has won and another has been defeated. The best polemicists are, precisely because of this realism, deeply allergic to moralism, correctly recognizing that the moralist is driven by sentimentalism.

Because the polemicist is relentlessly partisan, because she is a realist, and because she is exhilarated by the taste of combat, her weapons of choice differ from that of the pedagogue and the scholar. The polemicist's tools are those of exaggeration, caricature, ridicule, mockery; all of these deployed with merciless and devastating effect. The polemicist's métier is the lightning-quick *piece d'occasion* tossed as one would a grenade to break up the obscene tête-à-tête of the chattering classes. If there is something of the eliminationist war whoop in the polemicist rounding on a hapless opponent, it is a qualified adversarialism. For one, the polemicist's relentless friend or foe worldview is inflected by an appreciation and delight in the worthy opponent who matches her in wit and ruthlessness. But it is even more the case that the polemicist is often something of an aesthete and thus takes a secret, subversive pleasure not just in the joy of victory but in defeating an opponent with devastating style.

But already these attributes speak to the vices of the polemicist.[194] At his worst, the polemicist's relationship with truth is complex and contradictory. It is not so much that the polemicist has little use for truth or truthfulness. It is rather that the polemicist tends to have an idea of himself as the only true believer, the only true fighter on behalf of others, the only person with the courage to call the truth as he sees it. This speaks to the secret vainglory that beats just below the polemicist's indignation. The polemicist's vanity is manifested as a disturbing craving for spectacle and a hunkering for the stage. One result of this is that the polemicist is often a rebel in search of a cause, and if such causes cannot be found, is often led to convert minor hermeneutical differences of opinion into life-and-death doctrinal battles, petty tiffs and minor contretemps into mortal causes. At his worst, the polemicist is given to declaring that this or that cause is the "defining battle of the age," positioning himself as the spokesperson of the cause, and appointing himself the patron of victims of the cause. Another virtually predictable result is that the polemicist is almost always to be found a *disillusioned reactionary* in his senior years, his zeppelin-sized ego crashing and burning in self-consumed fury at being rendered irrelevant. Lacking a modicum of self-criticism, however, the polemicist is almost always led to blame his comrades and younger generations for betraying his cause. Thus it turns out that what often endears the polemicist to his faction in the early years of his rise—independence of mind, contrarianism—is the poisoned chalice of an incorrigible sectarianism and utter lack of loyalty to anything but himself. The dessicated polemicist does not die; he fades into the moralist he despised in his youth.

The Aesthete

> It is only shallow people who do not judge by appearances. The mystery of the world is the visible, not the invisible.
> —Oscar Wilde, *The Picture of Dorian Gray*

Embodiments of the aesthete include the *ephues*, the bohemian, the dandy, the *flaneur*, and the *sapeur*. The *ephues* was a distinctive intellectual figure in ancient Greece. He sought to embody physical, moral, and intellectual symmetry, balance, grace, and harmony. The sculpted and rippling body of the *ephues* symbolized youth, virility, strength, and beauty; it evoked desire, vitality, and triumph. The ancient Greek dramatist Sophocles, who assiduously sought to cultivate the figure of the *ephues*, is reported to have appeared naked when leading celebrations after the victory of Salamis.[195] The *ephues*'s body also held moral and intellectual symbolism. He was said to enact the ideals of *sophrosyne*—temperance, moderation, healthy-mindedness. The *ephues* was largely an intellectual figure of the ancient world. In contrast, the bohemian, the *flaneur*, and the dandy are arguably both the effect of the bourgeois revolution and reactions against bourgeois value. The bohemian, unlike the *ephues* who seeks to embody the ideals of society, lives on the fringes of bourgeois society.[196] The bohemian aesthete rejects bourgeois utilitarianism and instead champions *l'art pour l'art*, art for its own sake. The *flaneur* walked the streets observing the curiosities, consumer goods, and people in the booming metropolises of capitalist modernity. The *sapeurs* are Central African dandies known for their flamboyant designer suits (imported from the metropolitan capitals of the G8 countries).[197] The ideology of the *sapeur* is a bewildering kaleidoscope of contradictory drives: partly a *habitus* of imitation inculcated by European colonial false consciousness; partly a critique of European constructions of Africans as absolute alterity; partly a reaction against African nationalist governments and their ideologies of authenticity; partly a masculinist assertion of daring; and partly a feminist form of gender-bending.

At her best, the aesthete offers a radical *defamiliarization*, a shattering of society's oppressive and sanctified commonplaces. The aesthete through her art and life offers a distance-taking from society's morals, taste, duty, civic-mindedness. The aesthete disdains routinization, normalization, conformism, commodification, massification, and reification. Her life speaks, within the register of the aesthetic and the beautiful, to a perfectionism that is not satisfied with the catechism of the middle-brow, while, on the register of the ethical, it strips away the elaborate metaphysics of the peculiar institution of morality, revealing it to be no more than papered-over conventionalism. Like the polemicist, the aesthete dislikes cliché, and practically heaves at the slightest hint of the sentimental. Unlike the polemicist, the aesthete finds indignation vulgar; her response is always subtle—irony, the wrinkled nose, the clever put-down, the world-weary tone, the paradoxical aphorism, the turning away. Many aesthetes are insurgents and draw on insurgent institutions for resistance. Like the insurgent, the aesthete is a shape-shifter, a person who seems to reinvent herself right in the public eye. In doing so, the aesthete not only exposes the manner in which "nature" is a construct but also opens up possibilities for agency. The aesthete is deeply critical of *gnosis* (secret wisdom). For the aesthete, knowledge consists in seeing what is right before our own eyes rather than thinking that truth is always to be found somewhere else, hidden.

At his worst, the aesthete is completely unaware of how much the character he affects is derivative of the pathologies of the society he detests. "I used to rely on my personality," a sorrowful Oscar Wilde wrote in correspondence just a year before his death. "Now I know that my personality really rested on the fiction of *position*. Having lost position, I find my personality of no avail."[198] Moreover, if aestheticism rightly insists that notions of beauty and ugliness, play and entertainment, are as critical (that is essential) to the good life as any so-called "material needs," it is nevertheless true that there can be a temptation by aesthetes to subordinate such material realities to the aesthetic. This particular temptation to think of the aesthetic as somehow primary to or separate from the material is a temptation most often indulged by the *petite bourgeoisie*, which perhaps goes to show that in many (but not all) cases, aestheticism quite often just is a bourgeois reaction to a bourgeois society.

INTIMATIONS OF THE UTOPIAN IN INTELLECTUAL FORMS

> At their best, intellectuals do more than package their research
> into digestible bits for policymakers or the public. They force us to
> think beyond the limits of the day, to ask the questions no one is
> asking. They are an invitation to imaginative excess and political
> trespass. Academic experts in the mainstream media reassure us
> with their authority; young intellectuals in the little magazines
> arrest us with their divinations.
> —Corey Robin, "The Responsibility of Adjunct Intellectuals"

This chapter offers sketches of a variety of intellectual forms of life or embodiments that are emergent in institutions and social practices in the North Atlantic and African worlds. The intellectual figurations that I have sounded in this chapter are not advanced as "pure types," but rather as distinctive, signature assemblages of ways of imagining the world. As the discussion above makes clear, my purpose does not consist in elevating any single intellectual form as absolutely better than other forms. Rather, I sought to ask more fine-grained questions about how these intellectual forms create or delimit space for making or unmaking the world. Yet another value to this chapter, I hope, is in dramatizing the sheer diversity of intellectual forms that are available to the imagination—a diversity that is, alas, under severe pressure from the machineries of standardization and professionalization in the neoliberal geopolitical economy in general and in the academy in particular.

In the next chapter, I make a turn toward a sustained engagement with aesthetics. As will be clear, I conceive of aesthetic articulation as a form of intellectual practice. Nonetheless, such is the importance and distinctiveness of aesthetic creation and criticism that I think it rewards sustained attention as an autonomous practice.

CHAPTER 3

Radical World-building

Notes Toward a Critical Contextual Aesthetic

> What form do you suppose a life would take that was determined at
> a decisive moment precisely by the street song last on everyone's lips?
> —Walter Benjamin, "Surrealism"

This chapter articulates a critical contextual aesthetic ontology—
that is, a comprehensive, systematic account of the context and form
of aesthetic creation, performance, dissemination, and reception. My
goal in this chapter closely tracks the impulses in the first and second
chapters. First, I aim to establish that aesthetic practice is a constitutive dimension of any robust account of the intellectual life. Against a
powerful current in reigning philosophical traditions that imposes a
strict division—often opposition—between knowledge and aesthetics,
truth and art, understanding and imagination, I want to make a case for
their mutual imbrication. Second, I suggest that accounts of aesthetic
practice that begin by embedding artifacts and performances in thick
social ontologies offer deeper, more textured visions of actually existing
as well as utopian iterations of artistry and craft than those that begin
by stipulating normative principles of aesthetic analysis or criticism.
This is so in large part because these normative theories narrow the
range of aesthetics to the philosophy of the fine arts. Against this, I

endeavor to think about aesthetic creativity, sensibility, and criticism as *embedded* in actually existing ecological and historical contexts, as *entangled* in social relations of power and solidarity, as *embodied* by particular persons, as *encountered* in global flows of translation and transmission, and as *engendering* of particular, contested social practices and artifacts.

I also argue for a critically contextual account of aesthetic practice. Specifically, I argue that we can get a better understanding of aesthetics if we embed artifacts and performances in at least four contexts: emergence, performance, dissemination, and reception. Having established this contextual ontology, I then put forward a normative account of fully realized aesthetic artifacts and performances as *four-dimensional forms* oriented toward robust explorations of the following asymptotic horizons: participatory embodiment, knowledge, politics, and meaning. I will unpack this argument and then go on to explore its implications.

MAPPING AESTHETIC ONTOLOGY

The Form and Context of Aesthetic Articulation

All great works of literature found a genre or dissolve one.
—Walter Benjamin, "On the Image of Proust"

The term *aesthetics* can be defined as sensory, affective, phenomenological, and evaluative articulations and responses to particular artifacts (e.g., paintings, novels, or films); performances (e.g., plays, dances, and speeches); events (e.g., meetings, festivals, and wars); ideas (e.g., propositions, theories, and ideologies); practices (e.g., egalitarianism, spiritualism, and scientism); or environments (e.g., shopping malls, forests, and mountains). Aesthetic responses are *sensory* insofar as they involve various activations and stimulations of the senses (sight, hearing, taste, smell, and touch); *affective* insofar as these sensual responses take on distinct emotional valences (pleasure, fear, disgust, anxiety, resentment); *phenomenological* insofar as aesthetic responses are constitutive of experience and thereby orient dispositions and whet sensibilities; and *evaluative* insofar as aesthetic responses are value laden interpretations of artifacts, performances, and the world (beautiful or ugly, dangerous or safe, attractive or repulsive, etc.).

Aesthetic responses can thus be focal or diffuse, hypo-sensory or hyper-sensory. Focal aesthetic stimuli are the sort wherein a person's aesthetic reactions are caused by a specific—often concentrated—stimuli. In other words, the stimuli that causes the aesthetic response can be traced to a determinate etiology or cause. For example, a loud explosion can be easily identified as the cause of panic in a theater. Diffuse aesthetic stimuli, on the other hand, occur when it is difficult to narrow down the cause of an aesthetic response. These aesthetic experiences are the sort wherein a person's response is structured by either subliminal, peripheral, or ambient stimuli. For example, a reader may not be aware that her enjoyment of a book is mainly due to ambient stimuli such as the aroma of coffee, the music playing the background, and the warmth of a fireplace. Focal and diffuse aesthetic may either be experienced as hyper-sensory or hypo-sensory. Hyper-sensory aesthetic experiences are intense aesthetic experiences. For example, if a person pricks you with a needle, one's aesthetic experience will be a feeling of intense pain. Hypo-sensory aesthetic experiences are those that are not intensely felt—almost like a dull pain in the background of a person's consciousness. Aesthetic experiences such as boredom and lassitude are examples of hypo-sensory aesthetic experiences. Though it may be tempting to argue that most focal aesthetic stimuli are experienced in hyper-sensory ways and most diffuse aesthetic stimuli in hypo-sensory ways, this is not always the case. For example, a person may experience an intense bout of nostalgia without knowing exactly why. Aesthetic experiences such as the uncanny have the singular characteristic of being at once hypo- and hyper-sensory.

Such an account emphasizes the "aesthetic" as a practice. By *aesthetic practice*, I mean the resources, traditions, and repertoires of imagination, artistry, craft, and criticism that are constitutive of a whole range of artifacts, performances, styles, and contexts. An expansive definition of the aesthetic as a practice invites a thoroughgoing reassessment of traditional theories of the aesthetic. For one thing, it breaks with the practice of narrowing aesthetic discourse to a consideration only of aesthetic objects of contemplation (for example, artworks) or—its obverse—to aesthetic experiences. Rather, the aesthetic comes to be seen as interactive encounters with artifacts, performances, events, environments, and so on. Such diverse forms as wildernesses and wetlands, cities and suburbs, prairies and parking lots, styles and sensibilities may be rightly considered aesthetic formations not only insofar as they are subject to human evaluative judgments— for example, interpretations as to whether they are beautiful, sublime, enchanted, simple, complex, and so on—but also precisely because they are constituted by human imaginative agency. Additionally, my expansive definition of the aesthetic significantly accounts for the range and diversity of aesthetic responses. Against narrowly cognitivist accounts of aesthetic judgments as disinterested or contemplative, an embodied account of aesthetic response registers it as the interanimation of the cognitive, the affective, and the kinesthetic. It is also the case that such a comprehensive definition of the aesthetic allows for a robust critique of both *reductionist* accounts of aesthetic practice, which would limit aesthetic artifacts and practices to functional or utilitarian equations, and *inflationalist* theories, which claim a transcendental realm for aesthetic discourse and practice. Rather, aesthetic formations encompass both the evental and the everyday, the striking and the banal. It is also the case that an account of the aesthetic as practice marks a forceful break with the provincialism and class snobbery that has been a longstanding feature of aesthetic discourse. It is instead attuned to the historical depth and geographical breadth that make up the remarkable diversity from which aesthetic practices are emergent.

To be sure, as deeply phenomenological and evaluative interactive encounters, aesthetic practices are always already normatively charged. It is only that a robust normative account of aesthetic forms ought to emerge only after taking seriously its constitutive dimensions as a practice. Aesthetic practices form a complex ecology that include: *contexts*, the temporal and spatial relationships from which a practice is emergent; *embodiment*, the persons and subjects embedded within these contexts and that in turn create, perform, and critique aesthetic practices; *form*, the material and imaginative technologies and repertoires that constitute the imaginative art and craft of an aesthetic practice; and *imaginary*, the asymptotic horizon that every particular aesthetic practice latently or manifestly seeks to realize.

A brief elaboration of these constituents follows below. I would argue that there are at least four major contexts that constitute and are in turn constituted by aesthetic practices: the context of emergence, the context of performance, the context of dissemination, and the context of reception. The *context of emergence* refers to the political, economic, and cultural background (history or "tradition") from which an aesthetic practice is emergent. In other words, it is the social and embodied conditions of possibility for the invention of artifacts and performances. It includes the institutional interpellations—race, gender, class, sexuality, impairment/disability, and so on—that are constitutive of the emergence of the subjectivity of artists; the institutional relations, for example, an archive of artistic innovation; the existence of a clerisy of writers and critics that make up the horizon of a formal artistic tradition; and the institutional infrastructure, for example, the existence of musical instruments, a room to write in, a library, pen and paper, and so forth, that make up the resources for the empowerment or disempowerment of artists, inventors, and critics.

The *context of performance* refers to the time-space in which an artist or group of artists actually bring artifacts into being or enact a performance. It is the moment, in a manner of speaking, in which an association, image, story, narrative, idea, vision, and so on is actually brought to bear on a blank page (in the case of a novel), or stage (in the case of a dance), or canvas (in the case of a painting).

The *context of dissemination* tracks contestations over circulation, translation, and canonization of artifacts, performances, and practices. In the case of a novel, for example, this refers to the process of publication, dissemination to readers, and even canonization within a list or genre or type or syllabus. In the case of a painting, dissemination refers to the moment in space and time in which the painting is exhibited.

The *context of reception* refers to the interaction of the aesthetic artifact with interpreters (be they readers or viewers). Of course, these contexts are inextricably interanimated. That is, the context of emergence, performance, dissemination, and reception should be seen as layered, overlapping, dialectical, co-constitutive, and recursive continuums rather than a simple linear sequence. Moreover, these contexts are best seen as temporal reencounters rather than as singularities. For example, insofar as no artifact or performance is ever created *ex nihilo*, it may well be said that all contexts of emergence are reemergences; just as all contexts of performance are reperformances.

Moreover, these contexts ought not to be seen as necessarily sequential. The context of emergence and performance, for example, are so dialectically intertwined that seeing them as separate events is a category mistake. Moreover, in a late capitalist regime, the context of dissemination (the process in which an artifact or performance is exhibited, staged, or marketed) and the context of reception (the time and space in which audiences or readers encounter the artifact) are inextricably intertwined. For example, it is almost impossible for particular paintings to be disseminated outside of a network of established art gallery regimes. Depending on the aesthetic tradition, the context of performance and the context of reception can also be deeply intertwined—this is the case, particularly, with the African and African-American aesthetic traditions that emphasize a great deal of artistic improvisation during the performance of the artistic piece in response to interpreters' interaction with the performance. The interanimation of contexts means that they ought not to be seen as seamlessly flowing in a linear sequence. Contextualization ought to be seen not as a movement from one entirely self-contained context to another but rather as *recontextualization* and *decontextualization*. If certain meanings in an aesthetic practice are gained through its dissemination, others are lost. That gaining and that losing is by no means "natural" or "innocent." It is always contested by and for particular formal investments and social interests.

Just as context constitutes form, so form constitutes context. Form consists of an aesthetic practice's materiality, extension, type, and orientation. By materiality, I mean the aesthetic practice's mediatory technology. A distinction may be made between *epical* versus *evental* media. Epical media consist of those that have developed over the long arc of evolutionary history. These include language, musical or rhythmic sound, images, ideograms. Evental media consist of more recent technologies that extend, modify, or enhance epical media. These technologies include, for example, textual and electronic technologies such as paper, canvas, radio, and television. By *extension,* I mean the techniques or crafts that are harnessed in the making or enacting of an aesthetic practice, for example, the writing skills needed for the articulation of a novel or embodied skilled movement that is a vital component of dancing. By *type*, I mean the transfiguration of a medium by particular techniques into a meaningful or significant phenomenon—the transformation of a canvas into a painting, a wilderness into a forest, writing into a book. And by *orientation,* I mean the cognitive, affective, and kinesthetic sensorium constructed by a particular aesthetic practice.

Every aesthetic practice is charged with distinctive intensities, vibrates to particular sonorities and tropes, or turns toward certain horizons. I call this the aesthetic practice's *imaginary*—the asymptotic limit that an aesthetic practice seeks to realize. The imaginary encompasses an aesthetic practice's latent and manifest ambition. It can be utopian or dystopian, hegemonic or radical, singular or plural. The imaginary not only is deeply constituted by the interanimation of context and form but also dialectically reconfigures form and context. Aesthetic practices involve a dialectic of the contextual structure on an art-form with the art-form's agential response and reconfiguration of its context. In what follows below, I argue that a fully realized aesthetic practice is one that engages the possibilities and limits of form toward the robust exploration of a four-dimensional asymptotic horizon—*participatory embodiment, knowledge, politics,* and *meaning*—as these horizons are constituted in contexts of emergence, performance, dissemination, and reception.

Much follows from conceiving of aesthetic practices as the interanimation of contexts, embodiments, forms, and imaginaries. One immediate implication is that such a view refuses the opposed schools of reduction and transcendence that have dominated traditional aesthetic practices. Just as form is irreducible to context, so context is often reconfigured by form.

A deep examination of the imaginary, moreover, enables a re-visioning of vexed debates in aesthetic discourse. Four immediately come to mind: an exploration of participatory embodiment allows for a nuanced engagement of the tension between pleasure and disinterest as modes of aesthetic engagement; revisiting knowledge as an imaginary of aesthetic practice enables a rigorous critique of the vexed place of "truth" in aesthetic practice; investigating the political imaginary of an aesthetic practice makes space for grappling with how power inflects aesthetic practices; and, lastly, a critique of meaning as an aesthetic imaginary, insofar as it prompts a reckoning with the existential, also thereby illuminates the intersection of the particular and the universal in aesthetic practice.

Consider, for example, the vexed debate between contextualism and normativity in aesthetic discourse. On the one hand, an affirmation of a critical contextualism resonates with a robust pluralism about the glorious diversity of aesthetic practices. Thus, such an account rejects the notion that aesthetic practice is reducible to a single essence—such as significant form, universality, vivacity, or institutionaliza-tion. The impulse to a reductionism about what aesthetic practice is has long been a dominant—and pernicious—part of North Atlantic philosophical aesthetics. It is common to hear North Atlantic aes-thetic philosophers search for one covering law or essential element for *all* of art.[1] Clive Bell is paradigmatic of this impulse: "If we can dis-cover some quality common and peculiar to all the objects that pro-voke it, we shall have solved what I take to be the central problem of aesthetics. We shall have discovered the essential quality in a work of art, the quality that distinguishes works of art from all other classes of objects . . . [for] either works of art have some common quality, or when we speak of 'works of art,' we gibber."[2]

But to recognize the contextual embeddedness of aesthetic prac-tice does not entail denying the normative pulse of artworks. In other words, an exploration of how context, form, and the imaginary are interanimated makes space for the possibility of normative evaluations without the absurd positing of such judgments as conducing to a single scoreboard or entailing a simplistic rankings list. The problem with the North Atlantic aesthetic tradition, therefore, is not only that its quest for a single covering law for art is mistaken. It is also that North Atlantic theorists are far too liable to smuggle in the normative under the color of the descriptive—that is, to shirk from the hard work of the normative through exclusionary maneuvers, namely, declaring that bad art is simply not art. Note also the implication of understanding aesthetic practices as embedded in temporal and spatial resonances. Inasmuch as aesthetic practices gesture at an asymptotic horizon, no normative judgment of any single aesthetic practice can be final and absolute.

A robust aesthetic ontology—my argument therefore holds—prompts a reckoning of it as a *praxis*. If this is granted, it encourages us to conceive of the aesthetic as a thickly embedded *lived orientation* about the what, when, where, why, and how of invention, performance, sensibility, dissemination, and reception. Aesthetics, then, is constitutive of the well-lived life. It is to these asymptotic horizons as they are constituted in contexts of emergence, performance, dissemination, and reception that I now wish to turn. Though, as I have argued above, my definition of the aesthetic is expansive and refuses to narrow aesthetic practice to the philosophy of art, in what follows below I frequently invoke artistic practice as a shorthand for aesthetic practices. I do so in part for reasons of parsimony and in part because artistic work—when embedded within a critical practice—has the potential to offer some of the most sustained explorations of the possibilities and limits of aesthetic practice.

TOWARD A NORMATIVE AESTHETIC

Participatory Embodiment

To lend himself, to project himself and steep himself, to feel and feel till he understands and to understand so well that he can say, to have perception at the pitch of passion and expression as embracing as the air, to be infinitely curious and incorrigibly patient, and yet plastic and inflammable and determinable, stooping to conquer and serving to direct—these are fine chances for an active mind, chances to add the idea of independent beauty to the conception of success.

—Henry James, *Criticism*

A fully realized aesthetic practice is oriented toward the realization of a mode of being that I am referring to as participatory embodiment. Participatory embodiment has two major dimensions. The first is the extent to which the aesthetic practice awakens, articulates, and extends embodied capacities within the intersectional contexts of emergence, performance, dissemination, and reception. The second dimension of participatory embodiment is that practice's formal repertory in engaging and reconfiguring its contexts of emergence, performance, dissemination, and reception. The aesthetic practice's interaction with context is thus a dialectical knot: on the one hand, it refers to how the practice absorbs the trace of context from which it is emergent, enacted, circulated, and received; on the other hand, it refers to the practice's responsiveness to social context, its formal innovations in engaging the dynamic contexts that it traverses.

An aesthetic practice realizes a participatory stance within its context of emergence inasmuch as it fully extends human capacities of the imagination and insofar as it proffers a robust response to the social context from which it is emergent. A practice oriented by participatory embodiment engages its *context of emergence* by acknowledging its embeddedness in a particular ecological and social context and by acknowledging the embodiedness of artists and critics. A critical dimension of a fully realized aesthetic practice, then, is its formal responsiveness to these ecological and social contexts, the manner in which the practice's formal innovations are a palimpsest of embodiment. Embeddedness and embodiedness are acknowledged to the extent that the practice responds to and reconfigures its spatial and temporal context. In this rendering, spatial context refers to not only the physical space within which the artist works and the relational networks with and against whom the artist works, but also the practice's "imaginary" orientation to certain social formations, communities, and constituencies. Similarly, the practice's temporal context refers not only to the chronological time within which the artistic performance is embedded but also to the "imaginary" orientation that the artifact or performance articulates vis-à-vis its history and futurity.

Aesthetic realization is thus always already elusive. It has much to do with the particular social and ecological context within which the artist is embedded, including the forms of power and resources afforded the artist, as these intersect with artistic virtuosity, the artist's technical abilities in crafting of intricate dimensions of plot or design or notation, and the critical reception of the aesthetic practice. In acknowledging the embeddedness of aesthetic practice, it follows that realization of form is contingent on "aesthetic luck"—analogical here to moral[3] and epistemic luck[4]—that is, the fortunate exigence when a moment in historical time and space seems precisely felicitous for the emergence and flourishing of a particular artistic performance and its incitement of other artistic works.

Second, an aesthetic practice attuned to participatory praxis robustly engages its context of performance by the depth and breadth with which it brings into being a sensorium. By sensorium, I mean the capacity of the aesthetic form to articulate and transform the senses: the visual, auditory, olfactory, gustatory, tactile, proprioceptive, and the kinesthetic senses. On the one hand, form functions multisensually in bringing all the senses to life. At its best, the aesthetic form is a disclosure of cognitive embodiment, a synesthetic awakening. It thereby confounds the mind/body binary so deeply embedded in the North Atlantic tradition. On the other hand, such multisensuality is fine-grained rather than coarse-grained. That is, the aesthetic form is responsive to the particularity and irreducibility of each sense. Call this a *textured* or *fine-grained* participatory embodiment. In its attentiveness to formal precision, then, the aesthetic form also proffers a radical break with the aesthetics of spectacle and kitsch, that is, artifacts and performances that are designed to overwhelm the senses. For example, advertisement and pornography are coarse-grained not only insofar as their modes of interaction employ a kitchen-sink strategy to sensory arousal but also in their fetish-object of arousal qua arousal.[5]

The horizon of aesthetic participation involves the *articulation* of spatial, temporal, and performative form. Spatial form finds realization through the performance of relational imaginaries in the aesthetic practice. It is instantiated not only in and through formal techniques such as depth, dimension, volume, size, and distance, but also through artistic attentiveness to the materiality of form—the medium and technologies that the artist is working with—and the alchemical transformation of materiality into performativity. Moreover, spatial form also involves the intertextuality of the artistic performance, its resonance across space. Simultaneously, the artist realizes temporal form by enfolding time in the aesthetic form, making it resonate with tempo, pulse, movement, rhythm, and speed. Performative form is realized to the extent that the aesthetic practice stirs up existential and utopian energies and longings.

These dimensions—that of the spatial, the temporal, and the performative—gain even deeper richness to the extent that the aesthetic form dramatizes their intersections and dynamic tensions. Thus, for example, performative form inflects temporal and spatial form insofar as it makes particularly salient the incompleteness, unfinishedness, and underdetermined ontology of an aesthetic practice. This incompleteness is realized in the improvisatory and participatory space opened up by the aesthetic practice.

Just as the fully realized aesthetic form dramatizes the intersection of space, time, and performativity, it also offers a choreography of their tensions. If, for example, the spatial composition of an aesthetic form offers a particularly dramatic revelation of sheer capaciousness and possibility, its temporal movement may contrapuntally dramatize loss and finitude. Thus, the aesthetic form's realization is to be found only in the interanimation of the spatial, the temporal, and the performative. A sole focus on the spatial dimension may lend to the artistic performance an intricacy and an arresting singularity, but lacking in temporal unfoldment, it will struggle to realize qualities such as texture, versatility, and relationality. A focus only on the temporal dimension of form may lend to the artistic performance an extraordinary dynamism, but absent spatial depth and breadth, it will be lacking in subtlety, nuance, and delicacy. A focus on the spatial and temporal dimensions of form may endow the aesthetic practice with both elegance and power, but absent the performative, its content is likely to be sterile, nostalgic, and reactionary. The singularity of an artistic performance lies in its refusal to resolve the tensions involved in the activation of synesthetic embodiment. These tensions are *dramatized* rather than resolved by formal innovations.

To argue, however, that artistic performances realize the inter-animation of spatial, temporal, and performative form does not mean that form is achieved through "balance," "integration," or "proportion-ality" of these elements. One is reminded here of, say, a Willem de Kooning painting, which succeeds precisely because its temporal energy (that is, its riot of color) appears to be on the brink of bursting through its structural seams (that is, its lines, borders, figures). The upshot is that the precise manner in which the formal and the contextual are imbricated and inscripted in one another is not subject to formulaic stricture but rather is emergent in contextual choreography or play. Moreover, the fully realized aesthetic form does not have a singular *telos*. Insofar as form is embedded contextually, the specificity of the performative cannot be determined by a single rule. What this means, practically, is that it frees the artist to create a wide range of artworks, the evaluation of which depends on the manner in which form and the imaginary proffer subtle and powerful engagements with the contexts of emergence, performance, dissemination, and reception.

What follows is that a robust exploration of form as these are emergent and responsive to multiple contexts leads to the reimagin-ing of dominant aesthetic evaluations. On the one hand, attentive-ness to form, the imaginary, and context refuses the privileging of a single aesthetic category as the only proper value fitting of an aes-thetic artifact. Thus, for example, the Renaissance fetish of beauty, the enlightenment fascination with the sublime, or the postmodern privileging of minor aesthetic categories are historicized and opened up for critique. This expands the space for engaging with a wide variety of aesthetic forms, categories, and responses that have been seen as marginal or that have simply been subsumed under larger categories— aesthetic interests such as the intriguing, the difficult, the simple, or the playful.

On the other hand, a renewed attention to the imbrication of form, the aesthetic imaginary, and context also refuses any easy debunking or dismissal of longstanding aesthetic categories. For example, the beautiful and the sublime—once dominant aesthetic categories—came under withering fire in the twentieth century. For the modernist mandarin Clive Bell, any talk of beauty is so hopelessly confused that he excludes it completely from a rigorous response to artworks. He instead stipulates significant form as the aesthetic standard.[6] R. G. Collingwood, for his part, emphatically declares that "the words 'beauty,' 'beautiful,' as actually used, have no aesthetic implication. . . . To sum up: aesthetic theory is not the theory of beauty but of art."[7] Postmodern critics as well increasingly turned against what they perceived to be the grandiosity and immensity claimed by the beautiful and the sublime. But if there is much truth to the notion that the beautiful and the sublime have been fetishized within a certain privileged strain of philosophical aesthetics, it is no less true that blithe dismissals of these categories are just as much freighted with vulgar ideology. For the beautiful and the sublime—far from being simply categories of false consciousness—make up the fabric of spectacularly diverse aesthetic experiences. To listen to the oppressed is to awaken to forms of beauty undreamt by the powerful and invites involvement with depths of the sublime unfathomable to *bien pensant* cultural arbiters.

Rather than strained efforts to deny and evade the significance of these aesthetic categories, then, a critical contextual turn calls for their resignification. Here only brief notes toward such a project may be ventured. The beautiful, I want to suggest, is at least constituted—though not thereby exhausted—by the interanimation of the kinetic (grace, elegance of movement, dynamism), the configurative (proportionality, delicacy, nuance, and intricacy), and the performative (vitality, warmth, and color). The interanimation the kinetic, the configurative, and the performative incite multiply realized embodied responses to beauty. Kinetic dimensions incite cognitive and affective responses of anticipation, emergence, and possibility; configurative dimensions transfix auditors in disinterested appreciation, admiration, and contemplation; and performative encounters incite affects of desire, enchantment, delight, and joy. The phenomenology of beauty is thus constitutively characterized by tension. If its kinetic elements invite the subject to participation, its configurative elements in contrast keep the subject at a distance, encourage contemplation and veneration. For example, the subject in the grip of beauty feels at once as if she would be violating an artwork if she were to change it while at the same time is moved to complete the artwork, elaborate on it, immerse herself in it.

If beauty has almost certainly been centrally privileged as the quintessential aesthetic category, the closest second has been the sublime. The sublime designates performative forms and phenomena that radiate a sense of overwhelming magnitude or infinite force and thereby unleash affects of terror, insignificance, vertigo, helplessness, despair, or awe. If, on the one hand, an initial encounter with beauty has something of a strikingly focal encounter, sheerly singular in its particularity, encounters with the sublime are far more refractory, formless, and disorienting, all consuming in their totality. As such, the sublime dramatizes particularly forcefully the antinomy between determination and agency. If, on the one hand, encounters with the sublime are radically revelatory of all that lies beyond human ingenuity, rationality, and control—dreadfully demonstrating human existential insignificance—the sublime can also reveal the extent to which human agency troubles the limits of the possible, for good and ill.

One of the gains of insisting on a precise delineation of the contours and resonances of aesthetic categories is that it yields more subtle, nuanced evaluative responses beyond a tendentious conservative rankings index à la Plato or—the converse—a dismissive *ideologiekritik* that renders them illusory. If it is necessary to insist that there ought to be room within any robust aesthetic practice for the beautiful and the sublime, it is just as true to insist that they ought not to be fetishized as paradigmatic of aesthetic praxis. Beauty, for example, is just one of many aesthetic properties and ought not to be seen as the most significant one. Many artifacts and performances are aesthetically realized precisely because they are *not* beautiful.

Moreover, an adequate aesthetic practice cannot be satisfied with any vulgar opposition of the beautiful against the ugly, the sublime against the ordinary, or the uncanny against the real. Rather, aesthetic practices are at their most realized in noting the enfoldments and transfigurations of the beautiful in the scarified, the sublime in the everyday, the uncanny in the normative. Instead of a narrowing of notions of the aesthetic to reflection only on the beautiful and the sublime, or in instituting binary cleavages between and among these aesthetic forms, the field of aesthetic critique opens up to a richer, layered, transversal field—including subtle investigations of play as interanimated with seriousness, simplicity as dialectically entangled with difficulty, boredom as constitutive of creativity, and so on.

As with the context of emergence, an aesthetic practice's engagement with its context of dissemination is dialectical. A robust aesthetic critique ought to map the manner in which the contexts of emergence, performance, and reception inflect the context of dissemination and how, in turn, the context of dissemination inscribes the formal repertoire of artifacts and performances. The context of dissemination of a specific aesthetic practice can be so hegemonic that it determines the context of emergence. Similarly, the context of dissemination considerably shapes the meanings and reception of aesthetic forms. For example, the performance of music in a concert hall considerably modifies the musical form from that which obtains in musical records. The renowned composer, Glenn Gould, at least in part eschewed live performances, or so he claimed, because of the exaggerated stylistic tics that crept into his performances when performing in large concert halls. Anxious to reach and seduce listeners seated high on the balconies he exaggerated his performances of phrases in the Bach partita.[8]

It follows, then, that the fully realized aesthetic practice creates the space for a reimagination of how distribution and accessibility inflects the form of artifacts and performances. To think of the artifact as responsive to multiple audiences involves a radical rethinking of form and the imaginary. Specifically, it involves a radical challenge to the notion that the artifact is single-authored. Moreover, it demands that the performers frustrate audience desires for closure. Instead, the realized aesthetic practice seeks to abide in the tension between creative freedom and ruthless criticism. The relationship between author and critic is not only troubled, it is reconfigured as a critical dialogue.

Resources for a radical rethinking of what I am referring to as the context of dissemination are available in the writings of the cultural theorist Walter Benjamin. It is now a commonplace, thanks to the brilliant theoretical interventions of Benjamin, that the means of production of various artworks—not least the changes in technology that have made the reproducibility of artworks unremarkable—have wrought seismic effects on the dissemination and interpretation of aesthetic artifacts. Benjamin is however often misread as bemoaning the decline of the "aura" of works of art brought about by new technologies of reproduction. In fact, Benjamin deploys the notion of "aura" in a variety of different senses that glance against each other depending on the constellation within which he embeds them. He is also deeply ambivalent about some of the dominant meanings that ripple out from the term. Moreover, Benjamin's rumination on the medium of artwork encompasses the entire social and formal structure that governs the reception of artwork, not just the technologies of media (a la Marshall McLuhan).[9] One of the dominant glosses of the word "aura," of course, is that it refers to the halo around a work of art, radiating from its authenticity and uniqueness. And yet, even in his famous essay "The Work of Art in the Age of Mechanical Reproduction,"[10] Benjamin indicates that the auratic distance cast by works of art reflect cultic and theological reifications and ritual functions. Thus, in shattering the aura around works of art, mechanical reproduction makes possible the "exhibition value" of artwork, a development that clears the way for the mass appropriation and political understanding of artwork. Moreover, against any regressive valorization of painting in comparison with film, Benjamin insists on the manner in which film deepens "apperception" through techniques such as camera angles and close-ups and thereby enables the audience to participate as critics of the artwork.

But Benjamin does not lose sight of the dialectical underside of what he calls the "liquidation of the traditional value of the cultural heritage." A longstanding critique of his centers on how new technologies of perception had led to the death of experience. He distinguishes between two forms of experience: *Erfahrung* and *Erlebnis*. For Benjamin, *Erfahrung* is experience that is conveyed through story or narrative and is emergent through shared and repeated experiences. *Erlebnis*, on the other hand, refers to the kind of experience that seeks out the unique, the sensational, and the fleeting. The contrast, Benjamin's writings indicate, can be pictured by thinking of a person—perhaps a harried travel writer—intent on visiting a museum so that he can say he has been there, and that of a frequent walker in a city, so familiar with its streets and alleys and people that it has seeped marrow deep. Where *Erlebnis* is conveyed as bits of information, *Erfahrung* is a form of memory, but memory not as "dead tradition" but rather as a movement forward into a rediscovery of the past.

Benjamin's insightful articulation of the context of dissemination also underscores its deep entanglement with the context of reception. The institutionalization and canonization of aesthetic forms powerfully—though implicitly—inculcates dispositions on how the artifact or performance ought to be interpreted and responded to. Here one thinks of how paintings exhibited in a gallery can impose a unity—even perhaps a uniformity—to otherwise diverse works (for example, when museum exhibitions reductively frame diverse non-Western artworks under one sign such as "the primitive" or the "religious"). Beyond this, however, judgments of an artifact also ought to be informed by the capacities of the artifact to proffer a context for qualitatively valuable responses. Fully realized aesthetic forms ought then to anticipate a kaleidoscope of fruitful responses.[11] Such aesthetic forms do so through a subtle reading of the contexts traversed by the work and through the formal innovations that invite robust participatory engagement. Finally, aesthetic interpreters also have deep responsibilities in articulating critically fruitful modes of engagement. Insofar as one can speak of the aesthetic as a field of participatory embodiment, it means that aesthetic realization is a social practice.

What counts as a fruitful mode of engagement with an aesthetic practice is of course plural and contextual. North Atlantic critical institutions have relentlessly promoted contemplation as the privileged—indeed, in certain cases, as the only—mode of engagement proper to the appreciation of artwork. But this will not do. Indeed, insofar as contemplation has been constructed in the order of religious veneration and worship, a critical contextual hermeneutic offers salutary lessons on the importance of demystifying such forms of reification. The point is not, then, that contemplation ought to be opposed to other bodily responses—as if the mind and the body were two separate entities. The point is to proffer modes of response that articulate engagement as cognitive-affective embodiment (for example, one thinks of African-American "call and response" modes of engagement). If the specificities of how, when, where, what, and why embodied responses are rightly as various as the diversity of aesthetic practices, such responses ought to be *critical* insofar as they are capable of distinguishing among responses that proffer modes of engagement disabling of critical and ethical agency.

The account sketched out above of the aesthetic as participatory embodiment will already be seen to depart substantially from dominant aesthetic accounts. In aesthetic discourse, few have cast as large a shadow as Plato's aesthetic. Plato conceives of beauty as a Form—and therefore inextricably intertwined with the true and the good. Particular instantiations of beauty are beautiful insofar as they are manifestations of this ontic form. From this, Plato articulates a mimetic theory according to which art is problematic because it presumptuously purports to represent the really real while in fact it offers copies that are "two generations away from reality."

In making this move, Plato inaugurates the pernicious dualisms that have gone on to distinguish hegemonic aesthetic discourses: those between appearance and reality, the sensual and the formal, the particular and the universal, and the ephemeral and the eternal. Moreover, Plato's rage for order leads him to characterize beauty mainly in spatial ratios—as symmetry, proportion, and harmony.

The Platonic inheritance exerted a massive weight. His notion that beauty designates a metaphysical property that gravitates alongside the good and the true reverberates to this day in the pervasive moralization that saturates aesthetic discourse. Moreover—from Aristotle to Augustine, Plotinus to Aquinas—Plato's primarily spatialist account of beauty was elaborated into an extravagant metaphysical canopy that cemented aesthetics to a particular political economy of order and hierarchy.

The problem with the Platonic aesthetic is in the danger that such an aesthetic poses to creativity, innovation, and diversity. The notion that legitimate artwork ought to be in the service of order is destructive of creativity. One thinks of Plato's draconian stipulations and strictures in the *Laws* regarding music and dancing. Plato argues in the *Republic* that the guardians "must throughout be watchful against innovations in music and gymnastics counter to the established order. . . . For a change to a new type of music is something to beware of as a hazard to all our fortunes. For the modes of music are never disturbed without unsettling of the most fundamental political and social conventions."[12] Plato wants music and dance to follow orderly movement in much the same way as he believes the planetary heavens dance to an immutable order. This exerts pressure on the artistic imagination to conform to his inflexible metaphysics. Moreover, his aesthetic, in obdurately insisting on the orderly, the proportionate, and the immutable, is blind to other forms of beauty that are disorderly, disproportional, transient; indeed that simply cannot be accounted for in the terms of order, proportion, immutability. Think, for example, of the startling brilliance of white light and blue color aslant ocean waves or the blazon of color across a spring landscape or the golden silver light in the darkest of nights. None of these forms of beauty can be adequately explained by notions of proportionality or order. Plato's aesthetic theory has consequences as well for both the cognitive intelligence that is vital to the artistic imagination and to the critical sensibility necessary for its appreciation. His metaphysical account of beauty as Form translates into an acute discomfort with the particular and the singular.

If modernist aesthetic discourse in the North Atlantic world departed in some ways from the Platonic paradigm, it did so only in order to establish a universalist aesthetics on the purported refined sensibilities of the white male. Kant's aesthetic theory offers arguably the most influential aesthetic theory in the North Atlantic tradition. According to Kant, the aesthetic refers to a disinterested judgment of an object. By disinterested, he means judgments that are pure, that is, judgments that admit of no desire for the object and are not invested in any practical or moral interest in the object. Indeed, Kant's remarkable recoil against the sensuous and the functional lead him to champion an austere formalism. He speaks of "delineations *à la grecque*, foliage for borders or wall papers," "sea shells," and music "without any theme" as pure examples of "free beauty."[13] Moreover, according to Kant, the competent judge of beauty sees all of the components of the beautiful object as necessary rather than contingent—for example in tonal music, where a chord progression seems necessarily lacking without a tonic chord, or in poetry, where the poem appears incomplete without a particular stanza. According to Kant, disinterested judgments are universal, both in the sense that all those with disinterested judgments will assent to the judgment but also in the sense that such disinterested judgments apply to the evaluation of all aesthetic objects. As he puts it: "The judgment of taste itself does not *postulate* everyone's agreement (since only a logically universal judgment can do that, because it can adduce reasons); it merely *requires* this agreement from everyone, as an instance of the rule, an instance regarding which it expects confirmation not from concepts but from the agreement of others."[14]

Kant's notion of disinterested judgment proved to be deeply influential. It is the inspiration behind aesthetic theories as diverse as that of Arthur Schopenhauer and formalists such as Clive Bell. Nonetheless, Kant famously takes a further step. He also wants to find out why the making of disinterested judgments is a source of delight for competent judges such as himself. The antinomy reinstaurates Kant's earlier worries about the nature of aesthetic judgment, the very puzzle that had triggered his initial exploration of the conditions of possibility of aesthetic judgment. The antinomy, summarily stated, can be framed thus: on the one hand, there does *not* seem to be an objective brute fact—there is *no* fact of the matter about the objects themselves—that makes the disinterested judge come to a particular judgment. On the other hand, there *does* seem to be a determining ground that serves as the basis for the disinterested judgment, why the judgment is *not* purely subjective. Kant's answer is that it is not the objects themselves that prompt aesthetic delight; rather, the delight issues from the awareness of the "lively" and "indeterminate" "free play" of the imagination. It is the mental powers, then, that engage in delightful free play that has no end save an "internal feeling" of "harmony."[15] The imaginative faculties of the human, when unleashed in contemplating the aesthetic, exhibit what Kant famously describes as "finality without end." In other words, the aesthetic imagination conveys a kinetic purpose as if it has a predestined destination, and yet for all of that, has no discernible definitive end.

The formidable conservative, Edmund Burke, had a significantly different sensibility from that of the Prussian Aufklärer, but he remained true to the eighteenth-century European confidence in being the avatar of a universal aesthetics. For the conservative Edmund Burke, "the pleasure of all the senses, of the sight, and even of the Taste, that most ambiguous of the senses, is the same in all, high and low, learned and unlearned." This is self-evident, Burke thinks, from the fact that "all concur in calling sweetness pleasant, and sourness and bitterness unpleasant." Light, Burke declares confidently, is "more pleasing than darkness" for all people find summer "more agreeable than winter."

If for Kant sublime pleasure comes from a recognition of the competent judge's rational capacities, for Burke the delight of the sublime issues from tranquility that follows the terror of the sublime. According to Burke, the individual "on being released from the severity of some cruel pain" finds himself "in a state of much sobriety, impressed with a sense of awe, in a sort of tranquility shadowed with horror." Burke calls the feelings of delight or pleasure that well up in this state the sublime. If there is disagreement between Kant and Burke on this point, what is most striking consists in the resonance of their theories of the sublime. Faced with the prospect of encounters that shatter human capacities for representation, Kant subsumes the sublime to an "aesthetic idea."[16] Burke, on his part, celebrates the sublime as the thrill that comes from brushing shoulders with Thanatos. Both, then, are theories of triumph—Kant as the cognitive triumph of reason over sensibility; Burke as the triumph of vitality over passivity.

It is arguable that Kant and Burke set the stage for modernity's transmutation of the sublime to spectacle. Indeed, there is an argument to be made that spectacle is modernity's master aesthetic. The ocularcentrism of modernity is everywhere ubiquitous in Kant's language of "exhibition," "presentation," and, of course, "illumination." Burke's imagination—strikingly demonstrated in his outrage at the revolutionaries' *lèse-majesté* humbling of Marie Antoinette—is worshipful of the courtly spectacle of Versailles. It is for this reason that Kantian and Burkean accounts of the sublime are at their most insidious precisely because they render a critical praxis of the sublime hollow. For if a critical praxis of the sublime most insistently reveals the abyss, the aporia, the χώρα (khôra) at the very core of agency, spectacle is the aesthetics of megalomania.

Knowledge

> Instruction in the arts of life is something other than conveying
> information about them. It is a matter of communication and
> participation in values of life by means of the imagination, and
> works of art are the most intimate and energetic means of aiding
> individuals to share in the arts of living.
>   —John Dewey, *Art as Experience*

Knowledge is the second imaginary of aesthetic practice. The extent to which knowledge characterizes an aesthetic practice is best evaluated in light of how an aesthetic form interacts with its contexts of emergence, performance, dissemination, and reception. A conception of knowledge as a value of aesthetic practice prompts an understanding of the context of emergence as a space of inquiry. One ineluctable consequence of conceiving of invention thus is the manner in which this shatters the myth of *ex nihilo* notions of creation and of absolute originality in the invention of aesthetic artifacts and performances. Rather, a view of the context of emergence as a space of inquiry reconfigures it as a space of radical *re*-imagination, *re*-articulation, *re*-petition, *re*-vision, *re*-formation.

Dialectically, the reimagination of the context of emergence as a space of inquiry vividly demonstrates that no form of artistic rearticulation is ever absolutely coincident with what is being rearticulated. Rearticulation reveals the faultlines, seams, fissures, even chasms and abysses of invention. Institutions and structures that determine the context of emergence—such as institutions of socialization, educational institutions, social networks, publishing houses—are therefore inevitably a field of contestation on the specific modalities that aesthetic reinvention takes. The notion of invention as rearticulation also embeds creativity in an embodied context—and hence embraces creativity as the intertwinement of the everyday with the new, the mundane with the extraordinary, ritual with exploration, repetition with crisis. To think of invention as the articulation of contextual inquiry therefore involves a double critique: it rejects the exaltation of invention in the order of religious inspiration but it also proffers a critique of materialist theories of invention as vulgarly reflective of anterior social determinations.

Fully realized aesthetic artifacts and performances also evince knowl-edge in the context of performance through an exploration of the epistemic dimensions of aesthetic practice. At least four problematics emerge at the nexus of knowledge and aesthetic practices: the problematic of artistic rationality and agency, the problematic of technique, the problematic of representation, and the problematic of ignorance. The fully realized artifact or performance stages an artistic dramatization of the tensions between and among these problematics. The *problematic of artistic rationality* and agency involves the irreducibly performative dimension of aesthetic practice. Artworks, arguably more than any other dimension of human practice, dramatize particularly saliently the tensions between performative knowledge and representational knowledge. An art-form is performative insofar as the action that it dramatizes manifests an *imaginative rationality* rather than an *instrumental rationality*. Artistic work is not only subject to the collision of chance and plan, intention and serendipity, but at its best it dramatizes and reveals the tensions and gaps that open up whenever the artist performs. An irreducible aspect of imaginative rationality consists in the attempt to inhabit impulses that no one has put a name to, desires that are either too amorphous or too imperceptible for representational articulation. Michael Wood evocatively describes the particular kinds of knowledges that literature yields as "the knowledge of the very gap between knowledge and life, between what can be said and what can't; of what takes the place of thinking when we encounter or engineer the unthinkable; of an array of scarcely nameable forms of loss and regret."[17]

Imaginative rationality also consists in attention to actions whose motives and causes are opaque or too multifarious to lend themselves to a single narrative. The consequence is that the artistic performance often outstrips the knowledge the author consciously apprehends. This is in at least two senses. In the most straightforward sense, it does mean that the artist's knowledge of various dimensions of the artistic performance is only intelligible in retrospect; that is, that the artist's intentions underdetermine the horizons of the art-form. But it also means—more mysteriously—that the artist is not as knowledgeable about the art-form as the art-form is knowledgeable about itself; that is, that the art-form has a richer vein and depth of knowledge than the artist's knowledge of it. This, however, is not a matter of anthropomorphizing the art-form. Rather, it just means that every performance is inscribed with a deeper history than the artist can possibly plumb, sometimes especially so for the artist enacting the performance. It also means that the medium of communication is neither private nor personal but rather is a public artifact. Thus, for example, the novelist who employs language can never plumb the histories of the language she is using and the performative force of that language.

Few wrestled with the pressures and tensions of these impulses like the writer Joseph Conrad, who states in his autobiography: "The conception of a planned book was entirely outside my mental range when I sat down to write."[18] Edward Said argues that "both in his fiction and in his autobiographical writing Conrad was trying to do something that his experience as a writer everywhere revealed to be impossible. This makes him interesting as the case of a writer whose working reality, his practical and even theoretical competence as a writer, was far in advance of what he was saying."[19] Conrad, Said reports, saw his "narratives as the place in which the motivated, the occasional, the methodical, and the rational are brought together with the aleatory, the unpredictable, the inexplicable. On the one hand, there are conditions presented by which a story's telling becomes necessary; on the other hand, the essential story itself seems opposite to the conditions of its telling."[20]

The *problematic of technique* involves the mastery of craft by the artist.[21] For all that invention is not a linear process, the artist has to command particular techniques of artifice. What must the artist know about technique and craft? To begin with, the artist ought to evince an attentiveness to the *particularities* and *spectrums* of the medium she is working with. For example, a writer ought to be deeply immersed in language (its morphology, phonology, and syntax) and deeply conversant with its potentialities (for example, in poetry, one thinks of an attunement to, say, meter, rhyme, and generic forms). This writer also ought to have a sensitivity to the distinct differences between written and spoken language, to the intonations and inflections of dialect, to the uses and abuses of idioms, cliché, voice. Similarly, a figural painter ought to be responsive to the texture of the canvass, the rules of perspective, the gradations of scale. The artist ought not only to mine the potentialities of the medium and traditions of the art-form but also to be cognizant of and responsive of its limits—that is, what the medium cannot do or what the genre is unable to accomplish. Second, an artist also ought to be keen to the resonance of a particular artifact or performances with other artifacts and performances. For example, to write a novel in the twenty-first century not only involves a recognition of the resonance of a particular genre with other genres of the novel, but also involves writing in the context of an engagement with the resonances of other technological media (film, television, and photography) with that of the novel. Third, these knowledges are cultivated in bodily dispositions and habits of mind. A good painter ought to have a lightness and steadiness of hand and the keenness and accuracy of eye.[22] A good writer must be willing to go through multiple drafts, must have the patience of waiting for the thoughtful response, must have the endurance to sift fruitful responses from bad-faith critiques. All forms of artistry demand a stance of experimentation and improvisation, of vulnerability to chance and risk, and all involve a measure of failure and loss.

Questions of technique cannot of course be mastered in the abstract. Form is intertwined with content and context in such a manner that the particular challenges faced by the artist come from engaging a particular scene, theme, concept, character, color as these intersect with various contexts of dissemination and reception. Every artist must respond to the peculiar challenges of representational content through the mastery of form. Wayne Booth describes Jane Austen as an unquestionable master of the "rhetoric of narration" because she set out to invent plots "where the chances for technical failure are great indeed."[23] For example, in *Emma*, Austen invents a character with a great deal of intelligence, wit, beauty, wealth, and position, but who is, at the same time, excessively prideful and disposed to interfere in the lives of others in the belief that she knows what's best for them. The challenge, then, for Austen, was to write a character who would evoke sympathy and love from the reader—and indeed that this love would increase as the book progresses—even as the reader understood all the more deeply how flawed she (Emma) is and how grave her harmful actions are. Austen solves this technical conundrum by having Emma narrate the story in the third person from the vantage point of having learned from her experience. The reader thus experiences the story through Emma's eyes, with the result that her flaws evoke sympathy rather than the harsher rebuke they would be inclined to trigger from an external viewpoint. And yet Austen was just as keen that the reader not be seduced into overlooking Emma's faults. Thus, even as the inside perspective draws the reader closer to Emma, Austen uses the critical judgments of George Knightley as a mode of distancing the reader from Emma. Knightley's corrections allow for the delicate equipoise between sympathy and distance because they are motivated by love for Emma.

The *problematic of representation* involves the tension between belief and disbelief incited by representations of the aesthetic practice. It occurs at the intersection of artifice and realism in aesthetic practices. On the one hand, good artistry invites interpreters to "suspend disbelief," to surrender to the practice, to invest self and affect in the performance. On the other hand, good artistry engenders a critical engagement with representation, a sensitivity to the manner in which the performance came about and achieves its effect, a knowledge about the subtleties and nuances of fictionality. The hard task for any performance is to articulate and then hold in tension two powerful energies circulating through the art-form. The first is to make salient and render deep the *immediacy* of the art-form—its materiality, affectivity, particularity, and performativity. At the same time, a fully realized art-form dramatizes itself as *mediatory*—that is, that the art-form *mediates* a historical context, is *affiliated* with particular artistic and intellectual traditions, *references* certain political and cultural events, and is *oriented* toward some thematic dispositions.

This work of immediacy and mediation takes place in and through the artifact or performance's form (that is, its genre, tone, texture, volume, rhythm, meter, pace, diction, syntax, point of view, address, and so on). For example, the literary text (of whatever form— poem, play, epic, treatise, essay, novel) achieves full realization of immediacy by deploying the full array of pragmatic and performative speech acts. Moreover, through the subtle deployment of specific formal techniques—for example, the stream of consciousness deployed by novelists most especially in the nineteenth and early twentieth centuries—the text enables access into distinctive mental states (*qualia*).[24] But if artifacts and performances enable an encounter with the blooming, buzzing confusedness of the world, they just as much *stage* this encounter and thereby awaken a realization of how being in the world is always already mediated through socialization, language, media, ideology and so on.

Even at their most "realist," every aesthetic practice draws upon some medium (language, signs, text, film, etc.). Thus, even artifacts and performances that aspire to realize a one-to-one correspondence with "reality" by minutely recording every detail about a moment in space-time evince a form of *chirality*—that is, like the left hand when superimposed upon the right hand, the content of an artwork cannot be made to coincide with what it seeks to represent. Contra Plato, however, this is not because the art-form is a poor substitute for the real. Rather, the art-form strives for chirality in order to emphasize the non-identity and asymmetry of every encounter. Against the desire for unity, integration, and dissolution with the infinite that Platonists and Neoplatonists long for, it emphasizes irreducible difference, recalcitrant *otherness*. For the Russian formalists, the aesthetic text ought to evince a strenuous self-reflexivity, a "literariness" that invites the reader to relish and savor the sound, taste, sight, and texture of signs. Their name for this is estrangement or *ostranenie*, the manner in which the literary text—through its powers of defamiliarization, intensification, deflation, obliquity, vivacity, and so on—forces the reader to attend to the materiality of word, sentence, and page; wrenches the reader from preconceived hermeneutical assumptions; or simply clears a path for the reader to encounter the world afresh.

The aesthetic practice, then, at its most sophisticated and realized, involves a deployment of form—symbols, signs, narrative, media, genre—in a manner that is attuned both to the higher and lower frequencies of immediacy and estrangement, alienation and homeliness. This is, for example, why the skillful deployment of *free indirect style* in literature is devastatingly compelling. At one register, the free indirect style enables the reader to experience the narrative through a character's eyes. But at another register, it also enables a seamless entry of the reader into the author's point of view.

A fully realized aesthetic practice, then, tarries in the abyss between alienation and homeliness—conjures the inhabitation of the uncanny. It will be recalled that the *uncanny* designates performative forms and phenomena that are at once utterly familiar and yet so utterly alien that they constitute hair-raising, nausea-inducing experiences. If encounters with the beautiful and the sublime have the feel of immediacy[25]—in the sense of a lack of mediation and in the sense of a deep cut or incision in the body—the *uncanny* is encountered as a surreal reencounter and repetition. The uncanny then does more than simply unsettle the familiar: it foregrounds the border between the homely and the alien precisely in order to question how it came to be instituted. Moreover, insofar as the border between the familiar and the strange is socially instituted, the uncanny enacts a double juxtaposition. From one end, the uncanny makes explicit the horror of the normal, the manner in which it has been naturalized and normalized into the background white noise of the evening news. But even as it does so, it also forces an encounter with how the perfectly mundane and ordinary came to be exoticized, stigmatized, othered.[26] The uncanny, it is clear, involves an acute troubling of the intersection of time and space. The reencounter with the repressed destroys the desire for a linear narrative of progress; but even as it does so, the traumatic past that reemerges strips the past of sentiment and nostalgia.

The history of the problematic of representation has of course been worked out in pitched debates over genre—most recently seen in debates over realism and magical realism. It should not have to be said—though it remains unfortunately necessary to say it—that there is no essence to either realism or magical realism that grants them a unique artistic imprimatur.[27] The choice over whether an artist ought to draw on realism or magical realism is of course not only a matter of the repertoire and versatility possessed by the artist, but it is also a matter of the historical intersection that marks the intervention of the artifact or performance. Such historical engagement marks all genres as rich with possibilities but also weighed down with limitations. As an intervention in an aesthetic field marked by a hegemonic will to idealization, realism proffered a bracing reengagement with actually existing forms of lived experience. But by naturalizing its formal innovations—its attempts to make the mediations of text transparent—realism also often distorted the complexity of encounters with worldliness.

The *problematic of ignorance* involves an engagement with how aesthetic practices explore the limits of knowledge and challenge reigning *konoi topoi* about the value of knowledge. Critical aesthetic practices do more than reveal the gaps and contradictions between beliefs and action. And they do more than map the inevitable partiality and perspectivism that mark the outer limits of any knowledge claim. That is, the aesthetic practice goes beyond rehearsing what is by now a familiar skepticism about truth, justice, meaning, and so on. Rather, fully realized practices dramatize the far harder question about whether there exist knowledges that are best not known. It may be that such knowledges may deliver devastating truths about individuals that would unravel the self. Or it may be that such knowledges are the kinds of political and existential truths that collectives find unthinkable because too costly.

For James Baldwin, "The two roles [preaching and writing] are completely unattached. When you are standing in the pulpit, you must sound as though you know what you're talking about. When you're writing, you're trying to find out something which you don't know. The whole language of writing for me is finding out what you don't want to know, what you don't want to find out. But something forces you to anyway."[28] Baldwin's statement articulates particularly well the space the writer inhabits, assailed by relentless desire to know even though such knowledge portends the unraveling of the self.

But against the Aristotelian notion that all humans desire to know, fully realized aesthetic practices demonstrate that humans often desire not to know and will often sacrifice everything not to know. That is, against traditional philosophy's popular commonsense that humans by nature want to know, there is just as powerful a case—most irrefutably articulated in the best aesthetic practices—that humans strive mightily against knowledge.[29] John Rawls makes this point in reference to John Stuart Mill's sunny argument that social institutions and public attitudes that guarantee freedom of thought and liberty of conscience would necessarily issue in the discovery of truth in all subjects. To this Rawls comments: "He [Mill] . . . supposes that we have a permanent interest in knowing the truth. He doesn't entertain the dark thought that one finds in Russian novelists such as Dostoyevsky: witness Ivan's tale of the Grand Inquisitor in the *Brothers Karamazov* that knowing the truth would be horrible, making us disconsolate and ready to support a dictatorial regime to preserve our comforting and necessary illusions."[30]

The context of dissemination also gives rise to an exploration of what knowledges are gained and lost in and through the distribution, institutionalization, and canonization of an art-form. Certain artistic traditions and, in a few cases, particular art-forms, are considerably resistant to translation across media, languages, and historical and spatial structures. One thinks here of some kinds of music, poetry, or fashions, for example, and the difficulty of bringing about a felicitous execution of meaning, verse, tone, music, imagery, or cachet across linguistic speech communities. Paul Celan essentially declared the process of translating poetry as hopeless, famously stating that "poetry is the fatal uniqueness of language."[31] All the same, this did not stop him from translating poetic works across a stunning range of languages (Russian, Romanian, French, German, among others).

Knowledge acquisition in the context of reception is, of course, deeply entangled with the contexts of emergence, performance, and dissemination. It involves an exploration of the kinds of knowledges that audiences are able to articulate in encounters with an artifact or performance. The power of an art-form consists in the extent to which it can anticipate various ways in which it is going to be interpreted (read, listened to, engaged) and the manner in which it challenges and extends various "literacies." For example, in a context where literacy is construed narrowly as the ability to "read," a fully realized aesthetic practice would demand an attentiveness to the full panoply of literacies—visual, tactile, auditory, olfactory, gustatory, kinesthetic, technological, and quantitative literacies. It is important, moreover, that an aesthetic open up space for the widest possible attentiveness to various interpretive stances and a corresponding critique of the limitations of each—*explication de texte* (descriptive, classification, contextualization, exegesis), understanding (elucidation), critique (analysis, clarification, archeology, genealogy), and evaluation (appreciation, contemplation, engagement).

My account of aesthetic practice as knowledge articulation proffers a critique of the aesthetic theories that have dominated academic discourse. Some of the arguments drawn upon from ancient sources such as Plato and Aristotle do not offer a particularly illuminating account of the nexus of knowledge to aesthetic practice. Plato, it will be recalled, is deeply ambivalent about the status of art as a form of knowledge. In the dialogue *Ion*, Plato characterizes poetry as a divine "madness," a sort of frenzied production inspired by the gods. In other dialogues, Plato appears to conceive of music and painting as forms of *techne*—which, though specialized crafts, he ranks lower than *sophia*. In the *Republic*, Plato goes as far as expelling poets from the *polis*. As Stathis Gourgouris has aptly observed, "It is fair to say that since Plato's famous decision, there has been an implicit but consistent association of the poetic act with a peculiar, mysterious, and even dangerous sort of knowledge."[32]

If Aristotle is inclined to take a much more benign view of poetry than Plato does, he does so on decidedly dubious grounds. Aristotle follows Plato in conceiving of art as *mimesis*, but he departs from Plato in believing that even works of art that are not at first glance edifying— such as visual representations of corpses and the entrails of animals— are useful because educational. For example, Aristotle thinks that by contemplating the insides of animals as depicted in art, we learn that nature is so designed that parts fit perfectly into wholes. Aristotle—no more than Plato—does not think of mimesis as a simple one-to-one visual likeness. Often he has in mind how art follows the teleological principles of nature—which, strictly speaking for Aristotle, reflects an ideal order and thereby differs from the contingency and disorder of history. Indeed, for Aristotle, poetry is superior to history because poetry deals with the universal while history pertains to the particular.

In the modern era—and, specifically, because of the emergence of scientism as a reigning ideology—aesthetic discourse becomes contested precisely on the grounds of the particularity and singularity of art-forms. At least two powerful currents would determine the trajectory of the art-form's relation to knowledge. Kant's contribution in the *Critique of Judgment* articulates the notion of disinterested judgment, but in claiming that his notion of the aesthetic idea is "free" and "independent of natural determination,"[33] he at once sacralizes and makes irrelevant encounters with actual aesthetic objects. The aesthetic idea, Kant argues, "prompts much thought, but to which no determinate thought whatsoever, i.e., no [determinate] *concept* can be adequate, so that no language can express it completely and allow us to grasp it."[34] Art here occupies the ethereal realm to which Kant had earlier consigned God in his *Critique of Pure Reason*. Poetry, he states famously, "engage[s] in mere entertaining play with the imagination . . . it does not seek to sneak up on the understanding and ensnare it by a sensible exhibition."[35] If the aesthetic idea—like God, souls, and immortality—constitutes thought about the ineffable, Kant also bestows on aesthetic discourse its own clerisy, composed of geniuses: "Genius is the exemplary originality of a subject's natural endowment in the free use of his cognitive powers. Accordingly, the product of a genius (as regards what is attributable to genius in it rather than to possible learning or academic instruction) is an example that is meant not to be imitated, but to be followed by another genius. (For in mere imitation the element of genius in the work—what constitutes its spirit—would be lost.) The other genius, who follows the example, is aroused by it to a feeling of his own originality, which allows him to exercise in art his freedom from the constraint of rules, and to do so in such a way that art itself acquires a new rule by this, thus showing that the talent is exemplary."[36]

The second major force of modernist aesthetics is Romanticism. If the force of Kant's *Critique of Judgment* likely renders aesthetic discourse as interesting primarily for its analogical resonances and illustrative potential, Romanticism spearheaded a movement that held that art—just by virtue of its essence—is revelatory of a special form of knowledge. According to Romantics, art is distinctive because—alone among other modes of knowledge—it has an immediate contact with nature. For the Romantic Samuel Taylor Coleridge, the poet alone possesses a privileged perception that "partakes of the reality which it renders intelligible."[37] In time, this claim came under pressure, thanks to the cultural force of science. No wonder then that its iteration in the work of someone like Joseph Conrad is articulated in stridently defensive tones: "Fiction is history, human history, or it is nothing. But it is also more than that; it stands on firmer ground, being based on the reality of forms and the observation of social phenomena, whereas history is based on documents, and the reading of print and handwriting—on second-hand impression. Thus fiction is nearer truth. But let that pass. A historian may be an artist too, and a novelist is a historian, the preserver, the keeper, and the expounder, of human experience."[38]

The Platonic, Kantian and Romantic traditions are in large part responsible for instituting—or at least reentrenching—many of the most intractable dualisms that have set the terms of debate for aesthetic discourse in its relation to knowledge: invention as originality versus mere copying/imitation, poetry versus rhetoric, symbol versus allegory. It is a measure of the striking force of Romanticism that even those who self-consciously repudiate it nevertheless retain much of its vocabulary and idioms.[39] Twentieth-century modernist artistic and critical movements often were at pains to disavow Romanticism, but did so in idioms that resounded with Romantic yearnings. Thus Victor Shklovsky repudiates Romantic symbolism and instead champions an art that would "make the stone *stony*."[40] But perhaps the most fascinating legacies of the Platonic/Kantian and Romantic philosophies of art is the schizophrenic binary that at once announced the absolute noncognitivism of art and at the same time sacralized art and offered un-abashed self-aggrandizing claims about the genius of artists or critics.

Politics

> But poetry is not a pure stream. It will never be sullied by partisan
> argument.
> —Eavan Boland, *Letter to a Young Woman Poet*

The exploration of politics is the third imaginary of a robust aes-thetic practice. By politics, I mean how power inflects the form of the artifact or performance and, in turn, how the artifact or performance orients itself and is responsive to institutional and embodied exer-cises of power. To think of aesthetic practice as a politics is to de-fine its context of emergence as a space wherein power circulates. The inscriptions of power in contexts of emergence have varied historically. Premodern societies proliferated with differing stratifications of artistic production. These included the "tribal bard professionally authorized to produce for his king or chieftain; the 'amateur' medieval poet presenting to his patron a personally requested product for private renumeration; the peripatetic minstrel housed and fed by his peasant audience; the ecclesiastically or royally patronized producer, or the author who sells his product to an aristocrat patron for a dedication."[41] The various subjectivities interpellated for artistic production were also determined by gender, religion, ethnicity, and body morphology or ableism.

The capitalist revolution ruptured much of the premodern con-text of aesthetic invention and reception. Two inextricably intertwined developments are particularly notable. First, in North Atlantic societies, a system of classification developed that grouped certain sorts of artistic practices—for example, painting, poetry, dance, music, drama, and sculpture—as fine arts (or simply the Arts) while deeming other creative practices (shoe-making, carpentry) as mere crafts.[42] Second, modern capitalism instituted a cleavage between *l'art pour l'art* and commercial art. Avatars of art for art's sake claimed that theirs was primarily a movement aimed at disavowing the market and proclaiming the autonomy of art. But as Theodor Adorno pointed out, "It was hardly accidental that the slogan *l'art pour l'art* was coined polemically in the Paris of the first half of the nineteenth century, when literature really became large-scale business for the first time."[43] Art for art's sake, as the critical theorist Pierre Bourdieu has brilliantly shown, became the most potent strategy of *distinction* in societies where branding was the difference between success and failure. In his subtle study, *The Rules of Art*, Bourdieu offers a brilliant excavation of the structural forces inscripted on the work of the novelist Flaubert. Working at a time when patronage from the aristocracy was petering out, Flaubert and his bohemian cohorts positioned themselves as the creators and arbiters of the new cultural capital, all the better to then seek out funding from a bourgeoisie desperate to launder their primitive accumulation in the aura of pedigree. This, Bourdieu intimates, is the real impetus behind the "cult of disinterestedness," and it gives rise to a curious rhetoric of disavowal at the heart of North Atlantic aesthetic discourse: "This discourse which speaks of the social or psychological world as if it did not speak of it; which cannot speak of this world except on condition that it only speak of it as if it did not speak of it."[44]

For the critical artist, to invent is to come to terms with the social conditions of possibility of one's work, determinations that are intersectional in cross-cutting webs of race, gender, body, class, sex, religion, and national power and status. Moreover, these forms of power are particularly potent when invisible, as precisely when Virginia Woolf pined for a room of her own. Masterful at evocatively bringing notice to the mute, inglorious life of Shakespeare's sister, what Woolf cannot imagine—what her class upbringing prevents her from imagining—is the world of her servants, such as that of her cook, Nellie Boxall, and her maid, Maud Chart. In one of the many vicious excoriations of Nellie Boxall, Woolf writes: "I am sick of the timid spiteful servant mind."[45]

The inscription of ideology in the context of performance is emergent at the intersection of political subjectivation (class, race, religion, gender, sexuality, able-bodiedness, nationality, generation, and so on), institutional strictures on the artist (that is, explicit and tacit logics or rules at work on the artist from, say, artistic peers, critics, publishers, or art galleries), biography (the artist's relative distinctiveness), the form of the artwork (language, genre, media), and the contextual exigencies of performance. The upshot is that ideological inscription in aesthetic practice is deeply complex. It follows, then, that ideology in any single art-form is best seen not in absolutist terms but rather in terms of its inscription and resonances at a variety of levels and dimensions— these include the contextual institutions from which the art-form is emergent, performed, and received; the individual artist's imaginary and technical repertoire; and the contextual exigencies of the moment. Moreover, the ideological vision of an art-form is emergent far more keenly in its formal dimensions than in its content. These formal dimensions include artistic vision, the overall aura cast by the art-form when its various dimensions are evaluated; theme, the elements that constitute an art-form's vision such as plot, characters, mood; genre, the historical tradition that it intervenes to contest or extend; and tropes, the devices used by the artist as technique.

It follows that given the concatenation of context and form, no art-form exhaustively or totally articulates a singular ideological vision. No art-form can ever be simply declared "reactionary" or "radical" without remainder. A novel, for example, may be deeply reactionary in its artistic vision but may proffer otherwise radical and empowering innovations in formal technique, language, or thematic energy. Art-forms, no matter how extraordinarily radical or execrably mediocre, are sites of contradiction and contestation rather than integral unities unto themselves. It is not possible then to exhaustively document the protean forms of ideological performance since that requires a deep immersion in the particularities of context, form, and temporal and spatial reception.

The impress of ideology in aesthetic practice then is therefore not— at least not in all but the most mediocre aesthetic artifacts—a matter of examining the doctrines and beliefs of the author as expressed in the contents of an artwork. It is at precisely those moments when form encounters the politically and existentially unthinkable that ideology bursts through. Thus, to encounter ideology in artistic form is to witness the contortions that form is placed in service of, the torture that it performs in order that it not see, feel, or confront what enables the artwork to function. Toni Morrison offers a brilliant articulation of this point in her pathbreaking essay *Playing in the Dark*. The very form of American literature, Morrison argues, is constituted by what she calls an Africanist presence. This Africanist presence is the creative source for the American imagination; the surrogates on whose bodies the plot, conflicts, characters, themes, and tropes play out; and, perhaps most importantly, the frame and background that figuratively and materially renders whiteness all at once pervasive and yet invisible, natural and yet distinctive. "It is as if," Morrison says, "I had been looking at a fishbowl—the glide and flick of the golden scales, the green tip, the bolt of white careening back from the gills; the castles at the bottom, surrounded by pebbles and tiny, intricate fronds of green; the barely disturbed water, the flecks of waste and food, the tranquil bubbles traveling to the surface—and suddenly I saw the bowl, the structure that transparently (and invisibly) permits the ordered life it contains to exist in the larger world."[46]

Morrison offers as an example a devastatingly brilliant close reading of Hemingway's *To Have and Have Not* (1937). Hemingway wants the black character to occupy impossibly contradictory embodiments: to be a slack-jawed ape on the one hand and yet, on the other hand, ready-to-hand and serviceable to the white protagonist; to be a nameless nigger—Hemingway is particularly eager to call him by this epithet—and at the same time one to whom the white hero is solicitous and compassionate; to be dependent on the white hero and at the same time set off and defined as everything the white hero is not; to be infantile and cowardly and at the same time posing a sexual and violent threat to the hero's proprietary hold over womanhood and the monopoly of violence. Hemingway employs extraordinarily "strenuous" measures to achieve this singularly impossible task:

> Only ten pages into the novel we encounter the Africanist presence. Harry [the white protagonist] includes a "nigger" in his crew, a man who, throughout all of part one, has no name. His appearance is signaled by the sentence, "Just then this nigger we had getting bait comes down the dock." The black man is not only nameless for five

chapters, he is not even hired, just someone "we had getting bait"—a kind of trained response, not an agent possessing a job. . . .

Something very curious happens to this namelessness when, in part two, the author shifts voices. Part one is told in the first person, and whenever Harry thinks about this black man he thinks "nigger." In part two, where Hemingway uses the third-person point of view in narrating and representing Harry's speech, two formulations of the black man occur: he both remains nameless and stereotyped and becomes named and personalized. Harry says "Wesley" when speaking to the black man in direct dialogue; Hemingway writes "nigger" when as narrator he refers to him. Needless to report, this black man is never identified as one (except in his own mind). Part two reserves and repeats the word "man" for Harry. . . .

The choice and positioning of the naming process ("nigger," "Wesley," and, once, "negro") may seem arbitrary and confusing, but in fact it is carefully structured. Harry, in dialogue with a helpmate, cannot say "nigger" without offending the reader (if not the helpmate)—and losing his claim to compassionate behavior—so he uses a name. No such responsibility is taken on, however, by the legislating narrator, who uses the generic and degrading term: "The nigger blubbered with his face against a sack. The man went on slowly lifting the sacked packages of liquor and dropping them over the side." Once Wesley has apologized, recognized, and accepted his inferiority, Harry can and does use "nigger," along with the proper name, in direct dialogue—in familiar camaraderie: "Mr. Harry," said the nigger, "I'm sorry I couldn't help dump that stuff." "Hell," said Harry, "ain't no nigger any good when he's shot. You're a all right nigger, Wesley."[47]

It would be foolhardy to attempt then any exhaustive articulations of how ideology is woven in aesthetic practice absent a deep critical engagement with the particularities of context and form. Nevertheless, it may be helpful to articulate in skeletal ways a few examples of how ideological effects work in and through the forms of artwork. First, the art-form proffers direct or oblique articulations of a variety of *social worlds.* Radical form unfolds worlds, allowing us to trace sediments of emergence, lines of formation. Reactionary form encloses worlds. Politically reactionary form, for example, articulates the social world in the form of a *modèle réduit*—a scale model. The scale model is an instantiation of an ideology that is powered less by a specific political commitment than in an epistemological desire to master a complex world. It not only involves the reduction of the complex world into an enclosed set, but the naturalization of such a world. For example, novelists often find it convenient to set the plot within an enclosed world that serves as a microcosm of the larger society or world. This microcosm could be a village, a ship, a college campus, or a family. It is this desire that has driven many a novelist to resort to the bourgeois convention of using the family or the village as a synecdoche of societal relations. Terry Eagleton puts it well when he argues that George Eliot—for example in her novels *Adam Bede* and *Silas Marner*—chooses rural society as a "simplifying model of the whole social formation—a formation whose determining laws may be focused there in purer, more diagrammatic form." Rural society, Eagleton ventures, allows Eliot to stage a drama in conditions that allow for "transparency" and in doing so to recast the historical contradictions traversing her fiction "into ideologically resolvable terms."[48] The *modèle réduit* is problematic then because it fails to take into cognizance the performative dimensions of the aesthetic artifact—that the artifact does things and, at least in this case, reduces a far more complex and richer terrain to a one-dimensional map.

Two examples of the *modèle réduit* are *organicism* and *privatization*. Organicism describes the naturalization or biologization of hierarchical relationships. Organicism is politically reactionary insofar as it naturalizes this synecdochic substitution, for example, by rendering it exhaustive of any other possible world. It is also problematic because it then underwrites the hierarchical relationships in the plot. Organicism—as with all modalities of artwork—occurs both formally and representationally. Formally, it takes place when the artwork purports (unconsciously or implicitly) to offer an unmediated access to the real, as is the case with many Romantic aesthetic ideologies. Representationally, organicism lays claim to be articulating certain social relations by naturalizing the power circulating between and among various subjectivities through the use of tropes that harmonize the tensions and conflicts within the polity described. Powerful examples of organicist ideology include the Romantic elegiac poem, pastoral literature, and the landscape painting. Within these genres, the landscape aspires to a totalizing representation of the world. Such totalization, John Guillory astutely notes, is accomplished "by depopulating the 'landscape,' by reducing the laboring many . . . to a metonymic sign, the 'smoke' of the villages on the horizon."[49] As Guillory points out, the valuation of the landscape is predicated upon "the transformation of the traditional 'common' into private property as a result of a long process of what was described at the time as agricultural 'improvement.'"[50]

The narrowing of the social world can also occur through *privatization*. Of the forms of privatization, the two most common in capitalist art are *domestication*, the reduction of the social world to familial relations, and *psychologization*, the reduction of the social world to the psychological workings of the mind. Both are of course an effect of capitalist *compartmentalization*, specifically the emergence of the middle classes and with it the articulation of bourgeois leisure as taking place in a sphere separate from the public domain of the state and the commercial space (work). Both are engaged in the fetishism of the normal insofar as they articulate "conflict" as the eruption of crisis into the routine and proffer endings as resolutions to conflict.

The last example of politically reactionary articulation of social worlds I want to engage is *scripturalization*. I will describe scripturalization as aesthetic artifacts that draw upon or invoke mythic or supernatural imprimatur toward the end of authorizing violently hierarchical relationships of power. Scripturalization is emergent in various dimensions and levels—artistic vision, thematic elements, genre, trope, and so forth. It occurs at the level of artistic vision when an art-form imperialistically imposes a religious or cultural myth as universal. This is the case for example with the three texts of the world's most dominant monotheistic religions—the Hebrew Bible, the Christian Bible, and the Koran—which demarcate texts that are otherwise emergent from a specific time and place as holding for all possible social worlds. Scripturalization may also work at the level of medium.

For example, a particular artistic text may fetishize a language within which it is instantiated as the privileged medium in accessing supernatural truth. One thinks for instance of claims that have been made by some traditions within Islam to the effect that Arabic constitutes the privileged medium for accessing Koranic truth. Scripturalization can also work at microlevels within the art-form, such as through tropes and techniques. The justly *deus ex machina* trope constitutes the most vulgar examples of scripturalization at the level of technique. In this case, scripturalization is used to extricate the artist from an imaginative cul-de-sac within the plot or as a convenient trope for closure. It cannot be reiterated enough that scripturalization is not reducible to a single form or genre. Thus, for example, scripturalization—as I am using the term—should not be taken as privileging realism as a genre. Toni Morrison's *Beloved*, for example, conjures the supernatural toward the end of desacralizing the so-called real and the realistic. Conversely, Dickens's realism functions to scripturalize the real in part through its unremitting sentimentalism. Scripturalization, then, need not be seen as genre specific.

Another important dimension of how art-forms are ideologically inflected consists in direct and oblique articulations of subjectivity and objectivity. Subjectivity occurs when an art-form interpellates or hails subjects into being. Certain art-forms proffer direct forms of interpellation—the hailing of certain sorts of subjectivity. Artwork, at its most ideologically vulgar, hails subjectivities into being through *identification* (for example, through the valorization of a protagonist), *abjection* (for example, through bestializing or objectifying or stereotyping social-cultural others), and *reification* (for example, through the naturalization of historically constructed relations and the instrumentalization of sensuous relational interactions). Identification and abjection are relatively blatant appeals to racial, gendered, class, or religious interpellations. Reification is far more subtle and sophisticated. For example, Hemingway's attempt at interpellating white male readers into identifying with the protagonist Harry in *To Have and Have Not* is quite obviously far more vulgar in execution than Conrad's sophisticated and subtle reification of race in *Heart of Darkness*.

Vulgar art-forms seek pure unmediated identification, as is evidenced by Hemingway's fantasy of the transparency of language and his masculinist anxiety that the substantiality of his hero must depend on the erasure of other characters. More sophisticated art-forms strive for more nuanced forms of subjectivation. In North Atlantic eighteenth-century novels, the characters that readers were encouraged to identify with often straddled a fine line between being portrayed as commoners—and therefore like the middle-class reader—and yet at a slight remove, indistinct enough to compel the reader to project certain wishes and fantasies that round out the gaps in the character's identity. Thus, the ideological interpellation of readers was achieved in two registers. The first register involved inviting the reader to project fantasies of identity onto the characters—thus, for example, constructing white, male, heroic characters that flattered the putative reader. But the second register ensured that readerly encounter with the other proceeded without risk—for example, by constructing the other as purely instrumental. Thus such artworks are precisely successful insofar as they promise to offer a risk-free encounter.[51] The (white) reader's world is buffered from without against the risks of confronting its racial, gendered, class-embedded, able-bodied imaginaries. Virginia Woolf's novels, for example, offer rich phenomenological accounts of members of her class but fall flat and thin when she attempts to engage working class characters. If her novels brilliantly trouble the divide between the "real" everyday and the "make-believe" of fiction, they brutally render insubstantial the lives of the other.

Yet another major dimension of how ideology structures aesthetic practice consists in direct and oblique ways that the art-form imagines ethical and meta-ethical ontology. *What* the art-form constructs as the ethical is as important as *how* it constructs the nature of ethical relationality. The ethical, as I am articulating the term, refers to the ensemble of practices emergent and embedded in relational encounters with human and nonhuman creatures. Ethics, construed in this sense, entails rejecting the practice of evaluating an artwork according to abstract moral imperatives. Rather, ethics is lived orientation. In other words, no art-form can escape the ethical, though of course various art-forms may more or less instantiate better forms of ethical living than others. My definition of the ethical is therefore radically different from the dominant articulation of the ethical by Platonic, Aristotelian, and Kantian traditions.

Indeed, given my understanding of the ethical, it follows that influential critical accounts of how art-forms ought to engage with the ethical can be considered politically reactionary because many such commentaries are demands for moralization rather than invitations to ethical engagement. For example, the Platonic account of morals is debilitating to the very idea of aesthetic practice because it constructs the ethical as transcendental order. Satisfied that ethics is a matter of reflecting preestablished, pregiven morals, Plato can only see in aesthetic artifacts as, at worst, a threat to his established order and, at best, useful tools for disseminating his preestablished, pregiven morality. The same point holds for a Kantian ethic: unlike Plato, of course, Kant is eager to sequester aesthetic judgments from moral judgments. But it should be borne in mind that this compartmentalization of the ethical from the aesthetic holds up precisely because Kant's idea of the ethical is severely impoverished. Artists ought to take little comfort from Kant's recusal of the aesthetic from ethics because his characterization of morality as rule-following forecloses a far more complex understanding of the ethical as embodied imaginative relationships. It is not then that Kant's firewall between the aesthetic versus the ethical offers freedom; it is rather that the portrait he paints of morality is rather too shriveled up to be worth fighting for in the first place.

The strident denunciation of all things ethical in art by the modernist avant-garde is best understood, then, as just the other side of the Kantian dialectic. For all its self-congratulatory rhetoric about upending the philistinism of the middle-brow, avant-garde *epater la bourgeoisie* is imprisoned in a dialectic of reaction against the values it purports to be repudiating. Its determination to scandalize the middle-class by avidly spurning its conformity, common tastes, and respectability is actually far more notable for its acceptance of the bourgeois demarcation of ethics as reducible to the spectacle of scandal. In this, it indicates a failure to understand the embeddedness of behavioral norms in wider political and economic logics. A wider attention to these logics reveals that capitalism thrives in spectacle, scandal, and the desire for the new. Avant-garde morality turns out, more often than not, to be at the leading edge of capitalist *habitus*.

Finally, ideology also structures aesthetic practice by proffering oblique and at times direct articulations of how an art-form ought to be interpreted and engaged with. Politically reactionary aesthetic practices have historically cultivated three modes of engagement. The first is *fetishization*—which is when an art-form imposes the demand for absolute cathexis. The impulse to fetishization springs from a conception of artworks as property to be possessed and owned, not practices that demand a broad range of critical responses. The second mode of engagement appealed to by politically reactionary artifacts is *aestheticization*—which is when an aesthetic praxis, in claiming a disinterested gaze, disavows embodiedness and embeddedness. The third mode of engagement of politically reactionary artifacts is *kitsch*—which involves the commodification of affect.[52] These ideological forms are inextricably entangled. Moreover, some are more sophisticated formally than others.

Attempts to engage and respond to politically damaging aesthetic forms will of course be multicontextual—involving a deep sensitivity to the contexts of invention, performance, dissemination, and reception. Moreover, artistic response involves a dialectical engagement with often contradictory aesthetic ideologies. For example, given that modern capitalism has relentlessly exerted pressure toward the production of kitsch, a *prima facie* response would seem to demand that the artistic challenge—one taken up by the greatest modern artists—ought to be toward cultivating an aesthetic of difficulty, depth, and abstraction. But it cannot be so simple. For if one side of the capitalist dialectic has involved the relentless churning out of kitsch, its androcentric counterpart has been just as relentless in the stigmatization of affect, in the labeling of emotion as the "sentimental" effluent of women and people of color. Thus, a robust artistic response would seem to demand a dialectical engagement of both kitsch and a reengagement with what was too easily dismissed as "sentiment." The point then is that there can be no fetishizing of any aesthetic, except in a rigorous engagement with the contexts in and through which the artwork traverses.

An attentiveness to the workings of politics in aesthetic practice also yields insightful engagements about its context of dissemination. Aesthetic practice within an overwhelmingly gendered, raced, class-based context requires an attentiveness to how power determines the dissemination of artifacts and performances. On the one hand, the context of dissemination radically structures contexts of emergence. Capitalism functions according to logics of *commodification, mass production*, and *obsolescence*. As Nicholas Brown has shrewdly noted, "the museum . . . only becomes necessary in a society predicated on the tendential annihilation of all other cultural forms. . . . [It] is therefore not only an institution for the preservation of a multitude of different cultural forms but, like the antiquities market it superficially opposes, also a symptom of one thing, namely their eradication."[53] Moreover, the demands of commodification and mass-production proffer a causal mechanism for churning out of kitsch.

The articulation of capitalism with racial and gendered power imbalances demands an attentiveness, then, to how the context of dissemination structures the context of reception of aesthetic artifacts. For example, reading is framed as much by paratextual elements (cover, title, front matter, back matter, blurbs, font, and so on) as its textual content. It is not for nothing, for example, that women—from George Eliot to Elena Ferrante—have had to resort to pen names. To think of power as imbricated in reception also involves an attentiveness to how pleasure is political. Reception within a context of power involves a deep attention to how aesthetic pleasure is extracted from the cruelty of racism, sexism, homophobia, and class exploitation.[54]

Articulations of the embeddedness of aesthetic praxis in politics have of course been deeply contested. I want to focus briefly on three prevailing modern traditions: art as *civilizational*, art as *apolitical*, and art as *socio-political*. The notion of art as civilizational found its modern apostle in the British educator, poet, and cultural critic Matthew Arnold. He diagnosed the era he lived in as one in which the *ancien regime* of church and aristocracy was in decline. But he worried that the bourgeoisie in ascendancy was unprepared for the task of governing the lower classes. It was, he thought, one of his missions to clear space for the bourgeoisie to assume its rightful place as the new aristocracy. In the event that they failed, Arnold believed, the lower classes' embrace of "Jacobinism" would be complete. For Arnold, this meant the unraveling of English order and subsequent descent into anarchy. Arnold's major recommendation is that English schools ought to be established with a mandate for sweeping social reform. Specifically, at the heart of the English curriculum would be an education in which poetry would take the place of religion as the principal means for cultivating English culture. Arnold saw in poetry not only an adequate substitute for the dry and dusty dogmas of religion, but also as superior to the prevailing mechanistic and materialist maxims of utilitarianism. Poetry's superiority lay in the fact that it cultivated a sensibility and therefore seeped deeper into the bones of a people than mere positivist propositions could. When grasped, it tutored the intuition, was formative of the inner self, and manifested itself instinctually, in a manner that rendered established systems and institutions moot.

Arnoldian humanism took deep root in North Atlantic intellectual soil, inspiring disparate and ideologically opposed traditions of thought, such as the Toryism of T. S. Eliot, the progressive organicism of F. R. Leavis and *Scrutiny*, the agrarian conservativism of the New Critics in the United States, and, into the twenty-first century, the liberal feminist humanism of Martha Nussbaum and the secular humanism of the popular critic James Wood. Whatever the differences among these diverse group, they are bound together by a *faith*—and this is true especially of the sublimated religion of the likes of Wood— in the salvific power of a select canon of literary works. It is, first of all, the *fetishistic* nature of this devotion that makes it dubious. The literary text is said to be inherently and essentially of a singular *nature*, and the reading experience is privatized as an individualistic encounter in a room of one's own with propositions in narrative or poetic form.[55] No wonder then that once this has been stipulated and established, other texts are seen as not "really" literary. There is moreover a whiff of self-aggrandizement that follows from such fetishism. For all the claims to urbane cosmopolitanism that these forms of humanism (Tory,

Christian, Liberal, Secular) claim, the canonical texts that they take seriously and the critics and criticism with which they deign to engage are overwhelmingly those that have achieved hegemonic ubiquity in North Atlantic institutions.[56]

To be sure, there has long been a minority report in North Atlantic aesthetic discourse that has proffered an apologetic for art's entanglement in politics. In the nineteenth century, the British poet Percy Bysshe Shelley famously concluded his apologia *A Defense of Poetry* (1820) with the sentence: "Poets are the unacknowledged legislators of the world." Shelley's title and tone bear witness to his defensiveness; a defensiveness, moreover, that is itself a form of resignation. As Raymond Williams aptly puts it in *Culture and Society*, Shelley's "bearers of a high imaginative skill become suddenly the 'legislators,' at the very moment when they are being forced into practical exile; their description as 'unacknowledged,' which, on the theory, ought only to be a fact to be accepted, carries with it also the felt helplessness of a generation."[57] Twentieth-century humanism can be fairly characterized as the transformation of what was for Shelley a cause of despair into a reason for pride. Thus, to Shelley's notion that poets are unacknowledged legislators, W. H. Auden would contemptuously respond with a zinger of his own: "'The unacknowledged legislators of the world' describes the secret police, not the poets." Auden's retort itself reflects a helplessness of its own, but only this time it is a resignation to the notion that politics is always and already vulgar and corrupt. That is, politics just is ideological dogma, reducible to explicit policy soundbites, and conveyed in rapid-fire hortatory rhetoric by bullhorn-bearing Stalinists. But like the Christian humanists of the twentieth century, Auden cannot resist converting the melancholy of marginality into a paean for the purity of poetry. It is this curious tone of existential resignation to the vulgarity and anarchy of politics coupled with an aloof patrician ode to the to the purity of (poetic) isolation that resounds in his "In Memory of W. B. Yeats":

> For poetry makes nothing happen: it survives
> In the valley of its own saying where executives
> Would never want to tamper...

This simplistic opposition between politics and art continues to be remarkably widespread within the humanist set. Consider Howard Jacobson's famous categorical avowal:

> I still believe that no good joke is ever racist. And I believe it for the same reasons that I believe no good play or novel is ever racist, regardless of the politics of its author. The discourse of racism is bald, monotonous, unquestioning, single-voiced and desolate. Art, when it is good . . . is none of those things. Art is dramatic, and by dramatic I mean that it holds everything in opposition and suspense.
>
> The moment art forgets it is dramatic and grows tendentious, the moment it begins to formulate a programme for the amelioration of mankind, or for spreading faith of disbelief, or for promoting racial disquiet or racial harmony, it ceases to be art. Call it a little novel, comprising voices at intellectual and moral odds with one another, taking you by surprise and told, vertiginously, by a narrator it would not be wise of you to trust.
>
> Thus in art, do matters of morality wait upon aesthetics.[58]

This statement is deeply misleading, and not simply because its Platonism allows it to define away any instance of racist or sexist art as not "really" art. Beyond this, however, what is misleading is its unimaginative understanding of ethics. Specifically, it fails to understand that ethical and unethical actions exist along a continuum of subtlety and are performed in more or less complex forms. Consider Bernard Williams' insightful exploration of the ethical, the counterethical, and varieties of the unethical:

> [T]he idea of the ethical, even though it is vague, has some content to it; it is not a purely formal notion. One illustration of this lies in a different kind of nonethical consideration, which might be called the *counterethical*. Counter-ethical motivations, a significant human phenomenon, come in various forms, shaped by their positive counterparts in the ethical. Malevolence, the most familiar motive of this kind, is often associated with the agent's pleasure, and that is usually believed to be its natural state; but there exists a pure and selfless malevolence as well, a malice transcending even the agent's need to be

around to enjoy the harm that it wills. It differs from counterjustice, a whimsical delight in unfairness. That is heavily parasitic on its ethical counterpart, in the sense that a careful determination of the just is needed first, to give it direction. With malevolence it is not quite like that. It is not that benevolence has to do its work before malevolence has anything to go on, but rather that each uses the same perceptions and moves from them in different directions. (This is why, as Nietzsche remarked, cruelty needs to share the sensibility of the sympathetic, while brutality needs not to).[59]

What Williams is concerned to show is the manner in which philosophy—he means the dominant North Atlantic philosophies of Platonism, Kantianism, and Utilitarianism—has monomaniacally sought to reduce ethics and ethical consideration to a metaphysical essence, principle, or unit (the Forms, the categorical imperative, utility). This is why Williams often thought literature offered more complex engagements with the variety and complexity of ethics than philosophy. But Jacobson's statement above also indicates that there are a great many artists invested in this reduction of ethics to a grey moralism—"bald, monotonous, unquestioning, single-voiced and desolate"—while inflating and sacralizing art as always and everywhere inherently and transhistorically complex.[60] Jacobson's claims about racism is based on the liberal conceit of prejudice as vulgar, performed by massed ranks of hooded KKK fascists hurling racial slurs (e.g., "nigger," "Jew," "Paki," etc). Art is on the other hand sacralized as metaphysically transcendent. This self-congratulatory account of racism is not just a failure to understand racism, it is a failure to understand art—or rather, the rich histories and diverse forms of art.[61] Antony Julius points to one of those examples in his careful engagement with T. S. Eliot's poetic *oeuvre.* Eliot's anti-Semitism, Julius argues, is "creative" and cannot be easily dismissed as reflective of the casual prejudice of his era. Rather, Eliot is so virtuosic in putting his anti-Semitism to imaginative use that Julius declares that his poetry is "one of anti-Semitism's few literary triumphs."[62] This virtuosity lay in Eliot's considerable resourcefulness in transfiguring a "cluster of literary and anti-Semitic clichés . . . conventions exhausted through overexposure, and abuse staled by repetition" into resonant, charged, and discursively rich articulations of hatred.[63]

The upshot, then, is that the ethical as such can be more or less understood as having more or less *artful* dimensions—provided art is not understood in traditional ways as spectactorial but rather understood as participatory. It follows from this understanding of *ethical form* that artworks can explore ethical and unethical actions in more or less complex, more or less subtle, more or less multidimensional ways. In other words, artworks can fail to be good artworks precisely because they are *formally* inadequate to the complexity of the ethical.

Not all aesthetic theories, of course, have sought to build a firewall between the social and the aesthetic. Hegel argues that art "in its highest human vocation" aims at the reconciliation of a people to their society.[64] Art, as the realization of what Hegel calls "absolute spirit," is a rival of philosophy and religion in being forms of activity that make a people at home in the world in which they live. To be sure, Hegel held that of the three—philosophy, religion, and art—the highest activity was philosophy. Or rather, in terms of Hegel's relentless dialectical idealism, art is superseded by religion which in turn is superseded by philosophy. Art's vocation to represent absolute spirit means that, for Hegel, the essence of art lies in its affirmative character. Of course, that does not mean that Hegel conceives of art in vulgarly propagandistic or moralistic ways. Art does not offer propositional commandments of what we ought to do in every given situation so much as it draws inhabitants of a society into grasping the logic or rationality of the cunning of reason. It is arguable that by articulating the embeddedness of art in the flow of sociality, Hegel puts paid to the Kantian disavowal of the social. But he does so at a steep cost. Hegel valorizes content in artworks and is notoriously indifferent to form. Moreover, there is reason to be suspicious of his notion that the content of artworks ought to evince an affirmative character. In societies such as Hegel's own where social injustice is systemic, this amounts to the ratification of these injustices.

The hegemony of humanist apoliticism aside, the twentieth century did have a prominent advocate for art's possibilities in the making of democratic culture. This was the American pragmatist John Dewey. According to Dewey, "works of art are means by which we enter, through imagination and the emotions they evoke, into other forms of relationship and participation than our own."[65] For Dewey, art proffers a means of communication that goes beyond the mere conveyance of information. It articulates politics as the art of friendship: "Every intense experience of friendship completes itself artistically. The sense of communion generated by a work of art may take on a definitely religious quality. The union of men with one another is the source of the rites that from the time of archaic man to the present have commemorated the crises of birth, death, and marriage. Art is the extension of the power of rites and ceremonies to unite men, through a shared celebration, to all incidents and scenes of life."[66] If the problem with much of the humanism of the twentieth century is that it figures politics as always already a Stalinist boot grinding the face of (humanist) art, then the problem with Deweyan aesthetics is that it conjures the horizon of art as a Norman Rockwell painting. "That which distinguishes an aesthetic is conversion of resistance and tensions, of excitations that in themselves are temptations to diversions, into movement toward an inclusive and fulfilling close."[67] There is little room for a genuinely *radical* art in Dewey's aesthetics, let alone for the disruptive possibilities of the uncanny and the sublime.

Existential Meaning

Men build their cultures by huddling together, nervously
loquacious, at the edge of an abyss.
                    —Kenneth Burke, *Permanence and Change*

The existential is the fourth imaginary that a robust aesthetic practice ought to explore. By the existential, I mean an exploration of the enduring formations that characterize the human condition— suffering and joy, failure and triumph, life and death—and that profoundly constitute human senses of the good life. The context of emergence for the exploration of the existential in aesthetic practice begins by placing context itself under question. Every context is a layered intersection of the transhistorical, the political, and the phenomenological. The *transhistorical* context describes the transversal conditions of creaturely life—for example, suffering and death. But the transhistorical is striated through with the *political*—that is, how power relationships shape and inflect transhistorical encounters. These structures determine who, where, why, when, and how particular populations and individuals suffer, live, and die. The *phenomenological* describes how the existential is understood, how it shapes subjectivity and experience. Of course, the transhistorical, the political, and the epistemological are all inextricably intertwined. It is thus part of the task of the artist in the context of emergence to exercise against the grain readings of the existential. In one direction, the artist has to refuse the reduction of the political and the phenomenological into the transhistorical. This cuts against the grain of conservative ahistoricism and liberal humanism. In the other direction, the artist has to refuse the erasure of the transhistorical in the name of the political and the phenomenological. This cuts against the grain of separatist tribalism and radical transhumanism.

The exploration of the existential in the context of performance involves attentiveness to how form and the imaginary are responsive to the deepest and widest currents of conscious experience. An aesthetic practice is at its most self-realized when it engages—through form and the imaginary—the spectacular diversity of experience across social contexts and species-being; the remarkable nuances of these experiences—the ghoulish laughter of the concentration camp, the sorrow of victory, the absurdity of sexual intercourse; and, not least, the elusive *form* of experience, the manner in which it runs ahead but also subverts belief, genre, intelligibility. It is for this reason that the existential puts into question the very notion of form even as form must wrestle with and trouble the existential. The art-form at its most realized places the existential and the formal in fruitful tension. Conversely, an art-form is in bad faith when its investment in form takes the shape of existential fetishism, existential imperialism, existential totalism, and existential redemptionism.

Existential fetishism occurs when a particular artistic form—a genre, a medium (drama, novel, film, photography)—claims hegemonic space as the principal mode for articulating human experience. For example, much of the elite critical commentary in the North Atlantic tradition has been dedicated to the fetishization of tragedy as superior to every other mode of artistic production. The causal reasons for the fetishization of tragedy are various. Tragedy has often been seen as more profound—because more serious and solemn—than comedy, which is marked by revelry and laughter. The dismissal of comedy is thus at least in part marked by a certain disapproval of pleasure qua pleasure. Of course, that does not mean that comedy ought to be fetishized any more than tragedy has been. Commentators have pointed out that the shift from feudal societies to modern capitalism—an era that also marked a transition from the dominance of the play to the novel—signified the shift from tragedy to romantic comedy as hegemonic artistic genres. For capitalism, the impulse to the fetishization of a certain kind of comedy lies in its relentless interest in the manufacture of a "positive psychology."[68]

If the fetishism of tragedy in select pockets of critical opinion was in part a salutary oppositional stance against the depthlessness of capitalism, it was not wholly so. A great deal of the fetishism of any form involves an ideological erasure, diminishment, and exclusion of other experiences. *Existential imperialism* names the practice wherein the privileging of a particular artistic form has the implication of erasing experiences that cannot be articulated in the privileged medium. A genre can be imperial when the very manner in which it is articulated excludes or diminishes huge swathes of other social experiences. Raymond Williams has argued that if the greater majority of North Atlantic theorization about tragedy is to be believed, a work of art only qualifies as a genre of tragedy if misfortune befalls a certain kind of powerful person whose life catechizes a metaphysical or theological destiny. States Williams: "War, revolution, poverty, hunger; men reduced to objects and killed from lists; persecution and torture; the many kinds of contemporary martyrdom; however close and insistent the facts, we are not to be moved, in a context of tragedy. Tragedy, we know, is about something else."⁶⁹ Williams is concerned to critique this exclusivist definition of tragedy, which he rightly sees as stemming from a contempt for ordinary lives and common experiences.

Existential totalism names the ideology that experiences can be exhaustively represented through a particular artistic form. What is problematic about such totalism is that it constitutes a disavowal of the extent to which existential limit-experiences—such as searing pain, *jouissance*, death—pose a challenge to the very adequacy of representation, that is, shatters the very possibility of artistic form. Attempts to represent existential limit-experiences take the form of clichéd and sentimentalized imagery—the constant recourse to certain metaphorical, allegorical, and analogical tropes such as flowers, for example, to represent death or blinding light to represent pain. Or such attempts at representation gesture ineffectually and evasively at the sublime. Other equally troubling responses to existential totalism seek refuge in the aestheticization of violence through spectacle. Against existential totalism, the realized art-form resists both the closure and unity of the generic as well as the abstractionism of allegory. Instead, the realized art-form stages the crisis of representation as materially particular, only partially communicable—though not containable—in symbol and image.

Existential redemptionism names the ideology that all experiences are in the last instance recuperable. It involves, on the one hand, a furious denial of the intractability of trauma—incurable illnesses, chronic pain, and ultimately death. It also represents a profound refusal of the random, of how luck and chance does not discriminate the deserving from the undeserving. Existential redemptionism is sometimes motivated by good intentions, as when artists seek to represent a melancholic desire for justice or equity in a world in which the majority lead lives of quiet desperation, solitary, poor, nasty, brutish and short. But even when well motivated, existential redemptionism is in bad faith, not only because of its epistemological vices (wishful thinking, cowardice) but also because it fails ethically in its denial of finitude. The major ideologies that have been committed to existential redemptionism have been, of course, the major monotheisms and

North Atlantic philosophy. The monotheisms bestowed on North Atlantic philosophy the now familiar dialectical gesture of claiming to face up to the full horror of death but only in order to sublate these horrors in a redemptive *Aufhebung*. It would be left to Hegel, of course, to schematize this in his rambling theory. For all that he thought that tragedy was a superior genre to any other artistic mode, Hegel's teleology is *the* modern theodicy.

It is part of the task of the fully realized art-form to proffer articulations of existence that break with fetishism, subvert imperialism, repudiate totalism, and give up on redemptionism. No single genre—much less story—can do everything, of course. Moreover, the most realized fictions will tend to be those that do not seek after existential solutions anyway. Rather, artworks fully alive to the protean forms of existential being will be those that are subtly attuned to form's possibilities and limits. Bernard Williams's remarkable and brilliant essay "The Women of Trachis," in my view easily one of the best essays of the twentieth century, offers one possibility to think narrative form away from existential redemptionism. Williams's essay is written to contest North Atlantic philosophy's attachment to what he calls "good news"—that is, the notion, as exemplified in the theodicies of Leibniz and Hegel, that ultimately horrendous suffering will be redeemed. Against these blandishments of philosophy, Williams argues, fiction offers far better treatments of what it means to be human in the world. Williams distinguishes two kinds of fiction. The first is what he calls "dense fictions." These kinds of fictions provide "a depth of characterization and social background which gives substance to the moral situation and brings it nearer to everyday experience."[70] The paradigmatic form of dense fictions is the realist novel, such as Dickens's novels. For Williams, dense fictions are rife with dangers that may mislead about existence. For one, "the notorious deceptions of narrative closure can impose an ethical significance which would not be available in reality—unless, as often happens, reality itself is interpreted in terms of such deceptions."[71] Moreover, "some of the most sharply delineated reminders of bad news in fiction are presented when necessity comes to the characters in the form of unmanageable chance, and the attempt to deploy this in the context of dense fiction runs the danger of coming too close to the territory that such notions equally supply to comedy and farce. (Some of Hardy illustrates this, including ... the climactic disaster in *Jude the Obscure*.)"[72]

Williams contrasts dense fictions with what he calls "stark fictions," the paradigmatic form being the work of the ancient Greek playwright, Sophocles. Williams states of these fictions that "it is not merely that [in] style and structure [stark fictions] avoid the anecdotal and incidental, but that these resources are typically directed in a concentrated way to displaying the operations of chance and necessity."[73] The force of stark fictions—Williams highlights Sophocles's *The Women of Trachis* as illustration—"is directed to leaving in the starkest relief" the existence of "extreme, undeserved, and uncompensated suffering."[74] Stark fictions, by their very form as an engagement with the eruption of chance and the in-breaking of luck, are necessarily obscure in that they ruthlessly critique the theological desire for a bedrock unmoved mover. But what they do particularly well, Williams argues, is offer a devastating "limitation to the tireless aim of moral philosophy to make the world safe for well-disposed people."[75]

The articulation of the existential in the context of dissemination is a question of what happens to the existential when a work or performance is disseminated or travels across space and time. A long-running conceit of many an artist is that they create for immortality. As Horace famously proclaimed, *non omnis moriar* (I shall not completely die). It is a battle cry that artists across the centuries have echoed. Indeed, one of the conceits of North Atlantic critical discourse is that a work is canonized if it is monumental and perdures through time. Museums are then said to exist to preserve works of art, but such preservation is often in practice the embalming of these works of art. Against this insistence on the monumental, a critical aesthetic praxis must insist on its transience—that is, its embeddedness in time and therefore its receptiveness to the affective and the participatory. From this perspective, the work of art is not an object work to be gazed at but a responsiveness to existence. Such timeliness of the art-form should not be equated with presentism. Transience is a full articulation of the temporal, in other words, of the intersection of the past, present, and future.

Lastly, the articulation of the existential in the context of reception involves drawing interpreters into the deeps and breadths of the variety of experience. At its best, the art-form refuses the sop of escape from the realities of death, suffering, and pain. But if death, suffering, and pain are irreducible elements of embodied lives, play, pleasure, and frivolity are no less part of the texture of that experience.

These brief notes on the existential work of the art-form cut against dominant aesthetic theories. For Kant, the Aesthetic Idea is that which moves beyond the ordinary or the commonplace (*alltäglich*). Kant can be credited with contributing to a body of work within North Atlantic aesthetics that recoils from the ordinary and the everyday, deeming it boring and trite. Romanticism provides an almost completely opposite vision to Kant's. For the Romantics, reality is enchanted. Indeed, for Romantics, the artist uniquely possesses a sensitivity for the real—so much so that the artist embodies the suffering of the world.

Nietzsche occupies both an appropriative and oppositional stance to both the Kantian aesthetic and Romanticist aesthetics. For Nietzsche, the real is a swirling vortex of terror and horror. As such, there are two major artistic responses to this reality. The first is the Apollonian artist who veils the terror at the core of being and thereby saves humans from staring it full in the face. The power of Apollonian art, Nietzsche says, is that "before our eyes it transforms the most terrible things by the joy in mere appearance and in redemption through mere appearance."[76] Nietzsche points to Raphael's *Transfiguration* as an example of the Apollonian. Toward the bottom half of the painting are images of helplessly frightened disciples and despairing porters, their faces and bodies contorted with pain. The upper half is the figure of Christ, his face and body transfigured with the purest and painless joy. Dionysian art, on the other hand, intoxicates, flings revelers into "ecstatic rapture." Under the spell of the Dionysian artist, the *principium individuationis* collapses, "the subjective fades into complete forgetfulness of self." According to Nietzsche, the Dionysian artist rips the "veil of Maya," and out of the yawning abyss comes the terrifying truth of Silenus: "The very best thing is not to have been born, the second best thing is to die soon." Nietzsche understands the Apollonian and the Dionysian as revelatory of a reciprocal necessity, the beauty and moderation of the Apollonian as necessarily rooted to the hidden underground of suffering and death latent in the Dionysian.

The Nietzschean aesthetic does well to reject the bad faith of Kantianism and Romanticism. But it compels questions of its own. It is blithely indifferent to the specificities of form, content to point to the effects of the Dionysian and the Apollonian. Moreover, it participates in a longstanding—if minority—conceit that pain and power, despair and death account for the real, whereas play, frivolity, and the beautiful constitutes the illusory. This may at times offer a salutary metaphysic in the face of North Atlantic theodicy, but it is no less fetishistic for what it denies.

ASYMPTOTES OF FORM: PARTICIPATORY EMBODIMENT, KNOWLEDGE, POLITICS, AND MEANING

> I want to draw a map, so to speak, of a critical geography and
> use that map to open as much space for discovery, intellectual
> adventure and close exploration as did the original charting of the
> New World—without the mandate for conquest.
> —Toni Morrison, *Playing in the Dark*

This chapter seeks to articulate an aesthetic ontology; specifically, if we take seriously the notion that aesthetic invention and criticism is embedded in historical structures, and, moreover, is emergent from embodied persons, how then ought we to think of the normative horizons of aesthetic practices? I argue that there are at least four dimensions of robustly realized aesthetic practices: participatory embodiment, knowledge, politics, and meaning. An aesthetic practice realizes *participatory embodiment* insofar as it deepens and expands sensory capacities: visual, auditory, olfactory, gustatory, tactile, proprioceptive, and kinesthetic senses. It realizes *knowledge* insofar as it explores to the very limits the problematics of the imagination, rationality, technique, representation, and truth. It realizes the *political* insofar as, through an extended fossicking of form, it registers the trace of its conditions of possibility; inscribes its ontological status as practice or object or gift or commodity through its relational enunciations; interpellates or annihilates particular subjectivities through its mode of addresses; and proffers a palimpsestic intimation of alternative worlds. It realizes meaning insofar as its form instantiates the deepest and widest encounters with phenomena that have wrought the human condition—for example, how transhistorical existential experiences (joy and pain, love and hate, desire and revulsion) are expanded as well as confounded by irreducible particularity and irrepressible eccentricity; how the emergency, the crisis, and the tragedy is lived in and through the everyday, the mundane, and the banal; and, finally, the utter ineliminability of contingency, the inevitability of suffering, and the irreversibility of death.

In the next chapter, I examine these questions by offering a close analysis of African aesthetic practices. As with chapter two, my argument in the next chapter not only seeks to expand the range of conversations on all matters aesthetic by demonstrating the entanglement of aesthetic forms of creativity, performance, dissemination, and criticism in global flows and contestations, but also shows how the aesthetic is critical to larger questions about what constitutes the good life and the good society.

CHAPTER 4

Geographies of the Imagination

Figurations of the Aesthetic at the Intersection
of African and Global Arts

There are more things in heaven and earth, Horatio,
Than are dreamt of in your philosophy.

—William Shakespeare, *Hamlet*

In this chapter, I make a turn toward a critique of major African aesthetic practices. As with earlier chapters, my aims in this chapter are both particularistic and global. A consideration of African aesthetic practices is rewarding in its own right insofar as it takes seriously the particularity and agency of African intellectual practice. But it is just as true that a close engagement with African aesthetics reveals the knots that entangle African creativity and criticism with that of other geopolitical and social formations—from the hegemonic North Atlantic world to those in the Middle East, the Far East, Australia, and the Americas. To be clear, I want to emphasize that my meditations below are properly seen as sketches rather than exhaustive cartographies of African aesthetic practices. The value of such sketching is that it leaves room for a radically new analytic of the aesthetic imagination while at the same time proffering a synoptic vision of what it could be.

Below, I outline five visions of African aesthetic practices: a communalist aesthetics, particularly as emergent in the long African quincentenary that marks precolonial, colonial, and postcolonial encounters on the continent; an elemental aesthetics, largely the product of North Atlantic discourses about Africa; a pedagogical aesthetics, with a particular focus on the doyen of African letters, Chinua Achebe; a mythopoeic aesthetics, championed by the Nobel laureate Wole Soyinka; and a late modernist aesthetics, which I shall illustrate through a close reading of the South African turned Australian, J. M. Coetzee. This chapter also stages an encounter between the aesthetic theory articulated in chapter 3 with some of the most acclaimed artifacts and performances on the African aesthetic landscape.

Articulations of African Aesthetic Practices

Communal Aesthetics

A mask in Nso, for example, is made by artists to be used in association with a costume made with the same artistic configuration as the mask. It is made by the artist to be accompanied by music and a specific group of dancers. A mask alone may be elegant and moving. But what is more important is the creativity that is involved in bringing the mask together with xylophones, dancers, drums, flutes, songs, etc. to a high resolution, to a harmony. When it is done properly, when the heterogeneity of the parts is thus harmoniously resolved, we get what in Nso we describe as *kinsetti shuu ke ki nyo*, or the indescribable. As the masks, xylophones, songs, drums, and dancers burn the hearts of everyone participating in the drama with joy and delight like wild fire in the harmattan, one might well think that the gods are visiting us. This represents one of the highest forms of art, as diverse and at times conflicting and incommensurable elements of art are proactively given an organic unity by an artist. These

aspects of the drama change the meaning of the mask looked upon as an entity in itself.
—Ajume Wingo, "The Many-Layered Aesthetics
of African Art"

I begin with a discussion of what I shall describe as communal aesthetics, which I consider to be a major motif of African creative work and criticism in the long quincentenary of precolonial, colonial, and postcolonial periods. These practices were of course spectacularly diverse. A few distinctive characteristics of African communal aesthetics, however, can be sketched out in broad strokes. First, communal aesthetic practice is multilayered.[1] The context of invention is emergent from a metaphysical structure that construes the imagination as endowed by the gods. For the Yoruba, the gods came down to earth and endowed humans with *ashe*, the ability to command and the power to make things happen.[2] Ashe is often portrayed in the shape of animals, most notably the royal python (*ere*), the gaboon viper (*oka olushere*), the earthworm (*ekolo*), the white snail (*lakoshe*), and the woodpecker (*akoko*). Yoruba aesthetic praxis thus conceptualizes the imagination (*ashe*) as not only incarnational (that is, material) but also as profoundly multidimensional. Like the gaboon viper, *ashe* is dangerous (hence its representation in the shape of the curved venomous fangs of the viper). But it is also life-giving (*ashe* has a performative denotation, as it literally means "so be it" or "may it happen"). Moreover, *ashe* is portrayed as elusively fast (hence often represented in the shape of zigzag patterns that suggest a lightning strike) and as slow and deliberate (much like the white snail).

The context of invention for many artistic practices was the social guild, one that had deep ties to royal and priestly cults. Ajume Wingo articulates one such context of invention among the Nso, a people in the North West province of Cameroon:

To create an artwork . . . is a task for a specialized set of people and can be as difficult as thinking about God. People know this in Nso. It is not uncommon to hear people saying that only those who are inspired by the Supreme Being can make art. This is a way of acknowledging the artist's creativity. Nso artists undergo a lifelong apprenticeship. In fact, most artists come from families with a lineage of venerated traditions of art. Most Nso artists are born and raised within the ethos of art creativity. The effect of being brought up in such a family tradition should not be underestimated in the enterprise of art creation.[3]

Second, the context of performance of African aesthetic performance and the context of dissemination and reception are inextricably intertwined. These contexts are emergent within social practices. Music, for instance, is embedded in certain social practices—funeral dirges, work songs, weddings, and so on. Social practices, of course, are themselves seen as embedded in communal identities that are anchored in particular metaphysical beliefs. But precisely because communal artistic work is embedded in social practices, the context of performance emphasizes social *participation.* As Kofi Agawu has noted of African communal music, African "oral texts have a kind of expanded existence, one that encourages performers to explore a range of alternatives in realizing the work. The work, in other words, enshrines a set of possibilities: it is emphatically not a fixed text."[4] An element of this participatory responsiveness is that the distinction between artist and audience is permeable and flexible. African music, for example, is responsive to the call and response pattern of engagement, with frequent interpolations from artists and listeners. Another element of participatory engagement is that there is an interplay of formal repertories with improvisational innovation.

Third, the formal dimensions of African aesthetic praxis emerge at the intersection of the artwork's performativity as a signifier of metaphysical and moral properties; as serving a distinct function in a social practice; as a compelling artifact or performance intended for admiration and awe; as a complex discourse of appreciation and competition within an artistic guild; and as a focal point of communal interaction and participation. Thus, it is precisely because African artwork is responsive to these diverse currents that it evinces an unusual attentiveness to formal innovation. Let us examine each of these in turn. To begin with, the artwork was often seen as the repository of deep metaphysical verities. According to Thompson, among the Yoruba, "a thing or a work of art that has *ashe* transcends ordinary questions about its makeup and confinements: it is divine force incarnate."[5] For example, among the Yoruba, ceramic bowls were often inscribed with various intricate avatars of deities, while the color red signaled *ashe* and potentiality.[6] Such was the spectacular diversity of deities in the Yoruba pantheon that the metaphysical resonances of Yoruba art did not spell a narrowing of the artistic imagination. Indeed, one of the great muses of Yoruba creativity was the Eshu-Elegba, the trickster god, spirit of the crossroads, master of potentiality, change, and creativity. The lore, legend, and inspiration of Eshu endowed Yoruba artists with a wide latitude for creative exploration.

African communal artwork was also resonant with moral values. For the Yoruba, artwork ought to exhibit character (*iwa*). Salient among prized virtues of character was "coolness," defined and practiced as seriousness, grace under fire, practical wisdom, magnanimity in a moment of triumph, finely calibrated and modulated *habitus*. The formal articulation of coolness occurred in sculptures, carvings, and paintings that emphasized symmetry, balance, and a regal posture. Yoruba artists also often represented coolness in the form of carvings and sculptures that presented the face with a serious mien, with sealed lips and composed features. The colors blue, indigo, and green were also seen as the salient formal features of coolness. Other manifestations of character in Yoruba art emphasized purity (which is represented by the color white).

African communal artwork also often—though not always—served a distinct role in social practice. African art historians have pointed to the Asante gold-weights as particularly illustrative of the multiple functions of African art in a social context. The gold-weights not only served as a means of measuring gold dust currency but also were deeply prized in their own right for their elegance and beauty. The embeddedness of artistic work in social practices has the implication that communal artistic practices cut against presuppositions that carve a sharp binary between aesthetic contemplation and functional purposes. Perhaps it is important to make clear—against the grain of much functionalist anthropology—that social practices such as funeral rituals are not themselves reducible to the functional. But more precisely, the embeddedness of artistic work in social forms does not make the artistic work itself vulgarly utilitarian. That is in part because the role of the artistic work in the social practice is overdetermined. Songs sung at funerals are responsive to the grief of mourners and are sung in memory of the deceased, but precisely because the *form* of the song—its metrical organization, rhythmic texture—is constitutive and performative, it is not just a conduit for the transmission of an a priori emotion. Similarly, the gold-weights served a function but were also valued for their own sake.

Formal virtuosity and superior artistic craftsmanship counted deeply in the realization of communal artwork. Because audiences were attuned participants and trained listeners, form was evaluated in much more demanding ways than contemplative engagement involved. African communal artworks often traversed genres and were often deeply resistant to aesthetic notions of unity and integrity. What was emphasized, for example, was antiphony or polyrhythm that struck a discordant note against exquisitely harmonious beats or tunes; incompleteness, protuberation, or grotesquerie erupting from breathtakingly beautiful sculptures; jagged scarifications inscribed on superlatively supple and glowing bodies. Agawu offers an invaluable articulation of this complexity in drawing out the rhythmic features of the Southern Ewe dance *Gahu*: "Gahu's fully activated texture features four or five contrasting rhythmic layers unfolding within a polyrhythmic matrix. The bell provides a referential pulse for the whole ensemble within its own distinctive pattern. A rattle reinforces this pattern as well as the pattern of hand-clapping that invariably accompanies ensemble musics that involve dancing, singing, and drumming. Smaller drums respond to and contrast with the bell, trade motifs with the lead drummer, or articulate a consistent off-beat pattern that never migrates to the beat. Stylistic choices such as the preference for asymmetric time lines, the assumption of a downbeat rather than its external articulation, and the preference for musical patterns that seem to originate and terminate within metrical units rather than at their beginnings or endings."[7]

Communal artwork straddled a tension between secrecy and openness, simplicity and complexity. Ajume Wingo refers to African communal artwork as the realization of an aesthetics of "hiding and revealing."[8] This is insofar as an irreducible layer of African aesthetics often performatively represented interventions and conversation within an artistic guild. The inscriptions on Asante gold-weights, for example, resonated with allusions to proverbs heavy with the significance of the artistic tradition. In many communities in precolonial Africa, the complex patterns on masks often conveyed a secret discourse within particular guilds, cults, or societies. Ajume Wingo notes that the abstract patterns and arabesque motifs on the masks of the Nso of Cameroon constituted a language of cohesion, participation, solidarity, continuity, tolerance, and mutual respect. But if one layer of African communal aesthetics was secret and complex, another layer was open and simple. This is because the context of performance of African artwork was participatory and invitational.

The upshot then of African communal art is open-textured. The hermeticism of the context of invention and the free-wheeling, improvisatory texture of the context of performance are held in exquisite tension in the realization of artistic performance. The elitism of the context of invention is in tension with the democracy of artistic criticism. The rigors of genre are stretched almost beyond the breaking point by the permeability and free-flowing dance of spontaneity. According to Agawu, "African conceptions of music are more holistic than modern European notions, closer perhaps to those of ancient Greece." Thus, for example, "In Ewe, as in a number of African languages, there is no single word for 'music.' There is, in other words, no word that would enable us to describe a funeral dirge, a children's play song, and a recreational dance as forms of music. . . . The distinction between vocal and instrumental music does not register in Ewe discourse."[9]

African communal aesthetic praxis offers a far more complex and richer account of aesthetic praxis than that offered by dominant North Atlantic aesthetic theories. Nevertheless, the limitations of communal aesthetic practices are not insignificant. The attribution of artistic abilities as endowment from the gods is not that different from North Atlantic discourses of artists as geniuses. Moreover, for all the diversity that African communal aesthetic practice fosters and encourages, the most dominant discourses conceive of discordance and dissent as falling under the umbrella of an overarching metaphysical harmony. In other words, African communal aesthetic practice allows for a great deal of difference and disunity, but dissent is tolerated in the understanding that there is an ultimate metaphysical unity or harmony that subsumes or absorbs the manifest disunity. The upshot is that African communal art is a fairly robust political aesthetic praxis with a sophisticated apparatus for exploring knowledge, but its existential horizons remain constricted.

To be sure, the account sketched out above of African communal aesthetics is far from exhaustive of the diversity of African aesthetic praxis. These traditions were far from monolithic. For example, the *ugolochamma* statues among the Igbo did not have any religious or ancestral significance.[10] Often they signified a family's affection for a daughter or bride. Moreover, as Nkiru Nzegwu has helpfully pointed out, the central concept of *ikenga* in Igbo aesthetic practice troubles any easy assumption that there is a singular communalistic discourse of aesthetics in Africa. *Ikenga* denotes the virtue of individuality or assertiveness. Artists in Igbo society often represent *ikenga* in the form of a wooden sculpture whose human features are idealized.

Elemental Aesthetics

Who is the Tolstoy of the Zulus? The Proust of the Papuans? I'd be glad to read them.
—Saul Bellow, *New York Times Magazine* (1988)

Tolstoy is the Tolstoy of the Zulus—unless you find a profit in fencing off universal properties of mankind into exclusive tribal ownership.
—Ralph Wiley, *Dark Witness* (1996)

Elemental aesthetics is a discourse and practice of aesthetics emergent from the changes wrought on artistic practices in Africa following encounters with North Atlantic nations—most markedly, the experience of the trans-Atlantic slave trade and, later, the invasion and colonization of Africa. What followed was the fracturing of the context of communal aesthetics. Two large trajectories can be readily discerned. In one direction, a discourse of unremitting contempt for African creativity and aesthetic production burst forth from their European conquerors. Hegel is illustrative of this discursive othering of Africans:

> If finally we look beyond single individuals and their capricious taste to the taste of *nations*, this too is of the greatest variety and contrariety. How often do we hear it said that a European beauty would not please a Chinese, or a Hottentot either, since the Chinese has inherently a totally different conception of beauty from the negro's, and his again from the European's, and so on. Indeed, if we examine the works of art of these non-European peoples, their images of the gods, for example, which have sprung from their fancy as sublime and worthy of veneration, they may present themselves to us as the most hideous idols; and while their music may sound in our ears as the most detestable noise, they on their side will regard our sculptures, pictures, and music, as meaningless or ugly.[11]

If the Hegelian pole of North Atlantic encounters with African aesthetics stressed the *incommensurability* between and among aesthetic discourses, another—a far stronger pole—sought to *appropriate* African aesthetic artifacts and performances into North Atlantic aesthetic praxis. At the material level, this involved the widespread looting of African aesthetic artifacts and the transfer of these artifacts to North Atlantic museums and private collections. Perhaps one of the most notorious examples of this occurred in 1897, when a British expeditionary force burned and sacked Benin City and plundered the city of its finest art.[12] Some of these pieces are now owned by Europe's best museums while others are in the private collections of North Atlantic art connoisseurs. The discursive justification for engagement with African artifacts was riddled with contradictions. The Benin bronzes, for example, were received in Europe with consternation and disbelief, so stunned were they by the highly technical skill and craftsmanship required in their making. Early European art criticism spent considerable time and effort denying that Africans had made them. Some claimed that the bronzes had been manufactured by the Portuguese while others claimed that the Africans who had made them were under Portuguese tutelage and instruction. Thus was initiated a long-standing critical motif of Africans as imitators of Europeans.

Another line of discourse offered a backhanded concession to African originality. According to this discourse, African aesthetic practice consisted of a primordial *ursprung* from which Europeans could draw upon to reignite their atrophied critical virility. This is the line of discourse articulated by early-twentieth-century modernists. These artists saw in Africa an authentic primitivity and pure exoticism that they wanted to leverage against what they saw as European decadence.

The illegitimate acquisition of African art objects along with modernism's discourse on primitivity opened a market for certain kinds of African art-objects. Capitalism thus further fractured the field of African aesthetic practice by introducing a compartmentalized field among arts intended for collectors in the North Atlantic world; a domestic commercial art intended for Africa's middle to upper class market;[13] and "traditional" art emergent from Africa's rural communities. These diverse forms of art of course influenced one another and exert differential pressure on forms of cultural production.

Pedagogical Aesthetics—Chinua Achebe

"I want Okonkwo to answer me," said Uchendu.
"I do not know the answer," Okonkwo replied.
"You do not know the answer? So you see that you are a child. You have many wives and many children—more children than I have. You are a great man in your clan. But you are still a child, my child."

—Chinua Achebe, *Things Fall Apart*

"Why do you want a job in the Civil Service? So that you can take bribes?" he asked.
Obi hesitated. His first impulse was to say it was an idiotic question. He said instead: "I don't know how you expect me to answer that question. Even if my reason is to take bribes, you don't expect me to admit it before this board. So I don't think it's a very useful question."

"It's not for you to decide what questions are useful, Mr. Okonkwo," said the Chairman, trying unsuccessfully to look severe. "Anyhow, you'll be hearing from us in due course. Good morning."

—Chinua Achebe, *No Longer At Ease*

"I have one question I want the white man to answer." This was Nweke Ukpaka.
"What's that?"
Unachukwu hesitated and scratched his head. "Dat man wan axe master queshon."
"No questions."
"Yessah." He turned to Nweke. "The white man says he did not leave his house this morning to come and answer your questions."

—Chinua Achebe, *Arrow of God*

By pedagogical aesthetics, I mean a practice of aesthetics oriented toward the educational form and its potentialities. Few have been as influential in articulating this aesthetic as the doyen of African letters, Chinua Achebe; it is to a close reading of his work that I turn in this section toward the end of illustrating the riches and limitations of pedagogical aesthetics. To his credit, Achebe was often the first to decry the oft-repeated notion that he was the "father of African literature."[14] For he was not of course the first African novelist. As numerous commentators have pointed out, there is a literary tradition that long preceded Achebe, some of it in vernacular languages (such as the work of D. O. Fagunwa) and others in the English language (such as the work of Amos Tutuola). Rather, his extraordinary influence is in significant part attributable to how his novels seemed to capture the wishes and dreams of a new Pan-African bourgeoisie just feeling out what it meant to be African in postindependence countries. Additionally, his novels were then institutionalized in the syllabi of Anglophone Africa's postindependence countries—and, later, in Anglophone North Atlantic countries—as the quintessential postcolonial literary texts. Of course, Achebe's influence was also in no small part a result of his inimitable literary style.

Achebe himself thought of his literary *oeuvre* as an instantiation of pedagogical aesthetics: "The writer cannot expect to be excused from the task of re-education and regeneration that must be done. In fact, he should march right in front. For he is, after all—as Ezekiel Mpha-hlele says in his *African Image*—the sensitive point of his community."[15] Achebe's notion that the task of the novelist is to be a teacher in his society is sufficiently complex, however, to demand unpacking. He rejects the North Atlantic romanticization of the artist as a fringe outsider to his own society, a rebel without a cause. Indeed, for Achebe, nothing quite underscores the bad faith undergirding this Romantic image than the racist portrayal of Africa by North Atlantic artists—such as Joseph Conrad's *Heart of Darkness*. But if Achebe rejects the notion that the artist is unmoored from any society, he just as vehemently stands against the notion that the artist uncritically reflects the views of his society: "It is important to say . . . that no self-respecting writer will take dictation from his audience. He must remain free to disagree with his society and go into rebellion against it if need be."[16]

The tensions that crisscross Achebe's best fiction reflect this dual perspective. On the one hand, Achebe is quite clearly anxious to challenge representations of Africa as a heathen heart of darkness. But on the other hand Achebe is well aware that there is no single Africa that can be held over and above the European version as the authentic Africa. Indeed, for Achebe, the novelist's task as pedagogue involves as much a reeducation of Africans as a reeducation of Europeans. He sees his novels as speaking to the *nouveau* African bourgeoisie who—under the tutelage of Christian missionaries—had learned to thoroughly hate what they took to be "indigenous" or "traditional" African culture: "Here . . . is an adequate revolution for me to espouse—to help my society regain belief in itself and put away the complexes of the years of denigration and self-abasement."[17]

Achebe then has a sophisticated understanding of the relationship of the artist to his audience. He is just as concerned that our understanding of teaching—especially the aesthetic education imparted by the artist— be understood in all its nuanced dimensions. He rejects the notion that novels are "how-to" manuals of information. As he puts it: "[A] reader in Ghana . . . wrote me a rather pathetic letter to say that I had neglected to include questions and answers at the end of *Things Fall Apart* and could I make these available to him to ensure his success at next year's school certificate examination. This is what I would call in Nigerian pidgin a 'how-for-do' reader and I hope there are not very many like him."[18] But he also rejects the notion that novels teach by a simple one-to-one representation of certain characters and values as "good" and other characters and values as "bad."

Achebe's formal mode of engagement is realism. But it is just as important to note that his is a very particular, distinctive form of realism. *Naïve realism* makes efforts at presenting the narrative as a transparent window into reality. One thinks here of Hemingway. Its focus is on the writer as objective. *Reflexive realism* is focused on simultaneously making one see as vividly and as intensely as possible while constantly drawing attention to the instability of what one is seeing. One thinks here of Conrad.[19] *Embedded realism* emphasizes that one is encountering a prior reality that existed before one arrived on the scene. This is Achebe's realism. He wants, in a sense, to provincialize the reader's perspective, to remind the reader that he or she has happened upon an event or situation that long preceded the reader's existence and will likely exist in some form after the reader leaves. If the reader is fortunate to arrive just when the tree is falling in the forest that does not mean that no trees fall in the reader's absence. Unlike reflexive realism, which is deeply "epistemological," embedded realism is in a sense "ontological."

Achebe's embedded realism is constituted by a perspicacity of vision the likes of which have few precedents in novel writing. His pellucid sentences and supple syntax are paradoxical in that they make for *pleasurable reading* and thus, for that reason, are *not* precisely transparent—and yet also make for *absorbing reading* and thus, for that reason, tempt his readers to take his prose for granted. He embeds his distinctive style in a context that—to borrow Auerbach's famous phrase—is fraught with background. There is therefore a deep tension—one that Achebe dramatizes forcefully—between his deliberately simple prose and the vexingly difficult meanings that his texts wrestle with. That is, his felicitous prose is precisely aimed at amplifying the enigmatic depths of his characters and the complexity, even ineffability, of the societies within which his stories are embedded. His style poses a challenge to naïve realism as much as to reflexive realism. It should be remembered that the style of naïve realism constitutes the major accent of colonial anthropology. It is a stripped-down, austere style that does not so much speak as it *gazes*, constituting its authority and mastery of meaning and knowledge by its performance of clinical detail and masculinist detachment. Achebe's embedded realism refuses the illusion of objectivity.

Embedded realism also poses a challenge to reflexive realism. According to Francis Mulhern, the reflexivity of modernist art arose in part from a crisis engendered by the new media. If earlier modes of storytelling maintained a certain co-presence of storyteller and listener—a co-presence that allowed the storyteller access to phatic dimensions of communication[20]—modern art is wracked by a deep sense of existential loss for what it perceives of as the disappearance of a palpable, tactile audience: is an audience really out there, are they really reading, and what is their response when they read? According to Francis Mulhern, the modernist writer is driven by a compulsion "to restore the communicative guarantee that the novelistic is constitutionally unable to underwrite."[21] Mulhern calls this compulsion *hyperphasia*, and he thinks of it as an anxiety to abolish or outwit the mediated nature of the novel as a form—by undercutting its authority—and to rally a return to the perceived fullness of oral communication.[22] For Mulhern, the hyperphatic anxiety of a novelist such as Conrad is made in the interest of a disavowal of the terror and horror of capitalist imperialism and exploitation: "Conrad, as a novelist, has been brought to know something, but cannot accept what he knows or that he knows it. His novels find their form in the struggle to contain an unbearable acknowledgment. . . . The brilliant, opaque protagonists of *Lord Jim* and *Heart of Darkness* who so fascinate Marlow are fetishes in the psychoanalytic sense, prized images of empire that allow him to look, indeed to gaze, without seeing."[23]

We are now in a position to see that Achebe, often accused of inaugurating a dreary parade of realist novels in Anglophone Africa, had a far more sophisticated engagement with realism than critics have given him credit for. To be sure, there was always something dubious about these accusations leveled at him, for no one had been quicker to jump to the defense of many arealist African texts as Achebe often did. Witness his vigorous advocacy on behalf of Amos Tutuola's unconventional *The Palm-Wine Drinkard*. If Achebe's aesthetic merits criticism, it is not on account of forcing a nonexistent monolithic realism down African novelists' throats, but rather on account of the limits of his particular pedagogical aesthetic. For despite its Herculean efforts at banishing the ethnographic narcissism of naïve realism and reflexive realism, Achebe's aesthetic remains entirely beholden to a communitarian vision. Whatever the virtues of his aesthetic, it continues to privilege a *moralistic* mode of engagement with the world. And not just moralistic, but also a realist moralism—in the sense of morals as entities in the external world that categorically demand obedience.

Achebe, thankfully, is not a vulgar moralist. Still, a sophisticated moralist remains a moralist nevertheless. Because Achebe takes a certain Christian-inflected Igbo metaphysics as the ground for art and criticism, the very notion of the existential remains unintelligible to him—the existential conceived here as a fundamental *unhomeliness* about the world that is not necessarily occasioned by political or epistemological crisis. Indeed, one can go further. For all that he concedes a certain measure of alienation in his characters, Achebe is much more comfortable attributing this to the characters' alienation from settled communal ways. In the last instance, then, Achebe's vision remains pervasively affirmative. Faced by a writer like Ayi Kwei Armah who has an uncompromising excremental vision of the world, Achebe retreats to the worst of communal moralism. Armah's novel *The Beautyful Ones Are Not Yet Born*, Achebe argues, is "sick." Achebe goes on to dismiss Armah's existentialism as "foreign." It is here that Achebe's pedagogical aesthetic knots around African literature in a stifling stranglehold. His communalism leads him to assume that Igbo identity was once much more integrated than in fact it ever was. If Achebe's vision has been remarkably devoid of nostalgia, it has not been devoid of a certain measure of romanticization of Igbo cultural achievements.[24] His aesthetic, on its part, moves him to think that what is unassimilable—such as Armah's scathing, scatological vision—must obviously be foreign and therefore unworthy to be understood. In the end, Achebe's aesthetic may be as interesting for the limits of its imaginative horizons as for the vistas that it has powerfully unfolded.

Mythopoeic Aesthetics—Wole Soyinka

> Iyaloja: "You have betrayed us. We fed you sweetmeats such as we
> hoped awaited you on the other side. But you said, No, I must eat
> the world's left-overs. We said you were the hunter who brought
> the quarry down; to you belonged the vital portions of the game.
> No, you said, I am the hunter's dog and I shall eat the entrails of
> the game and the faeces of the hunter. We said you were the hunter
> returning home in triumph, a slain buffalo pressing down on
> his neck; you said wait, I first must turn up this cricket hole with
> my toes. We said yours was the doorway at which we first spy the
> tapper when he comes down from the tree, yours was the blessing
> of the twilight wine, the purl that brings night spirits out of doors
> to steal their portion before the light of day. We said yours was the
> body of wine whose burden shakes the tapper like a sudden gust
> on his perch. You said, No, I am content to lick the dregs from each
> calabash when the drinkers are done. We said, the dew on earth's
> surface was for you to wash your feet along the slopes of honor. You
> said, No, I shall step in the vomit of cats and the droppings of mice;
> I shall fight them for the left-overs of the world."
> —Wole Soyinka, *Death and the King's Horseman*

In this section, I consider mythopoeic aesthetics, perhaps best theorized and enacted by the Nigerian Nobel laureate Wole Soyinka. Soyinka's *oeuvre* constitutes one of the finest libraries in African literary production, consisting of plays, novels, poems, and essays. He seeks to root his aesthetic in a Yoruba cosmology. This cosmology delineates the matrix for the imagination, the inspiration for resonant symbols and images that the artist enacts and the limit cases against which the artist contends against: "The stage, the ritual arena of confrontation, came to represent the symbolic chthonic space, and the presence of the challenger within it is the earliest physical expression of man's fearful awareness of the cosmic context of his existence. Its magic microcosm is created by the communal presence, and in this charged space the chthonic inhabitants are challenged."[25]

Soyinka has argued that the African artist ought to draw from his cosmology in the making of his or her art. His point is both positive and negative. The positive point is that Africans can only articulate an authentic self-apprehension by drawing from their own myths and rituals. The negative point is double-edged. In one direction, Soyinka is critical of Europeans and North Americans who have denied that there exists a coherent and rich African worldview. In the other direction, Soyinka has attacked discourses such as Negritude that—in the name of an African racial essence—have ended up reifying African identity as the radical other of European civilization. Ultimately, for Soyinka, an African would take the measure of his or her identity to the extent that he or she takes for granted the richness of his or her heritage. The point holds particularly keenly for African artists. The African artist, he thinks, should convey the "replete reality" of his or her African self-apprehension. "Social emancipation, cultural liberation, cultural revolution are easier but deflective approaches, for they all retain external reference points against which a progression in thinking can be measured."[26]

For all its indubitable power and reach, Soyinka's aesthetic has troubling limitations. Granted that Soyinka's cosmology yields a bountiful harvest of the creative imagination, its limitations cannot be passed over. One significant dimension is the extent to which Soyinka's interpretation of Yoruba cosmology forecloses critical political and existential exploration. Recall Soyinka's guiding premises: humans exist within a cosmic totality, and Yoruba cosmology is a necessary and sufficient repertory of the (African) imagination. Soyinka emphasizes that his cosmology is neither Platonic nor Christian, and as such he insists that the goings on in the earthly realm are not separate from or subordinate to a separate metaphysical realm. Rather, human life is embedded within a cosmic context; the human condition is an episode within a larger cosmic drama of interaction between gods and men:

> The setting of Ritual, of the drama of the gods, is the cosmic entirety. . . . The dramatic or tragic rites of the gods are however engaged with the more profound, more elusive phenomenon of being and non-being. Man can shelve and even overwhelm metaphysical uncertainties

by epic feats, and prolong such a state of social euphoria by their constant recital, but this exercise in itself proves a mere surrogate to the bewildering phenomenon of the cosmic location of his being. The fundamental visceral questioning intrudes, prompted by the patient, immovable and eternal immensity that surrounds him. We may speculate that it is the reality of this undented vastness which created the need to challenge, confront and at least initiate a rapport with the realm of infinity. It was—there being no other conceivable place— the natural home of the unseen deities, a resting-place for the departed, and a staging-house for the unborn. Intuitions, sudden psychic emanations could come logically, only from such an incomparable immensity. A chthonic realm, a storehouse for creative and destructive essences, it required a challenger, a human representative to breach it periodically on behalf of the well-being of the community.[27]

If it is true that the realm of mundane human affairs is still an important dimension of this cosmic drama, they are important insofar as they are *indicators* of a deeper metaphysical conflict. The political is *incidental* in the face of a far more momentous reality; it plays a fundamentally *functional* role rather than being an end in itself. Soyinka says as much in offering a reading of his immensely powerful play *Death and the King's Horseman*. Soyinka is anxious that this play not be read as a political or cultural conflict between British colonizers and the African colonized:

The bane of themes of this genre is that they are no sooner employed creatively than they acquire the facile tag of "clash of cultures," a prejudicial label which quite apart from its frequent misapplication, presupposes a potential equality in every given situation of the alien culture and the indigenous, on the actual soil of the latter. . . . It is thanks to this kind of perverse mentality that I find it necessary to caution the would-be producer of this play against a sadly familiar reductionist tendency, and to direct his vision instead to the far more difficult and risky task of eliciting the play's threnodic essence. . . . The confrontation in the play is largely metaphysical, contained in the

human vehicle which is Elesin and the universe of the Yoruba mind—
the world of the living, the dead and the unborn, and the numinous
passage which links all: transition.[28]

Even if it were true that this statement is "disingenuous" and
"absurd"—as Kwame Anthony Appiah has declared it is—it would still
be important to explore how Soyinka's reading of his art filters into
its form and content. The *formal* power of Soyinka's plays lies in the
poetic and musical resonance of his plays, an achievement that can
be traced to Soyinka's emergence from an aesthetic tradition in which
poetry, music, and theater are seen not as distinct kinds of art but
rather as inextricably intertwined forms. Soyinka also has an uncanny
ability to capture—from the inside, as it were—the "logic" of culture
and dispositions, that is, the manner in which agents experience the
pressure of particular cultural imperatives. His art lies in his ability to
render these cultural logics as characters in themselves, interacted with
as necessities rather than simply "choices" or "options." The point is
that he does better than simply offer a convincing "psychology"; long
before philosophers of mind were talking about the "extended mind,"
Soyinka was mapping its forms and movements in myth and ritual,
dance and masque. It is notable that Soyinka's empathetic evocation of
cultural logics is not restricted to Yoruba society; *Death and the King's
Horseman*, for example, offers powerful renditions of the dispositional
habitus of British colonial administrators. Soyinka at his best lets us
into the crucible of sociocultural duty and individual *habitus* or will, or,
to use the language of social theory, shows how *verstehen* (interpretive
understanding) is continuous with *erklären* (causal explanation).

If those are the gains that Soyinka's metaphysics allow for his art, the
limitations are no less apparent. It is not just that Soyinka peremptorily
takes a very local mythology of the ancient Oyo kingdom as somehow
representative of African metaphysics. It is that taking his interpretation
of Yoruba metaphysics as synecdochal of the African aesthetic also
flattens the very traditions he claims to be championing. It is at the very
joints of power and agency—the precise points at which Soyinka's art
has been hailed for its genius—that Soyinka's omissions are revelatory

of what his imagination cannot extend. Part of the reason for this lies in Soyinka's fascination with the Yoruba deity Ogun, which leads him to valorize will, creation, self-creation, conquest, and mastery. Witness, for example, Soyinka's unmediated identification with Olunde in *Death and the King's Horseman*. In the same play, Iyaloja is no doubt one of the most striking characterizations of a woman by a male playwright of the twentieth century, and yet, at the same time, she fits into longstanding tropes of the woman as embodiments of tradition.

Soyinka's metaphysics contribute as much to the limitations of narrative architecture as of linguistic performativity. His art and criticism teeters precariously on the thin wedge of spectacle and farce. At its best, Soyinka's prose is a study in eloquence, extraordinarily vital in metaphor and proverb, irony, wit, and play. At its worst, his prose is overheated and histrionic, florid and baroque. Soyinka seemingly lacks the ability to dramatize how thoughts can go unspoken and how words may be unsayable. His flamboyant behaviorism increasingly takes on the look and substance of the piaculum, so much does he recoil from any hint of stillness and repose. His frenetic word count talks over any hint of silence. Affects of melancholy, hesitance, lassitude, weariness have no place in his theater of the grand gesture. His is a strict division between actors and the acted upon, the active and the passive, and he has the most trouble rendering figures that are neither straightforwardly strong nor straightforwardly victims—figures like Amusa, the native police constable—or scenes wherein power is in flux, with no one straightforwardly superior and the other inferior, such as the confrontation between Amusa and the market women. Soyinka's tendency is to render such liminal persons and scenes in the idiom of farce and parody. In the case of Amusa, for example, Soyinka reduces him to an emasculated,[29] shuffling, blubbering "Uncle Tom":

AMUSA: I am tell you women for last time to commot my road. I am here on official business.
WOMAN: Official business you white man's eunuch? Official business is taking place where you want to go and it's a business you wouldn't understand.

WOMAN [makes a quick tug at the constable's baton]: That doesn't fool anyone you know. It's the one you carry under your government knickers that counts. [She bends low as if to peep under the baggy shorts. The embarrassed constable quickly puts his knees together. The women roar.]

Soyinka is a political writer who desperately wants to be a metaphysical sage. The reasons for this desire would say as much about what he is against as what he is for. There are reasons to think it is a mistaken desire. Bernard Williams once offered a brilliant critique of the modern desire for "depth." He was referring to the tendency to dig deeply into such notions as the "voluntary," the "will," "responsibility," and "evil" in such a way as to find the essence of these terms, what "really" underlay them. Williams argues that such metaphysical digging is ultimately mistaken, for though such terms can be "extended or contracted in various ways," they "can hardly be deepened at all." Indeed, the very possibility of understanding these notions is threatened by attempts at "profundity." Against this desire, Williams counsels a Sophoclean attitude, the "gift for being superficial out of profundity."[30]

Late Modernist Aesthetics—J. M. Coetzee

I ought to go back to my cell. As a gesture it will have no effect, it will not even be noticed. Nevertheless, for my own sake, as a gesture to myself alone, I ought to return to the cool dark and lock the door and bend the key and stop my ears to the noise of patriotic bloodlust and close my lips and never speak again. Who knows, perhaps I do my fellow-townsmen an injustice, perhaps at this very minute the shoemaker is at home tapping on his last, humming to himself to drown the shouting, perhaps there are housewives shelling peas in their kitchens, telling stories to occupy their restless children, perhaps there are farmers still going calmly about the repair of the ditches. If comrades like these exist, what a pity I do not know them! For me, at this moment, striding away from the crowd, what has become important above all is that I should neither be contaminated by the atrocity that is about to be committed nor poison myself with impotent hatred of its perpetrators. I cannot save the prisoners, therefore let me save myself. Let it at the very least be said, if it ever comes to be said, if there is ever anyone in some remote future interested to know the way we lived, that in this farthest outpost of the Empire of light there existed one man who in his heart was not a barbarian.

—J. M. Coetzee, *Waiting for the Barbarians*

The South African–turned-Australian writer J. M. Coetzee occupies an ambiguous place in African letters, much of this ambiguity owing to apartheid South Africa's anti-blackness in pressing its claim to a piece of the continent. Coetzee's *oeuvre* is dense and complex. One foothold into his imagination is a close reading of a lecture that he delivered entitled "What Is A Classic?" Coetzee begins his address by reflecting on a lecture by the same name given by T. S. Eliot in 1944. According to Coetzee, the lecture aimed at "consolidating" and "rearguing" a case Eliot had been making with more and more urgency as he grew in cultural stature. The lecture's major thesis, to quote Coetzee, was "that the civilization of Western Europe is a single civilization, that its descent is from Rome via the Church of Rome and the Holy Roman Empire, and that its originary classic must therefore be the epic of Rome, Virgil's *Aeneid*."[31]

Coetzee argues that there are at least two major ways of reading Eliot's lecture. The first, which he calls the transcendental-poetic reading, reads Eliot sympathetically and takes him at his word on the goals he claims to espouse. This reading assents to his audacious claim that Virgil's *Aeneid* is the seminal text of the European canon:

This is an approach which would take seriously the call from Virgil that seems to come to Eliot from across the centuries. It would trace the self-fashioning that takes place in the wake of that call as part of a lived poetic vocation. That is, it would read Eliot very much in his own framework, the framework he elected for himself when he defined tradition as an order you cannot escape, in which you may try to locate yourself, but in which your place gets to be defined, and continually redefined, by succeeding generations—an entirely transpersonal order, in fact.[32]

The second way of reading Eliot would view his claims with suspicion. Coetzee calls this view a sociocultural reading:

> [The sociocultural reading treats Eliot's] efforts as the essentially magical enterprise of a man trying to redefine the world around himself—America, Europe—rather than confronting the reality of his not-so-grand position as a man whose narrowly academic, Eurocentric education had prepared him for little else but life as a mandarin in one of the New England ivory towers.[33]

The reading one employs will then deeply inform what one makes of Eliot's project in defining the classic. Eliot employs a series of allegorical resonances in interpreting Virgil's Aeneas that are intended to redound to his benefit. Like Aeneas, he implies in his lecture, he too was an exile. Like Aeneas, he too was a figure of destiny, not in spite of the skepticism and derision that this claim would inevitably provoke, but precisely because of the opposition it was ranged against. For if Eliot sees himself as heir to Virgil's tradition, he sees that tradition as opposed to another, at the head of which was Odysseus. If Odysseus represents aimless wandering and lack of rootedness, Aeneas represents what Coetzee describes as a "destiny-inspired trajectory."[34] The stakes for Eliot go beyond simply declaring that he is an Englishman, important as he found it to go on the offensive against attempts to caricature him as the "eager American cultural *arriviste* lecturing the English and/or the Europeans about their heritage and trying to persuade them to live up to it." Rather, what is at stake for Eliot is the struggle to "redefine and resituate" European identity. Hitherto, many had sought to place Virgil as the "poet of Latinity"—that is, as belonging to France, Spain, and Italy. By claiming that Virgil is the father of Christian Europe, Eliot performs a brilliant *peritrope*—he essentially provincializes England and America, declaring them satellites to the eternal metropolis of Rome. It is against this massive historical backdrop that Eliot wants to define the classic. The "Aeneid [is] a classic not just in Horatian terms—as a book that has lasted a long time (*est vetus atque probus, centum qui perfecit annos*)—but in allegorical terms: as a book that will bear the weight of having read into it a meaning for Eliot's own age."[35]

Coetzee then makes a turn, saying he wants to use "Eliot the provincial as a pattern and figure of myself." If Eliot claims that Virgil spoke to him across time, for Coetzee, that figure was Bach:

> One Sunday afternoon in the summer of 1955, when I was fifteen years old, I was mooning around our back garden in the suburbs of Cape Town, wondering what to do, boredom being the main problem of existence in those days, when from the house next door I heard music. As long as the music lasted, I was frozen, I dared not breathe. I was being spoken to by the music as music had never spoken to me before.
>
> What I listened to was a recording of Bach's *Well-Tempered Clavier*, played on the harpsichord.[36]

Years later Coetzee asks himself the sense in which Bach's music qualifies as "classic," or if this judgment was simply a contingent identitarian gesture:

> The question I put to myself, somewhat crudely, is this: Is there some nonvacuous sense in which I can say that the spirit of Bach was speaking to me across the ages, across the seas, putting before me certain ideals; or was what was really going on at that moment that I was symbolically electing high European culture, and command of the codes of that culture, as a route that would take me out of my class position in white South African society and ultimately out of what I must have felt, in terms however obscure or mystified, as an historical dead end—a road that would culminate (again symbolically) with me on a platform in Europe addressing a cosmopolitan audience on Bach, T. S. Eliot, and the question of the classic? In other words, was the experience what I understood it to be—a disinterested and in a sense impersonal aesthetic experience—or was it really the masked expression of a material interest?[37]

Coetzee's answer is that a work such as Bach's qualifies as a classic by virtue of the fact that it has survived testing by professionals:

If there is anything that gives one confidence in the classic status of Bach, it is the testing process he has been through within the profession. Not only did this provincial religious mystic outlast the Enlightenment turn toward rationality and the metropolis, but he also survived what turned out to have been the kiss of death, namely, being promoted during the nineteenth-century revival as a great son of the German soil.... Dare I suggest that the classic in music is what emerges intact from this process of day-to-day testing? The criterion of testing and survival is not just a minimal, pragmatic, Horatian standard (Horace says, in effect, that if a work is still around a hundred years after it was written, it must be a classic). It is a criterion that expresses a certain confidence in the tradition of testing, and a confidence that professionals will not devote labor and attention, generation after generation, to sustaining pieces of music whose life functions have terminated.[38]

Not just any professionals, however. Coetzee is clearly speaking of professionals with mastery of the North Atlantic canon:

What does it mean in living terms to say that the classic is what survives? How does such a conception of the classic manifest itself in people's lives? For the most serious answer to this question, we cannot do better than turn to the great poet of the classic of our own times, the Pole Zbigniew Herbert. To Herbert, the opposite of the classic is not the Romantic but the barbarian; furthermore, classic versus barbarian is not so much an opposition as a confrontation. Herbert writes from the historical perspective of Poland, a country with an embattled Western culture caught between intermittently barbarous neighbors. It is not the possession of some essential quality that, in Herbert's eyes, makes it possible for the classic to withstand the assault of barbarism. Rather, what survives the worst of barbarism, surviving because generations of people cannot afford to let go of it and therefore hold on to it at all costs—that is the classic.[39]

Coetzee's "What Is A Classic?" lecture is important because in form and content it captures the animating drive of his late modernism as a dialectical dance of incommensurables. His thought is dialectical insofar as he enacts a clash between form versus content, civilization versus barbarity, reason versus the imagination. But if Coetzee's thought is dialectical, it is decidedly that of Adorno rather than Hegel. What results from dialectical clash is a bleak remainder rather than a full-throated affirmation. Take, for example, Coetzee's political vision. If his thesis can be said to detail with clinical precision how hegemonic rulers exercise brutal power over subjugated peoples, his antithesis articulates with just as detached an eye the barbarousness of the subjugated. But the clash of thesis and antithesis does not result in the sublation of one into another, much less get preserved in the positive consciousness of *Aufhebung*. Rather Coetzee takes these two opposite poles as the ruthless pincers between which the individual tacks. If this resonates with Matthew Arnold's world-picture of the aesthete as gazing upon on "a darkling plain/Swept with confused alarms of struggle and flight/Where ignorant armies clash by night,"[40] it is not entirely a strained connection. Coetzee would likely renounce the single-minded programmaticism of Matthew Arnold and T. S. Eliot, but he is attracted to their account of the aesthetic as transfiguration of self and tradition.

Whatever the gains of the Eliotian-Coetzeean aesthetic, its reification of what it conceives of as the "barbarous" end of the dialectic is deeply conservative and reactionary. Coetzee for whatever reason does not mention it, but Eliot's juxtaposition of Odyssean rootlessness against Aeneidian "destiny" triggers longstanding anti-Semitic tropes. Adorno, for his part, infamously dismisses jazz as *Negerplastik*, his racial animus marking the outer limits of his aesthetic sensibilities. As for Coetzee, his attitude to African art has alternated between studious indifference and seething contempt. In Coetzee's meta-fictional novel *Elizabeth Costello,* the African novel is embodied in the figure of Emmanuel Egudu. In lesson 2 of the novel, Coetzee stages a debate between the protagonist, Elizabeth Costello, who "represents" the Western novel—but speaks in a universalist idiom—and Egudu, who speaks up for the African novel. Egudu's claims about the essence of the African novel—he claims that the African novel is by its very nature an oral novel—is skewered by

Costello as risible nonsense. The many failings of the African novel are embodied in Egudu himself, a lascivious figure who uses his oral gifts to seduce white women.[41] Prolifically inventive in extending modernist tropes, Coetzee here proves predictable in reiterating them—Africans and African art as one-dimensional, all-body and no-mind, sinister, amounting to nothing more than a "street-hustle."

THE FUTURE OF THE IMAGINATION: AFRICAN AESTHETICS AS A FORETASTE OF THE GOOD LIFE

> You read a historic writer not for what they failed to see, not
> for the ideological blindspots of their writing—too easy, too
> programmatic in the literary academy of recent years—but for the
> as-yet-unlived, still-shaping history which their vision—partially,
> tentatively, foresees and provokes.
>   —Jacqueline Rose, *Response to Edward Said*

This chapter offers an encounter with some of the most striking aesthetic practices on the African continent. The very diversity and complexity of the aesthetic practices that it sketches gives the lie to reductive claims about a singular African mode of creation and performance. Moreover, this chapter establishes the extent to which taking seriously African aesthetic practices necessarily consists in an exploration of what is now a global aesthetics.

The larger upshot of this chapter is its dramatization of the aesthetic as precisely a *practice* and therefore as emergent in and constitutive of a social imaginary. If that is granted, then this chapter invites critical engagements on how dominant aesthetic practices—in Africa and the rest of the world—demonstrate the limits of our imagination. But to put it thus also intimates otherwise—that is, that aesthetic practices may yet emerge that are constitutive of lives well lived, of just societies, sagacious knowledges, ethical relationships, and of creative artifacts and performances characterized by beauty and sublimity, the uncanny and the wondrous.

Theses on the Intellectual Imagination

Philosophy, which once seemed outmoded, remains alive because the moment of its realization was missed.
—Theodor Adorno, *Negative Dialectics*

A PROPAEDEUTIC TO INTELLECTUAL PRAXIS

In what follows, I attempt to assemble *theses*—a distinctive genre of writing that articulates an intervention in a political, economic, or cultural practice—on the form and animating vision of intellectual practice. For all of its distinguished and formidable pedigree—instantiated, for example, in Martin Luther's devastating *Ninety-Five Theses*, which arguably serves as a catalyzing exigence of the Protestant Reformation; Karl Marx's *Theses on Feuerbach*, which inaugurates his mature thought on epistemology and social ontology; and Walter Benjamin's *Theses on the Philosophy of History*, which simultaneously rings the death knell for a moribund historicism and unveils a radical cultural criticism—there has been remarkably little sustained deployment of the theses-text in academic writing. It may therefore be helpful to flesh out the contours of the theses toward the end of illuminating the goals, scope, and limits of what I have set out to accomplish in this book.

The theses-text is, perhaps most of all, an incorrigibly hybrid form as is attested to by its indeterminate quantitative status. On the one hand, it is disseminated as a single text. On the other hand, it consists of multiple theses. Moreover, the theses-text is numbered in such a way as to suggest a self-contained particularity to each thesis. And yet the very concept of number suggests multitude and thus evokes an expectation of additional theses to come. To get around its vexing defiance of singular and plural characteristics, I have coined the term the *thessay* as a provisional name for this most protean of rhetorical forms.

These fraught concerns about its ontology extend to its *telos*. Historically, the *thessay* has often been advanced in a provocative spirit to stake or clarify positions, spark debate, and summon interlocutors. The title of Luther's text, *Disputation on the Power and Efficacy of Indulgences*, casts his theses as an invitation to the scholastic practice of *disputatio*. Marx's *Theses*, similarly, was initiated as a space-clearing rather than definitive document. Engels characterizes Marx's *Theses* as "notes hurriedly scribbled down for later elaboration, absolutely not intended for publication, but invaluable as the first document in which is deposited the brilliant germ of the new world outlook."[1] Benjamin's theses also echoes the spirit of its predecessors. In a letter to Gretel Adorno that he enclosed along with the typescript of his *Theses on the Philosophy of History*, Benjamin writes: "I am handing them to you more as a bouquet of whispering grasses, gathered on reflective walks, than a collection of theses."[2]

But if the *thessay* advances its arguments as propaedeutic sketches that await more extended exposition, its terse, oracular form evokes an unquestionably summative, synoptic ambition. As an intervention to pitched debates, the *thessay* not only radiates an urgency to clarify the stakes of a historical moment, it is also swept forward by an oppositional momentum against entrenched commonplaces. Hence, Luther not only seeks to disambiguate what he takes to be a fateful conflation of temporal and eternal authority by the church but also pits himself in opposition to its sacerdotal hierarchy. Marx, for his part, not only shows that the insurgent Young Hegelians were still beholden to the idealist assumptions of Hegel but also stakes out a devastating indictment against philosophy as a disciplinary practice. And at time when the Soviet Union's pact with the Nazis had scrambled categories between left and right, Benjamin's *thessay* not only delineates the radical left imaginary but also mobilizes intellectual history against the fascist onslaught.

No wonder, then, that the *thessay* is less properly a "genre" than a meta-genre. It draws on the *essay* form to stage its contingent claims and structure its suggestive insights. It revs up *polemic* to ground-sweeping critiques and articulate expansive judgments. It exercises the *aphoristic* meter to marry the sagacious with the prophetic. It is erudite and therefore *scholarly* in sensibility, and yet it is also conversational and therefore *demotic* in temper.

And yet it is for precisely these reasons that the *thessay* has almost completely been missing from contemporary academic writing. Carole Blair, Julie R. Brown, and Leslie A. Baxter's devastating critique of the professional codes of academic writing offers a succinct explanation as to why this might be the case:

> Academic writing . . . is regulated by clear norms, usually among them the demand for a refined, ahistorical, smoothly finished univocality. . . . Our writings suppress our convictions, our enthusiasm, our anger, in the interest of achieving an impersonal, "expert" distance and tone. . . . [We] seek a coherent, authoritative, cleanly argued, singular and defensible position, devoid of "extraneous" or "tangential" details.[3]

The very form of the *thessay* cuts against these hegemonic professional codes of writing. Far from being univocal, it is irrepressibly polyphonous. Against an affectless tone, it vibrates with intensity. Moreover, in contrast to the conventional academic article that sets out a narrow thesis that it is then expected to defend—"a coherent, authoritative, cleanly argued, singular and defensible position"—the *thessay*, by definition, is fecund with ideas. It is not coincidental, then, that it is the preferred form for insurgent knowledges. This is the case not only because it is attuned to plurality, affect, and fugitivity, but because of the writerly economy that it affords. In this vein, Audre Lorde's comments on the material conditions from which writing is emergent can prove particularly instructive. Lorde was protesting a decision by a prominent women's magazine to publish only prose ostensibly because poetry was held to be a less "rigorous" and "serious" art form. Against this, Lorde writes:

> Yet even the form our creativity takes is often a class issue. Of all the art forms, poetry is the most economical. It is the one which is the most secret, which requires the least physical labor, the least material, and the one which can be done between shifts, in the hospital pantry, on the subway, and on scraps of surplus paper. Over the last few years, writing a novel on tight finances, I came to appreciate the enormous differences in the material demands between poetry and prose. As we reclaim our literature, poetry has been the major voice of poor, working class, and Colored women. A room of one's own may be a necessity for writing prose, but so are reams of paper, a typewriter, and plenty of time. The actual requirements to produce the visual arts also help determine, along class lines, whose art is whose. In this day of inflated prices for material, who are our sculptors, our painters, our photographers? When we speak of a broadly based women's culture, we need to be aware of the effect of class and economic differences on the supplies available for producing art.[4]

These comments, I suggest, may hold true as well for the *thessay*— and indeed, other forms of writing—in academic contexts. As Blair, Brown, and Baxter have argued, the notion that academic writing must fit into an objective, affectless idiom if it is to count as "professional" is best seen as "a masculinist disciplinary ideology, whose professionalized and seemingly liberal thematic motifs serve as a benign cover for a selectively hostile and exclusionary disciplinary practice."[5]

Below, I have set out to deploy this marginal genre as a pungent intervention on how we ought to imagine intellectual practice. My goal is both illuminative, a distillation of what I take to be the focal ideas argued for in this book, and invitational, a summons to a robust conversation on the futures of philosophy as a way of life.

FORTY THESES ON INTELLECTUAL PRAXIS

1. Intellectual practice is a craft, an art, and a praxis. It is a craft because it is an embodied apprenticeship in the performances of reading, listening, tasting, writing, and image-making—an exploration of the depth and breadth of the body as sensorium; an attunement to sound at its highest pitch and its lowest frequency; a connoisseurship in the textures of taste; an immersion in olfactory reception in all its pungency and subtlety; an attentiveness to line, to color, to shape; an abandonment to kinesthetic movement. It is an art because it is an adventure at the very outer edges—and limits—of the imagination. It is a praxis because it is the interanimation of mind and body, theory made flesh, and because it is a social practice, a study of and an engagement with power—from whence it is emergent; who, what, where, when, why, and how it is wielded; and, ultimately, an exercise in the arts of embodied and collective transformation.

2. Intellectual practice is a ground project. It is not a "calling" or "vocation," in the manner of the religious summons to enter a priesthood of proselytizers, but neither is it a career or profession, fashioned to the specifications of the capitalist corporation. If the religious "vocation" is apt to mystify and sacralize the very human interests of the intellectual—in both senses of the "human" as worldly and flawed—the idea of intellectualism as a "career" suborns criticism to the commodifying and compartmentalizing logics of capitalism. Against both "career" and "calling," intellectual practice ought to be seen as a "ground project," a social engagement that seeks to draw upon the breadth and depth of creaturely potentiality and meaning, that aims at realizing to the fullest limits possible articulations of truth, knowledge, justice, wisdom, and the imagination.

3. The stakes of intellectual practice are nothing less than what it means to live well—a perilous, decidedly mortal quest on the meaning and form of the good life. Intellectual practice is more than a skill or activity—it is an existential commitment to a way of life.

4. The intellectual has no discrete "text," for the intellectual's being is a worldliness, that is to say, a responsiveness to ecologies (wildernesses and wetlands, cities and suburbs, prairies and parking lots, malls and metros); societies (politics, economics, cultures); structures (social stratifications, social movements, social institutions); artifacts (texts, images, sounds); performances (plays, operas, persons); embodiments (gestures and postures, styles and strategems); and practices (rituals, rites, rules).

5. Intellectual practice is an orientation toward an asymptotic horizon of realization. For realization—if it has any meaning at all—surely denotes that which exceeds the measurable, the standardized, the quantifiable.

6. Intellectual practice is a secular *habitus*.[6] It involves tarrying in the tension between creating what endures and living with the occasional and the ephemeral. A desire for the eternal is a feeble denial of human mortality; it devolves into the epistemic closure of theology, metastasizes into the zealotries of religiosity. A pursuit after the momentary disfigures the critical task by making a fetish of the fashionable and conscripts the intellectual into complicity with the factories of planned obsolescence.

7. Intellectual practice is a *habitus* of interpretation. As such, it is an extended lesson in *hermeneutics*, the tradition of scholarship concerned with various theories and modalities of interpreting texts, performances, and practices. So what then is a theory of interpretation to the intellectual? It is not a lens, for that suggests a transparent window through which the intellectual gazes out. Theories of interpretation, far from being transparent, are grounded in particular histories, are oriented by particular politics, are delimited by particular imaginaries. Nor is critical theory a toolkit, for that conjures the fantasy of the intellectual as hovering above a toolbox, here dispassionately picking the screwdriver of historicism, there deciding between the wrenches of Marxism and feminism. Rather than a lens or a toolbox, critical theories ought to be seen as vibrant interlocutors, relentlessly skeptical of the intellectual's assumptions, interrupting the intellectual's illusion of unmedi-

ated communion with the text, attentive to the grain, detail, and turn of the text. But, insofar as theories are interlocutors, they are not simply applied, as if ready-made and self-contained. The encounter of critic, theory, and text lays all three open to the discovery of their limitations, to what they won't or cannot say, and to what about them remains stubbornly excessive and unassimilable.

8. The intellectual does not fetishize a "method," but refuses the occultism of romantic "inspiration" and "intuition." Critical "method" consists in an indefatigable contextualization and recontextualization. The intellectual proceeds by acknowledgments of *embeddedness, embodiment, entanglement, encounter,* and *engenderment* rather than a rule, a formula, or a map. *Embeddedness* because intellectual practice is an acknowledgment of emergence in the ecological and the social; *embodiment* because intellectual practice is a self-reflexive responsiveness to reason, affect, sensation, flesh, and imagination; *entanglement* because intellectual practice is constituted by ineliminable interdependence; *encounter* because intellectual practice is the risk, the danger, the provisionality of relationship, and because intellectual practice is as much inquiry as it is serendipity; and *engenderment* because intellectual practice is an intimation of alternative worlds.

9. The intellectual *describes,* and therefore aims at a perception keyed at its highest pitch, an attentiveness stretched to its widest scale, a sensibility whetted to a fine palate;[7] *understands,* and therefore aims at inhabiting the uncanny, the monstrous, the alien, the strange;[8] *analyzes,* and therefore traces the residual and the emergent, the grain and the break, the part and the whole;[9] *clarifies,* and therefore exegetes, explicates, and elucidates; *explains,* and therefore contextualizes, historicizes, and hypothesizes; *complicates,* and therefore persists in the question, perseveres in the aporetic abyss;[10] *translates,* and therefore retrieves the discarded, listens for the resonant, gathers the fragmented; *evaluates,* and therefore puts to work political, ethical, and aesthetic judgment; *argues,* and therefore invites, reasons, and responds; and *imagines,* and therefore unfolds transformations of the self, the text, and the world.

10. The intellectual does not wield, much less claim, a possession of knowledge. Rather the intellectual inhabits knowledges: *praxis*, or critical wisdom, the arts of living; *techne*, or the techniques and technologies of craft-making, tending, care-taking, and professing; *metis*, or the lore of survival, guile, wiliness, and cunning; and *pronoia*, or the artistry of maneuver, of foresight, ruthless realism, and flexible pragmatism.

11. Intellectual practice begins with radical self-reflexivity. History deposits in subjects "an infinity of traces, without leaving an inventory."[11] Thus, every intellectual practice starts with an *acknowledgment* of the violence that inhabits critical practice. It follows that it is precisely the intellectual task to persistently confront its investment in patriarchy, white supremacy, heteronormativity, religious fanaticism, ableism, and class exploitation. The labor of self-reflexivity is relentlessly recursive; disruptive of fantasies of linearity, transcendence, mastery; and ruthlessly critical of perverse ruses of reflexivity such as confession and representation. It follows, then, that such a radical self-reflexivity cannot be an individualistic, introspective process—it has to be social, and is only possible in sustained *encounter* with the poor, the weak, the vulnerable, the despairing.

12. The intellectual seeks to follow questions where they lead[12] and therefore transgresses the moated domains of discipline, field, and guild. She is no professional, for her movements are fugitive incursions, illegible against the cadastral registers of the state; but neither is she a dilettante, nor even an amateur, for the intellectual's crossings demand an intimacy with a terrain fraught with mortal stakes.

13. Intellectual practice tracks the movement of artifacts, performances, and practices across the four-dimensional contexts of emergence, performance, dissemination, and reception. The *context of emergence* names the political, economic, and cultural conditions of possibility for the invention of artifacts, performances, and practices. The *context of performance* refers to the time-space in which artifacts, performances, and practices are articulated or enacted, the temporal

and spatial fabric within which an association, image, narrative, idea, story, or vision takes shape on a page, a stage, a platform, or a canvas, or comes to fruition on the street. The *context of dissemination* tracks contestations over circulation, translation, and canonization of artifacts, performances, and practices. The *context of reception* is concerned with the forms in which interpreters interact with artifacts, performances, and practices. Of course, these contexts are inextricably interanimated and irreducibly entangled; they are layered, overlapping, dialectical, co-constitutive and recursive ecologies of authorship, performance, circulation, and sensibility.

14. The intellectual understands the context of emergence as *contingent.* For that reason, she is particularly responsive to the ecological and social conditions of possibility of authorship. Intellectual practice keeps its distance from the theology of "giftedness," the romanticism of "genius," and the patrimonialism of "auter theory." Instead, the intellectual registers how power coalesces in the production and distribution of legibility and enunciation and also, crucially, how alternative forms of authorship are enacted relationally and collaboratively, democratically and centrifugally. Perhaps more vitally, the intellectual seeks to be attuned to the multivalent meanings of silence, to the names that never rate footnotes and citations, to pro forma, perfunctory nods in acknowledgments pages, to the erased thinkers in the hinterlands of the metropole.

15. The intellectual works at the intersection of history, exigence, and the imagination. A fetish of traditionalism tumbles into a cobwebbed antiquarianism; a fixation with the relevant becomes a tyrannical presentism; a fascination with avant-gardism folds in on itself. The intellectual seeks, instead, to summon memory from the fugue of Traditionalism, to seize time for the urgency of the present, to ignite the imagination for the possibilities of tomorrow.

16. The intellectual understands the context of performance as an attentiveness to the imbrication of context, form, and the imaginary.

17. Intellectual practice is an extended exploration of the form, dimensions, meaning, and limits of a practice's *realization*. For the intellectual, realization is an orientation toward an asymptotic horizon.

18. The intellectual engages an artifact, performance, or practice as a contextual and formal exploration of a four-dimensional asymptotic horizon of realization: *participatory embodiment, knowledge, politics,* and *meaning.* A practice realizes *participatory embodiment* insofar as it deepens and expands sensory capacities: visual, auditory, olfactory, gustatory, tactile, proprioceptive, and kinesthetic senses. It realizes *knowledge* insofar as it explores to the very limits the problematics of imagination, rationality, technique, representation, and truth. It realizes the *political* insofar as, through an extended fossicking of form, it registers the trace of its conditions of possibility, inscribes its ontological status as practice and gift through relational enunciations, summons particular subjectivities into being through its mode of addresses, and proffers a palimpsestic intimation of alternative worlds. It realizes *meaning* insofar as its form instantiates the deepest and widest encounters with phenomena that have wrought the human condition, for example, how transhistorical existential experiences (joy and pain, love and hate, desire and revulsion) are expanded as well as confounded by irreducible particularity and irrepressible eccentricity; how the emergency, the crisis, and the tragedy is lived in and through the everyday, the mundane, and the banal; and, finally, the utter ineliminability of contingency, the inevitability of suffering, and the irreversibility of death.

19. Intellectual practice is an aesthetic practice—which is to say a cognitive, affective, and kinesthetic invention, performance, dissemination, and response to the inextricably intertwined dimensions of context, form, and the imaginary. The intellectual is attentive to the trace of the temporal and spatial imaginary on form; how form, in turn, reconfigures its spatial and temporal context; and how context and form is constitutive of the imaginary. Thus construed, aesthetic criticism involves a thoroughgoing repudiation of dualistic traditions of thought that pit aesthetics against politics, form against content, the imagination against the empirical, fiction against fact.

20. For the intellectual, the impress of ideology in art-forms is not a matter of examining the doctrines and beliefs of the author as expressed in the contents of an artifact or performance. Rather, ideology is precisely most potent when form encounters the politically and existentially unthinkable. Therefore, political criticism consists in tracing the contortions that form is placed in service of, the torture by which it is stretched in order that it not see, feel, and confront what enables the practice to function.[13]

21. Intellectual practice is a dialectical interanimation of the *deconstructive* and the *constitutive*. The intellectual rejects the notion that critique must issue in positive prescriptions and affirmative hosannas. "Positive thinking" is neoliberal capitalism's sibilant whisper, "positive energy" the self-satisfied woo of vulgarized mysticism. Nor does the intellectual regard as innocent the demand that criticism be "constructive" on pain of being stigmatized as parasitic on creativity. Intellectual practice is precisely deconstructive because it ruthlessly, relentlessly tests the limits of human experience and imagination. In so doing, criticism allows for *silence* insofar as it finds that language can break down and may not be adequate to the depth and breadth of existential and historical encounters, and demonstrates *finitude* insofar as it reveals the limits of human capability, the inevitability of human failure, the perversity of human agency. It is a striking fact about opposition to "negative" critique that it conceives of critique in the mode of procreation—"negative" critique is labeled "barren," "impotent," even "illegitimate." Intellectual practice urgently unravels the seams of such patriarchal and heteronormative language. It is, in any case, a category mistake to conceive of deconstructive criticism as pitted in a binary opposition to the "creative" or the "constructive"; rather criticism is dialectical and therefore constitutive. Consider, for example, that, to the critic, cliché and stereotype is more than congealed idiom and enervated syntax. Rather, just as cliché is the aestheticism of the philistine, so is stereotype the sociology of the aristocrat. Intellectual practice is precisely constitutive because it breaks into the tomb of tradition to reanimate memory and history, shatters the rictus of stereotype to revitalize form and content, and subverts cliché to enliven the imagination.

22. The intellectual sees language as deeply contextual and therefore striated by history and violence, but also constitutive and therefore an agency for creation. Because language is contextual, the Humpty-Dumpty theory of language is farcical. But because language is constitutive, the intellectual is alive to the wildness of language, its uncontainable variousness. The intellectual seeks precision without pedantry, creativity without contrivance.

23. Intellectual style is eloquence—as against miserliness or grandiloquence.

24. The struggle of the intellectual against power is the struggle of language against violence.

25. The intellectual is witness to a public culture whose evaluative vocabulary is a funhouse mirror of the lurid and the apathetic. On the one hand, the language of public culture is a vaporous hothouse of superlatives and exclamations. A person is "awesome!"; an event is "amazing!"; a listicle is "top ten!" On the other hand, communication across public culture has been evacuated of a critical lexicon of judgment—replaced by the Facebook "like" and the Twitter "fave." This is no paradox, however: the torrent of acclamation—"greatest," "best," "top"—and the treacle of the sentimental— 😊 , 👫 , 😌 —issue from the same fountainhead of therapeutic capitalism.

26. The intellectual diagnoses an enfeebled evaluative vocabulary as symptomatic of an ideological assault on the radical imagination, fallout from a corrupt public sphere that has traduced language across the aesthetic, the epistemic, and the ethical dimensions. In aesthetics, the beautiful has been reduced to the cute, the sublime to spectacle, the uncanny to horror, the difficult to the interesting, the comic to the zany, the enchanting to the sentimental.[14] In epistemology, cleverness has been substituted for wisdom, information for judgment, data for warrants. In ethics, subjectivity has been reified into authenticity, affect to feelings, kindness to sweetness, solidarity to patriotism, citizenship to consumerism. The impoverishment of evaluative vocabulary bespeaks

an existential recoil from the transfiguration of human capacities and powers, an antipathy to realization.

27. The ubiquity of an aesthetics of miniaturization and infantilization is a recoil from the utopian imagination. The investment in idioms of equivocation and prevarication is a retreat from radical commitment. The obsessive fixation with the statistical is a short-circuiting of judgment. The investment in postures of irony is an accommodation to political defeat.

28. The intellectual refuses the privileging of any single aesthetic form no matter how canonized and consecrated. To the intellectual, a society's cathexis in one single aesthetic category tells a deeper story of its disavowals. Hence, the Renaissance fetish of beauty says much about the consolidation of the absolutist state in the monarchical court; the enlightenment fascination with the sublime unveils the shock and awe of European imperialist slaveholding, rape, plunder, and conquest; the postmodern pastiche reveals the flattening properties of global capitalism. Intellectual practice instead is a widening of the space of aesthetic practice, an excavation of discarded aesthetic forms, a proleptic hint of aesthetic imaginations yet to be. The intellectual orientation is that of encounter, and thus an openness to the playful and the deadly, the intriguing and the banal, the difficult and the simple, the beautiful and the sublime, the uncanny and the abject.

29. Intellectual practice consists in a loosening of rigid evaluative categories and the revaluation of ossified aesthetic qualities. Against the hallowing of value, the intellectual seeks to *re*contextualize, to *re*connect, to *re*imagine.

30. Intellectual practice conceives of technologies as contextually constitutive. Against technodeterminism, the intellectual insists on the embeddedness of technologies, how ecology and politics shape their meanings, uses, possibilities, and limits. Against technophilia, the intellectual offers a reminder that technologies are not simply instrumental— rather, they are weighted with the path-dependence of historical use,

dovetail with particular tools, enable specific affordances, make possible certain imaginaries, and cut off other ways of being. Against technophobia, the intellectual theorizes in the long arc of human agency, open to the astonishment of serendipity.

31. The intellectual understands the context of dissemination as *generative* rather than as a transparent conduit for the transfer of finished artifacts to readers or audiences. For example, schools do more than simply inform students about books—they delimit possibilities for authorship. Galleries and museums do more than display artifacts—they radically define what counts as "art." Award-conferring institutions do more than recognize great performances—they determine what is canonized. Advertising agencies do more than persuade consumers to buy products—they generate desire.

32. Intellectual practice cuts against institutional forms of canonization invested in the consecration of selected artifacts as objects of veneration. It cuts against a traditionalism that conceives of artifacts as a patrimonial inheritance sired by Great Fathers, biologically reproduced by Great Sons, and solely possessed by Great Civilizations. It is skeptical of the invention of a counter-canon of artifacts that purports to represent minoritized identities. Rather than take as given the ahistoricism of canonization and its investment in genealogies of cultural supremacy and purity, criticism theorizes the context of dissemination as the induction of bodies into the deep structures of literacy—written, visual, and oral.[15]

33. What conservatives call "tradition," intellectuals know as the slaughter-bench of history at which entire peoples have perished in genocide, the remnant generations consigned to grinding and abject poverty, and their oral and written archives of learning and memory destroyed beyond retrieval. The conservative's "cultural heritage" are "spoils" in a "triumphal procession in which today's rulers tread over those who are sprawled underfoot." Tradition "owes its existence not only to the toil of the great geniuses, who created it, but also to the

nameless drudgery of its contemporaries. There has never been a document of culture, which is not simultaneously one of barbarism."[16]

34. The intellectual engages the context of dissemination as a site of translation—and therefore, as a practice of encountering the stranger, the traveler, the foreigner, the exile, the homeless.

35. "Always contextualize!" This is the single most urgent imperative for the intellectual in the age of Google algorithms, of Yahoo information aggregation, of Amazon search-engine optimization, of YouTube click-bait, of Wikipedia "expertise."

36. The context of reception, for the intellectual, is fraught with background. Critical reading demands an acknowledgement of the thick palimpsests upon which the text is written—its conscious and unconscious influences, its polyglot languages and idioms, its multiple authors and editors. It involves a recognition of the historical particularity within which the reading practice is embedded—its hermeneutical horizons, its social imaginary, its distinctive sensibility. It invites an attunement to the ecological texture of the event of reading—the temperature in the room, the smells of the book, the surrounding sound.

37. The intellectual understands the context of reception as an embodied practice. For that reason, reception is the interanimation of the senses—cognitive, affective, and kinesthetic. To receive is to *see*, not simply spectate; to *listen*, not simply hear; to *touch*, not simply feel; to *savor*, not simply taste; and to *participate*, not simply watch.

38. For the intellectual, reception is an embrace of vulnerability, an acknowledgment of loss, a revelation of incompleteness. The intellectual is neither a consumer, bullish after the latest bauble at the local bazaar, nor a tourist, shuttled through the flood-lit boulevards of vanity fair. She is a walker in the city's cobble-stoned backstreets, a traveler in the country's overgrown footpaths.

39. The intellectual responds not only to the summons of the text but also to audiences ignored and erased, to forgotten and unrealized publics.

40. Intellectual practice is a relentless refusal of narrative closure. It gathers the utopian in the face of the hegemony of *la pensée unique*: *remembering*, where genocidal amnesia seeks to erase its bloodied trail of tears; *witnessing*, where fascism seeks to shock with spectacle; and *imagining*, where capitalist realism beguiles with false choices. It is for precisely these reasons, moreover, that intellectual practice refuses the consolations of moralism. It gives the lie to the theodicean platitudes of the modern age: the fantasy that the arc of the moral universe bends toward justice; the ideology that everything happens for a reason; the wishful belief that good always triumphs over evil; the sentimentalism that love conquers all; the supernaturalism that "extreme, undeserved, and uncompensated suffering"[17] will be redeemed in the hereafter. Against this, the intellectual animates justice, practices wisdom, and instantiates the beautiful, the sublime, the uncanny, and the ordinary.

A FUTURE FOR THE INTELLECTUAL IMAGINATION

The *thessay* above does not aim for exhaustiveness. It is, instead, a summons to debate and therefore provisional; a response to exigence and therefore improvisational; a clarification of concepts and therefore pedagogical; a rearticulation of affiliations and therefore dialectical; a renarrativization of history and therefore imaginative; and a call to action and therefore performative. Thus this book is written to hail philosophy into a robust conversation on its ontology, epistemology, axiology, and *telos*.

NOTES

INTRODUCTION

1. For a striking example, drawn from the African context, see Odera Oruka's sage philosophy project as outlined in his book, *Sage Philosophy: Indigenous Thinkers and Modern Debate on African Philosophy* (Nairobi: African Center for Technology Studies, 1991).

2 Pierre Hadot, *What Is Ancient Philosophy?*, trans. Michael Chase (Cambridge, MA: Harvard University Press, 2002).

3. See, for example, Odera Oruka's striking distinction between the "mere philosopher" and the "sage proper" in Kai Kresse, "'Philosophy Must Be Made Sagacious': An Interview with Prof. Henry Odera Oruka, 16th August 1995 at the University of Nairobi," in *Sagacious Reasoning: Henry Odera Oruka in Memoriam*, ed. Anke Graness and Kai Kresse, 251–60 (Frankfurt: Peter Lang, 1997), 253–54.

4. Bernard Williams, *Ethics and the Limits of Philosophy* (Cambridge, MA: Harvard University Press, 1985).

5. Pierre Bourdieu, *Distinction: A Social Critique of the Judgement of Taste*, trans. Richard Nice (London: Routledge, 1984).

6. See, for example, Craig Steven Wilder, *Ebony and Ivy: Race, Slavery, and the Troubled History of America's Universities* (New York: Bloomsbury Press, 2013).

7. On a critique of Aryanist discourse, see Martin Bernal, *Black Athena: The Afroasiatic Roots of Classical Civilization* (New Brunswick, NJ: Rutgers University Press, 1987).

8. See, for example, Molefi Kete Asante, *The Afrocentric Idea* (Philadelphia: Temple University Press, 1998).

9. See, for example, Alasdair MacIntyre, *After Virtue: A Study in Moral Theory* (Notre Dame, IN: University of Notre Dame Press, 1981).

10. John M. Cooper, *Pursuits of Wisdom: Six Ways of Life in Ancient Philosophy from Socrates to Plotinus* (Princeton: Princeton University Press, 2012), 6.

11. Emile Durkheim, *The Rules of Sociological Method: And Selected Texts on Sociology and Its Method*, ed. Steven Lukes, trans. W. D. Halls (New York: Free Press, 1982), 126.

CHAPTER 1. RADICAL KNOWLEDGE

1. See Omedi Ochieng, *Groundwork for the Practice of the Good Life: Politics and Ethics at the Intersection of North Atlantic and African Philosophy* (New York: Routledge, 2016).

2. *Phaedrus*, trans. Alexander Nehamas and Paul Woodruff, in Plato, *Plato: Complete Works*, ed. with introduction and notes John M. Cooper (Indianapolis, IN: Hackett Publishing Company, 1997), 525.

3. Hilary Putnam describes this as "inflationary" ontology: "[T]he inflationary ontologist claims to tell us of the existence of things unknown to ordinary sense perception and commonsense, indeed things that are invisible. . . . Moreover, these invisible which the inflationary ontologist claims to have discovered are supposed to be supremely important. For Plato, in this reading of him, the existence of the Forms, and particularly the Form of the Good, explains the existence of ethical value and obligation." See Hilary Putnam, *Ethics Without Ontology* (Cambridge, MA: Harvard University Press, 2004), 17.

4. Ryle of course famously called this the "dogma of the Ghost in the Machine," the notion that in order to discern someone's behavior, one has to peer into the "secret grotto" of the mind. See Gilbert Ryle, *The Concept of Mind* (New York: Barnes & Noble, 1949), 15–16.

5. Ibid., 23.

6. Ibid., 17.

7. Ibid.

8. Ibid., 22.

9. Pierre Bourdieu, *Sociology in Question*, trans. Richard Nice (London: Sage, 1993), 86.

10. Ryle, *The Concept of Mind*, 26.

11. Ibid., 27.

12. Ibid., 31.

13. Ibid., 30.

14. Ibid., 32.

15. Ibid., 141.

16. Ibid., 118.

17. Ibid., 117.

18. Pierre Bourdieu, *Outline of a Theory of Practice*, trans. Richard Nice (Cambridge: Cambridge University Press, 1977), 8.

19. Ibid., 9, 15, 106.

20. Eva F. Kittay, *Love's Labor: Essays on Equality, Dependence and Care* (London: Routledge, 1999).

21. Erving Goffman, "Self-Presentation: The Presentation of Self in Everyday Life," in *The Goffman Reader*, ed. C. Lemert and A. Branaman, 21–26 (Oxford: Blackwell, 1997), 23–24.

22. Erving Goffman, *The Presentation of Self in Everyday Life* (New York: Doubleday Anchor, 1956), 8.

23. Barbara Ehrenreich and John Ehrenreich, "The New Left: A Case Study in Professional-Managerial Class Radicalism," *Radical America* 11, no. 3 (May–June 1977): 7–22.

24. John Austin, *How to Do Things with Words* (Cambridge, MA: Harvard University Press, 1962).

25. Judith Butler, "Gender as Performance," in *A Critical Sense: Interviews with Intellectuals*, ed. P. Osborne, 109–25 (London: Routledge, 1996).

26. Judith Butler, *Excitable Speech: A Politics of the Performative* (New York: Routledge, 1997), 48–49.

27. Ibid., 39.

28. Butler's poststructuralist view assimilates the body to the workings of language. Thus her account—at least in much of the work where she theorizes gender—melds a curiously fatalist account of human capability, functional contrivances in the metaphysical machine of language (in her account, agency is posited as inhering in the iterability of language), and an exuberantly voluntarist theory of agency (in Butler's account, change is coded as "resignification"). So intent have poststructuralists been in attacking an "essentialist" account of bodies that they fail to register the ineliminable materiality of the body. The neovitalist Deleuze, for example, reduces the body to a machinic energy. He argues that "the kinetic proposition tells us that a body is defined by relations of motion and rest, of slowness and speed between particles. That is, it is not defined by a form or by functions"; Gilles Deleuze, *Spinoza: Practical Philosophy*, trans. Robert Hurley (San Francisco: City Light Books, 1988), 123. He adds: "We will not define a thing by its form, nor by its organs and its functions, nor as a substance or a subject. Borrowing terms from the Middle Ages, or from geography, we will define it by longitude and latitude. A body can be anything; it can be an animal, a body of sounds, a mind or an idea; it can be a linguistic corpus, a social body, a collectivity" (127).

29. Butler, *Excitable Speech*, 15.

30. Judith Butler, *Bodies That Matter: On the Discursive Limits of Sex* (London: Routledge, 1993), 95.

31. Max Weinreich's witty line that a language "is a dialect with an army and a navy" captures the deadly seriousness of such categorizations. See Rosina Lippi-Green, *English with an Accent: Language, Ideology and Discrimination in the United States* (London: Routledge), 1997. One of the major justifications of "racial nationalism"—the notion that certain populations formed a particular "race"—was Johann Gottfried von Herder's notion of language as *sprachgeist*.

32. Mikhail Bakhtin, *Problems of Dostoevsky's Poetics*, ed. and trans. Caryl Emerson (Minneapolis: University of Minnesota Press, 1984).

33. Mikhail Bakhtin, *The Dialogic Imagination: Four Essays* (Austin: University of Texas Press, 1981).

34. Though linguistic determinism is often attributed to Benjamin Lee Whorf, this attribution comes from a misreading of him. Whorf held a far more modest claim: "The cue to a certain line of behavior is often given by the analogies of the linguistic formula in which the situation is spoken of, and by which to some degree it is analyzed, classified, and allotted its place in that world which is 'to a large extent unconsciously built up on the language habits of the group.'" Thus language does not so much forbid or prevent a certain way of thinking as it *frames* particular habits of thought. See Benjamin Whorf, "The Relation of Habitual Thought and Behavior to Language," in *Language, Culture, and Personality: Essays in Memory of Edward Sapir,* edited by Leslie Spier (Menasha, WI: Sapir Memorial Publication Fund, 1941), 75–93.

35. Arguments that are indebted to versions of linguistic determinism—for example, the notion that the absence of a specific word in a society implies the absence of a phenomenological state or the absence of a concept—are not limited to the fringes of journalism. Bruno Snell's influential progressivist myth that the ancient Greeks had no conception of individual autonomy and of the coherence of the self is based in part on the notion that the absence of a word in a society is evidence of the absence of a particular idea, belief, or understanding. Thus, the progressivist myth goes, because Homer did not have a word that corresponded to our phrase "decision making," then *ipso facto* the Greeks of Homer's time lacked the concept of individual agency. For the definitive critique of Snell, see Bernard Williams, *Shame and Necessity* (Berkeley: University of California Press, 1993).

36. "Signature Event Context," in Jacques Derrida, *Limited Inc.,* 1–23, (Evanston, IL: Northwestern University Press, 1988), 1.

37. "Structure, Sign, and Play in the Discourse of the Human Sciences," in Jacques Derrida, *Writing and Difference,* trans. Alan Bass (Chicago: University of Chicago Press, 1978), 280–81.

38. See *Gorgias,* in Plato, *Plato: Complete Works.*

39. Brian Vickers, *In Defense of Rhetoric* (Oxford: Oxford University Press, 1988), 95.

40. Before souls fell to earth and took on human bodies, Plato believes, they communed with the gods and possessed perfect knowledge. Knowledge consists in recollecting this perfect knowledge that humans possessed in the past.

41. See, for example, Austin, *How to Do Things with Words.*

42. Raymond Geuss, "Goals, Origins, Disciplines," *Arion* 17, no. 2 (2009): 1–24.

43. Such as Gorgias. But see Isocrates's views. He rejected both the absolutism of Plato and Gorgias's relativism.

44. Darryl Fears, "Exonerations Change How Justice System Builds a Prosecution," *Washington Post*, May 3, 2007, available at http://www.wash ingtonpost.com/wp-dyn/content/article/2007/05/02/AR2007050202304 .html.

45. John Locke, *An Essay Concerning Human Understanding*, vol. 2, ed. A. C. Fraser, (New York: Dover, 1959).

46. Examples abound, such as Shakespeare's indebtedness to other writers from which he derived his narrative plots and marvelous turns of phrase. See, for example, Arthur M. Z. Norman, "Daniel's the Tragedie of Cleopatra and Antony and Cleopatra," *Shakespeare Quarterly* 9, no. 1, (1958): 11–18.

47. It is now a well-known aspect of natural science that there is a profound difference between how scientists actually arrive at their judgments and how they describe the judgments that they arrived at. Positivist fantasies of direct observation aside, discoveries are not linear processes from hypothesis to a "Eureka" observation. Rather, scientific work involves a measure of engagement with previous work, much of it tacit knowledge that is accepted on the authority and credibility of the scientific institution, an "intuitive" inkling that pursuing a certain trajectory of work may be fruitful, and intense conversation with other researchers on how to interpret particular directions taken.

48. Consider that journals such as the influential scientific journal *Nature* often decide whether to publish a paper based on whether the paper is likely to make an "impact" on the rest of the field, with impact often measured by the "buzz" it creates not only within the scientific community but also in the wider society. For a fascinating case in point, see Sean Carroll, "Guest Post: Terry Rudolph on Nature versus Nurture," August 27, 2012, available at http://blogs.discovermagazine.com/cosmicvariance/2012/08/27 /guest-post-terry-rudolph-on-nature-versus-nurture/#.WULLBevyu70.

49. See Hilary Putnam, *Ethics Without Ontology* (Cambridge, MA: Harvard University Press, 2004).

50. MacIntyre, *After Virtue*, 187.

51. Ibid.

52. Ibid., 178.

53. See Larry Laudan, "The Demise of the Demarcation Problem," in *Physics, Philosophy and Psychoanalysis: Essays in Honor of Adolf Grünbaum*, ed. R. S. Cohen and L. Laudan (Dordrecht: D. Reidel Publishing 1983), 111–27.

54. MacIntyre, *After Virtue*, 181.

55. MacIntyre's *After Virtue* is written as if the author has never heard

of—let alone paused to consider—arguments by critical race theorists and feminists. It is a credit to MacIntyre that his book *Dependent Rational Animals* emerges from an engagement with feminist literature.

56. Donald Davidson, "A Coherence Theory of Truth and Knowledge," in *Truth and Interpretation: Perspectives on the Philosophy of Donald Davidson,* ed. Ernest LePore, 307–19 (Oxford: Basil Blackwell, 1986).

57. Immanuel Kant, *Critique of Pure Reason,* trans. Norman Kemp-Smith (London: Macmillan, 1929), A51/75.

58. Ibid., B160n.

59. Ibid., A293/B350.

60. Immanuel Kant, *Prolegomena,* tr. Paul Carus (Chicago: Open Court, 1902), section 18.

61. See chapter 3 below for a further elaboration of these contexts.

62. John Calvin, for example, writes that "All right knowledge of God is born of obedience." See John Calvin, *Institutes of the Christian Religion,* ed. John T. McNeill, trans. Ford Lewis Battles (Philadelphia: Westminster John Knox, 1960), 1.6.2.

63. In a widely circulated article within religious studies, Richard Hays characterizes faith as trust. It is not entirely clear why he does so given that he seems to hold to an inflationary view of faith as transcending ordinary reason. Nevertheless, his article is instructive insofar as it strikingly illustrates the difference between faith and trust. While, of course there are as many different definitions of trust as there are definitions of faith, conflating the two muddies these differences. I take it that trust is deeply dependent on (a) whether one judges the person *competent* enough to tell the truth about *t* and, (b) whether one has the ability to *verify* the statements made. In that case, simply christening faith as "trust" begs the question as to why a holy text is competent and whether its claims are verifiable. See Richard Hays, "Salvation by Trust? Reading the Bible Faithfully," *The Christian Century,* February 26, 1997, 218–23, available at http://www.religion-online.org/article/salvation-by -trust-reading-the-bible-faithfully/.

64. See Louise Antony, *Philosophers Without Gods: Meditations on Atheism and the Secular Life* (Oxford: Oxford University Press, 2007).

65. See Alvin Plantinga, *Where the Conflict Really Lies: Science, Religion and Naturalism* (New York: Oxford University Press, 2011).

66. Though Nietzsche purports to explain everyone else's base motives, he describes his own motives as "enigmatic." In *Beyond Good and Evil,* he states: "Whoever, like myself, prompted by some enigmatical desire, has long endeavored to go to the bottom of the question of pessimism and free it from the half-Christian, half-German narrowness and stupidity in which it has finally presented itself to this century . . . whoever has done this, has perhaps just thereby, without really desiring it, opened his eyes to behold the

opposite ideal"; See Friedrich Nietzsche, *Beyond Good and Evil: Prelude to a Philosophy of the Future*, trans. Helen Zimmern (New York: Macmillan, 1907), § 56.

67. Nietzsche's critical term, "genealogy," did much to keep alive retrograde articulations of cultural transmission as biological generation, reproduction, and transmission. Nietzsche is, of course, a notorious believer in Lamarckian forms of cultural transmission. The adoption of a critical term certainly does not involve the wholesale acceptance of its assumptions, but one notices that critics like Foucault who are enamored of Nietzsche's genealogy remain willfully disdainful of intellectual traditions in Africa, Asia, and the Middle East that would have significantly qualified their Eurocentric provincialism.

68. Hans-Georg Gadamer, *Truth and Method* (New York: Seabury Press, 1975), 258.

69. "On the Concept of History," in Walter Benjamin, *Selected Writings*, vol. 4, 1938–1940, ed. Howard Eiland and Michael W. Jennings, 389–400 (Cambridge, MA: Harvard University Press, 2006), 392.

70. Gadamer, *Truth and Method*, 250.

71. Ibid., 249.

72. This is chilling, particularly in light of the fact that Gadamer delivered a speech at the German embassy in Nazi-occupied Paris in 1942 where he spoke supportively of the New Europe under the Third Reich. See Raymond Geuss, "Richard Rorty at Princeton: Personal Recollections," in *Arion* 15, no. 3 (2008): 85–100.

73. Gadamer, *Truth and Method*, 268.

74. Edmund Husserl, *Ideas*, trans. W. R. Boyce-Gibson (New York: Macmillan, 1962), 100.

75. Notwithstanding Husserl's dismissal of Cartesian substance dualism as a "centuries-old prejudice." See Edmund Husserl, *The Crisis of European Science and Transcendental Phenomenology: An Introduction to Phenomenological Philosophy*, trans. D. Carr (Evanston, IL: Northwestern University Press, 1970), § 60.

76. See John Guillory, *Cultural Capital: The Problem of Literary Canon Formation* (Chicago: University of Chicago Press, 1993), 39–40.

77. Ibid., 18 (emphasis in the original).

78. Guillory puts it well: "A rather different pedagogy, one that emphasizes historical contextualization, would at the very least inhibit the assimilation of cultural works to the agenda of constituting a national culture, or the Western culture which is its ideological support;" ibid., 43.

79. Stuart Hall, "Encoding/Decoding," in *Culture, Media, Language: Working Papers in Cultural Studies, 1972–79*, ed. Stuart Hall, Andre Lowe, and Paul Willis (London: Hutchingson, 1986), 128–38. See also Wayne C.

Booth, *The Rhetoric of Fiction*, 2nd ed. (Chicago: University of Chicago Press, 1983).

80. Philip Wander, "The Third Persona: An Ideological Turn in Rhetorical Theory," in *Contemporary Rhetorical Theory: A Reader*, ed. John Louis Lucaites, Celeste Michelle Condit, and Sally Caudill (New York: Guilford Press, 1999), 357–79.

81. Stuart Hall's "Encoding/Decoding" essay remains a useful intervention in reception studies. He emphasizes the multiple readings of audiences to the news media. However, critics are right to point out that it overemphasizes responses to *propositional content* and pays scant attention to subliminal affective and libidinal ways through which audiences absorb and react against the news media. Hall's theory is however far more nuanced and insightful than the postmodern cottage industry that sprung up to critique him. If early mass media research erred on the side of portraying audiences as wholly in thrall to mass media messages, liberal and postmodern theorists such as John Fiske offer voluntaristic and individualist celebrations of "active audiences" that seem far more like wish-fulfilments than actual ways in which people interact with media forms and messages. As Ien Ang has argued, "the politics of reception analysis has all too often been one-sidedly cast within the terms of a liberal defence of popular culture, just as uses and gratifications research could implicitly or explicitly, in theoretical and political terms, serve as a decontextualized defence of the media status quo by pointing to their functions for the active audience"; Ien Ang, "Culture and Communication: Towards an Ethnographic Critique of Media Consumption in the Transnational Media System," in *What is Cultural Studies? A Reader*, ed. John Storey (London: Arnold, 1996), 237–54, at 242–43. For a representative piece of Fiske's work, see John Fiske, "Moments of Television: Neither the Text nor the Audience," in *Remote Control*, ed. Ellen Seiter et al. (London: Routledge, 1989), 56–78.

82. See Ochieng, *Groundwork for the Practice of the Good Life*, 194–99.

83. I'm also playfully punning on the phonological resonance of *kairotic* and the erotic. I'm trying to emphasize how the *kairotic* is deeply affective (specifically, on how it is interanimated with *eros* attachment).

84. For a brilliant instantiation, see Cornelius Eady, *Brutal Imagination* (New York: G. P. Putnam's Sons, 2001).

85. See also Johannes Fabian, *Out of Our Minds: Reason and Madness in the Exploration of Central Africa* (Berkeley: University of California Press, 2000).

86. Aristotle, *On the Soul*, trans. W. S. Hett (Cambridge, MA: Harvard University Press, 1957), II.12.424a17-25.

87. See Richard C. Lewontin, "Is Nature Probable or Capricious?" *BioScience* 16, no. 1 (1966): 25–27.

88. "The Nature of Mental States" and "Philosophy and Our Mental Life" in Hilary Putnam, *Mind, Language and Reality: Philosophical Papers*, vol. 2, 429–40 and 291–303 (Cambridge: Cambridge University Press, 1975); Jerry Fodor, "Special Sciences, or The Disunity of Science as a Working Hypothesis," in *Readings in Philosophy of Psychology*, ed. Ned Block, 120–33 (Cambridge, MA: Harvard University Press, 1980); Alan Garfinkel, *Forms of Explanation: Rethinking the Questions in Social Theory* (New Haven, CT: Yale University Press, 1981); Richard Boyd, "Materialism Without Reductionism: What Physicalism Does Not Entail," in Block, *Readings in the Philosophy of Psychology*, 67–106; Richard Boyd, "Scientific Realism and Naturalistic Epistemology," *PSA: Proceedings of the Biennial Meeting of the Philosophy of Science Association* 2 (1980): 613–62, and "The Current Status of Scientific Realism," in *Scientific Realism*, ed. Jarrett Leplin, 41–82 (Berkeley: University of California Press, 1984).

89. Philip Kitcher, "1953 and All That: A Tale Of Two Sciences," *The Philosophical Review* 93, no. 3 (1984): 335–73.

90. Elizabeth Anderson, "Feminist Epistemology: An Interpretation and a Defense," *Hypatia* 10 (1995): 50–84.

91. Richard Boyd, "How to Be a Moral Realist," in *Moral Discourse and Practice: Some Philosophical Approaches*, ed. Stephen Darwall, Allan Gibbard, and Peter Railton, 105–35 (Oxford: Oxford University Press, 1997).

92. Michael Weisberg, "Three Kinds of Idealization," *Journal of Philosophy* 104, no. 12 (2007): 639–59.

93. Putnam, *Ethics Without Ontology*.

94. Alvin Goldman, "The Need for Social Epistemology," in *The Future for Philosophy*, ed. Brian Leiter, 182–207 (Oxford: Oxford University Press, 2004).

95. Philip Kitcher characteristically puts it well: "We are finite beings, and so our investigations have to be selective, and the broadest frameworks of today's science reflect the selections of the past. What we discover depends on the questions taken to be significant, and the selection of those questions, as well as the decision of which factors to set aside in seeking answers to them, presupposes judgments about what is valuable. Those are not only, or mainly, scientific judgments. In their turn, new discoveries modify the landscape in which further investigations will take place, and because what we learn affects how evidence is assessed, discovery shapes the evolution of our standards of evidence. Judgments of value thus pervade the environment in which scientific work is done. If they are made, as they should be, in light of the broadest and deepest reflections on human life and its possibilities, then good science depends on contributions from the humanities and the arts. Perhaps there is even a place for philosophy." See Philip Kitcher, "The Trouble with Scientism: Why History and the Humanities Are also a Form of Knowledge," *The New*

Republic, May 4, 2012, available at https://newrepublic.com/article/103086
/scientism-humanities-knowledge-theory-everything-arts-science.

96. Bernard Williams comments on this phenomenon: "Paul Grice
used to say that we 'should treat great and dead philosophers as we treat great
and living philosophers, as having something to say to us.' That is fine, so long
as it is not assumed that what the dead have to say to us is much the same
as what the living have to say to us. Unfortunately, this is probably what was
being assumed by those who, in the heyday of confidence in what was being
called the 'analytic history of philosophy,' encouraged us to read something
written by Plato 'as though it had come out in *Mind* last month'—an idea
which, if it means anything at all, means something that destroys the main
philosophical point of reading Plato at all." See "Philosophy as a Humanistic
Discipline," in Bernard Williams, *Philosophy as a Humanistic Discipline*, ed.
A. W. Moore (Princeton, NJ: Princeton University Press, 2006), 181.

97. Emmanuel Chukwudi Eze, "The Color of Reason: The Idea of
'Race' in Kant's Anthropology," in *Postcolonial African Philosophy: A Critical
Reader*, ed. Emmanuel Chukwudi Eze (Cambridge, MA: Blackwell, 1997),
103–40.

98. It should be said that professionalization and specialization were,
however, already taking root in Kant's time, no doubt helped along by Kant's
own obsessive categorization. Kant himself was accused of being a dilettante
by some of his contemporaries! See Jonathan Rée, "Passions of a Prussian,"
Lingua Franca: The Review of Academic Life 11, no. 5 (2001): 53–66.

99. Nietzsche aptly notes: "only that which has no history can be
defined." See Friedrich Nietzsche, *On the Genealogy of Morality*, ed. Keith
Ansell-Pearson, trans. Carol Diethe (Cambridge: Cambridge University
Press, 1994), §13.

100. Eze, "The Color of Reason," 103.

101. Kristie Dotson, "How is this Paper Philosophy?" *Comparative Philosophy* 3, no. 1 (2012): 3–29.

102. Paul Krugman, "How Did Economists Get It So Wrong?" *New York
Times* (September 2, 2009).

103. Media scholars have long demonstrated the social systemic structure that undergirds "information asymmetry," as have those who have long
tracked the vicissitudes of rationality.

104. Gramsci's point is instructive. Whereas everyone in some sense is
an intellectual, not everyone has in a society the function of performing intellectual work. Being aware of the distinction is an important form of critical
consciousness. See "Intellectuals and Education," in Antonio Gramsci, *The
Antonio Gramsci Reader: Selected Writings 1916–1935*, ed. David Forgacs (New
York: New York University Press, 2000), 304.

105. See, for example, Robert Pippin, "*Critical Inquiry* and Critical Theory: A Short History of Nonbeing," *Critical Inquiry* 30, no. 2 (Winter 2004): 424–28.

106. Friedrich Nietzsche, *The Will to Power*, ed. Walter Kaufmann, trans. Walter Kaufmann and R. J. Hollingdale (New York: Random House, 1968), 428.

107. Ibid., 464.

108. Wayne C. Booth, *The Rhetoric of Rhetoric* (Oxford: Blackwell Publishing, 2004), viii.

CHAPTER 2. EMBODIED KNOWLEDGE

1. A dominant *telos* in many an ascetic's practices is *thanatos*, the desire for death and union with the divine.

2. Jan Assmann, *The Mind of Egypt: History and Meaning in the Time of the Pharaohs*, trans. Andrew Jenkins (Cambridge, MA: Harvard University Press, 2003), 125.

3. Ibid., 123–24.

4. Ibid., 123.

5. Ibid.,125.

6. Martin Bernal, *Black Athena: The Afroasiatic Roots of Classical Civilization*, vol. 1 (New Brunswick, NJ: Rutgers University Press, 1987).

7. Mary Lefkowitz, *Not Out of Africa: How Afrocentrism Became an Excuse to Teach Myth as History* (New York: Basic Books, 1996).

8. The homologies of the Philhellenic movement with that of U.S. conservative cultural warriors such as Lefkowitz are striking, both in their racial resentment at cultural others and in their claim to be guardians of specialized knowledge.

9. Edward W. Said, *The World, the Text, and the Critic* (Cambridge, MA: Harvard University Press, 1983), 226.

10. Nicholas Lobkowicz, *Theory and Practice: History of a Concept from Aristotle to Mary* (Notre Dame, IN: University of Notre Dame Press, 1967), 6.

11. Ibid.

12. According to Martin Bernal, Isocrates' *Bousiris* is the first extant use of the word *sophia* [philosophy]. Bernal argues that the Greek term *sophia* is likely derived from the Egyptian *sb3* (teaching, learning). See Bernal, *Black Athena*, 1:104, 1:458n137 respectively.

13. Ibid., 1:104.

14. According to Marx, "Plato's Republic, in so far as division of labor is treated in it, as the formative principle of the state, is merely an Athenian

idealization of the Egyptian system of castes." As cited in Bernal, *Black Athena*, 1:106.

15. For Plato's theory of knowledge, see *The Republic*, 509d6–511e5.

16. In the *Gorgias*, Plato condemns rhetoric, but qualifies his remarks in the *Phaedrus*, where he allows for a rhetoric that serves as an instrument of philosophical truth.

17. Aristotle, *Nichomachean Ethics*, 1139a27–28, 1178b20–21.

18. Aristotle, *Metaphysics* 1.2; see also Joseph Dunne, *Back to The Rough Ground* (Notre Dame, IN: University of Notre Dame Press, 1993), 238.

19. See Aristotle, *Nichomachean Ethics*, 1177a15–16.

20. Ibid., 1141a17–20.

21. See ibid., 1141b14.

22. Ibid., 1140a2–5.

23. Lobkowicz, 17–18.

24. Ibid., 18.

25. Ibid., 30.

26. Ibid., 22, 29.

27. Kwame Anthony Appiah, *In My Father's House: Africa in the Philosophy of Culture* (New York: Oxford University Press, 1992).

28. Lobkowicz, *Theory and Practice*, 20.

29. Aristotle, *History of Animals*, as cited in Steven Shapin, *A Social History of Truth* (Chicago: University of Chicago Press, 1994), 88.

30. Lobkowicz, *Theory and Practice*, 23–24.

31. Ibid., 7.

32. Mbiti's work thus follows in the footsteps of the Belgian missionary Father Placide Tempels, whose infamous work *La Philosophie bantoue* purported to disclose the mysteries of the "Bantu mind."

33. See Odera Oruka, *Trends in Contemporary African Philosophy* (Nairobi: Shirikon Publishers, 1990), 129.

34. Pierre Bourdieu, *Sketch for a Self-Analysis*, trans. Richard Nice (Chicago: The University of Chicago Press, 2004), 5–6.

35. Ibid., 5.

36. Michael H. Keefer, "The Dreamer's Path: Descartes and the Sixteenth Century," *Renaissance Quarterly* 49, no. 1 (Spring 1996): 30–76, at 34.

37. Descartes as cited in Michael Keefer, "The Dreamer's Path," 35.

38. As cited in Keefer, "The Dreamer's Path," 35.

39. Keefer, "The Dreamer's Path," 39.

40. George C. Caffentzis, "On the Scottish Origin of 'Civilization,'" in *Enduring Western Civilization: The Construction of the Concept of Western Civilization and Its "Others,"* edited by Silvia Federici, 13–36 (Westport, CT: Praeger, 1995).

41. Lobkowicz, *Theory and Practice*, 165, 167.

42. No one did better than Heidegger in cultivating his own mystique. According to Hannah Arendt, Heidegger's lectures circulated around Germany like "rumors of a hidden king"; Hannah Arendt, "Martin Heidegger at Eighty," *The New York Review of Books*, October 21, 1971, 50–54.

43. Martin Heidegger, *Being and Time*, trans. J. Macquarrie and E. Robinson (Oxford: Basil Blackwell, 1962).

44. Pierre Bourdieu, *The Political Ontology of Martin Heidegger* (Stanford, CA: Stanford University Press, 1991).

45. In a *Der Spiegel* interview, Heidegger attempts to explain his enthusiasm for the Nazis thus: "In the general confusion of opinions and political tendencies of thirty-two parties, it was necessary to find a national, and especially a social, point of view"; Martin Heidegger, *The Heidegger Reader*, ed. with introduction by Gunter Figal, trans. by Jerome Veith (Bloomington: Indiana University Press, 2009), 316.

46. Jacques Derrida, "The Purveyor of Truth," in *The Purloined Poe*, trans. Alan Bass, ed. John P. Muller and William J. Richards, 173–212 (Baltimore: Johns Hopkins University Press, 1988), 177.

47. Jacques Derrida, *Positions*, trans. Alan Bass (Chicago: University of Chicago Press, 1981), 105.

48. V. Y. Mudimbe, *The Invention of Africa: Gnosis, Philosophy, and the Order of Knowledge* (Bloomington: Indiana University Press, 1988), 69.

49. Ibid., 12.

50. V. Y. Mudimbe, *The Idea of Africa* (Bloomington: Indiana University Press, 1994), xiv.

51. Recall Heidegger's plaintive cry, "Only a god can still save us. I think the only possibility of salvation left to us is to prepare readiness, through thinking and poetry, for the appearance of the god or for the absence of the god during the decline; so that we do not, simply put, die meaningless deaths, but that when we decline, we decline in the face of the absent god." See Martin Heidegger, "Only a God Can Save Us: Der Spiegel's Interview with Martin Heidegger," in *The Heidegger Controversy: A Critical Reader*, ed. Richard Wolin, trans. Maria P. Alter and John D. Caputo, 91–116 (Cambridge, MA: MIT Press, 1993), 107.

52. Andrew Apter, "'Que Faire?' Reconsidering Inventions of Africa," *Critical Inquiry* 19, no. 1 (Autumn 1992): 87–104, at 97.

53. Ibid., 98.

54. Ibid.

55. See Kwame Anthony Appiah, *Cosmopolitanism: Ethics in a World of Strangers* (New York: W. W. Norton, 2006), xiv.

56. I am drawing this insight and much of the subsequent account on bourgeois philosophy from Raymond Geuss, *Politics and the Imagination* (Princeton: Princeton University Press, 2010).

57. Ibid., 169.

58. Ibid., 170.

59. Ibid.

60. Ibid., 174.

61. Appiah, *In My Father's House*, 134.

62. Ibid.

63. Timothy Brennan, "Cosmo-Theory," *The South Atlantic Quarterly* 100, no. 3 (Summer 2001): 659–91, at 659–60.

64. Appiah, *In My Father's House*, 17.

65. See also Joseph Massad, "The 'Post-Colonial' Colony: Time, Space, and Bodies in Palestine/Israel," in *The Pre-Occupation of Postcolonial Studies*, ed. Hamid Naficy, Fawzia Afzal-Khan, and Kalpana Seshadri, 311–46 (Durham, NC: Duke University Press Books, 2000).

66. Archie Mafeje, "Africanity: A Commentary By Way of Conclusion," *CODESRIA Bulletin*, nos. 3–4 (2001): 14–16.

67. "What Is Enlightenment?" in Michel Foucault, *The Foucault Reader*, ed. Paul Rabinow (New York: Pantheon Books, 1984), 45.

68. Ludwig Wittgenstein, *Tractatus Logico-Philosophicus*, trans. C. K. Ogden (London: Routledge & Kegan Paul, 1922).

69. Wittgenstein's ladder (i.e., his signature concepts "language game," "grammar," "forms of life") can paradoxically require as ruthless a dissolution as the philosophical language games it seeks to dissolve. As Stephen Mulhall has argued in a brilliant engagement with the "realistic spirit" of Wittgenstein's work, Wittgenstein's signature concepts "might on occasion stand between us and an ability simply to acknowledge how things really are; rather than helping to subvert our tendency towards the imposition of a philosophical 'must,' they may actually subserve its further expression." See Stephen Mulhall, "Realism, Modernism and the Realistic Spirit: Diamond's Inheritance of Wittgenstein, Early and Late," *Nordic Wittgenstein Review* 1, no. 1 (2012): 7–33, at 10.

70. Oruka, *Trends*, 52.

71. Oruka, *Sage Philosophy*, 35.

72. See Omedi Ochieng, "The Epistemology of African Philosophy: Sagacious Knowledge and the Case for a Critical Contextual Epistemology," *International Philosophical Quarterly* 48, no. 3 (2008): 337–60.

73. F. Ochieng-Odhiambo, "The Evolution of Sagacity," *Philosophia Africana* 5, no. 1 (2002): 19–32. I am also grateful to Gail Presbey for encouraging me to reexamine my stance on Oruka.

74. Gail Presbey, "H. Odera Oruka on Moral Reasoning," *The Journal of Value Inquiry* 34, no. 4 (December 2000): 517–28.

75. Ibid., 519.

76. Oruka, *Sage Philosophy*, 8.

77. Kresse, "Philosophy Must Be Made Sagacious," 254.

78. *Theaetetus*, in Plato, *Plato: Complete Works*, 155d.

79. Teri Merrick, "Teaching Philosophy: Instilling Pious Wonder or Vicious Curiosity?" *Christian Scholar's Review* 34, no. 4 (Summer 2010): 401–20.

80. Martha C. Nussbaum, *Upheavals in Thought: The Intelligence of Emotions* (Cambridge: Cambridge University Press, 2001), 54.

81. Luce Irigaray, "Wonder: A Reading of Descartes' *The Passions of the Soul*," in *Feminist Interpretations of Rene Descartes*, ed. Susan Bordo, trans. Carolyn Burke and Gillian C. Gill (University Park: Pennsylvania State University Press, 1999): 105–14.

82. Kresse, "Philosophy Must Be Made Sagacious," 253.

83. Burton J. Bledstein, *The Culture of Professionalism: The Middle Class and the Development of Higher Education in America* (New York: W. W. Norton, 1976), 4.

84. See chap. 1 for my critique of disciplinarity.

85. Paulin Hountondji, *African Philosophy: Myth and Reality*, trans. Henri Evans (Bloomington: Indiana University Press, 1983).

86. Paulin Hountondji, *The Struggle for Meaning: Reflections on Philosophy, Culture and Democracy in Africa*, trans. John Conteh-Morgan (Athens: Ohio University Press, 2002).

87. Kwame Anthony Appiah, "Foreword," in *The Struggle for Meaning: Reflections on Philosophy, Culture and Democracy in Africa*, by Paulin Hountondji, xi–xv (Athens: Ohio University Press, 2002), xi.

88. Hountondji, *African Philosophy*, 33.

89. Ibid., 103–4.

90. Ibid., 104.

91. Ibid., 189.

92. Hountondji, *Struggle for Meaning*, 47.

93. Ibid., 33.

94. Hountondji, *African Philosophy*, vii.

95. Ibid., 72.

96. Ibid., 104.

97. Hountondji, *Struggle for Meaning*, xvii.

98. Ibid., 39.

99. Ibid., 39.

100. Ibid., xvii–xviii.

101. Ibid., 53.

102. Ibid., 53.

103. Hountondji, *African Philosophy*, 42.

104. Ibid., 34.

105. See, for example, T. J. Clarke, "Origins of the Present Crisis," *New Left Review* 2 (March–April 2000): 85–96.

106. Hountondji, *Struggle for Meaning*, 49.

107. Ibid., 46.

108. Ibid., 7.

109. Ibid., 194.

110. For more on distinction, see Bourdieu, *Distinction*, 6.

111. Hountondji, *Struggle for Meaning*, 97.

112. Ruth Finnegan, *Literacy and Orality: Studies in the Technology of Communication* (New York: Basic Blackwell, 1988), 5.

113. Harvey Graff, "The Legacies of Literacy," *Journal of Communication* 32, no. 1 (1982): 12–26, at 13–14.

114. Finnegan, *Literacy and Orality*, 5.

115. As cited in Finnegan, *Literacy and Orality*, 6.

116. Walter J. Ong, *Orality and Literacy: The Technologizing of the Word* (New York: Methuen, 1982), 78.

117. Finnegan's apt name for the "literacy" industry.

118. See, for example, Wendy Belcher, "Medieval African and European Texts about the Queen of Sheba: Some Speculations about the Early Circulation of Ethiopian Discourse," *Newsletter of the UCLA Center for the Study of Women* (May 2006): 4–5.

119. See Guillory, *Cultural Capital*, 18 (emphasis in original).

120. E. A. Havelock and J. P. Hershbell, *Communication Arts in the Ancient World* (New York: Hastings House, 1978), 3.

121. Ong, *Orality and Literacy*, 78.

122. Finnegan, *Literacy and Orality*, 6.

123. Ong, *Orality and Literacy*, 78.

124. Finnegan, *Literacy and Orality*, 4.

125. Ibid., 55–58.

126. Ibid., 13.

127. Jack Goody, *The Domestication of the Savage Mind* (New York: Cambridge University Press, 1977), 150–51.

128. A. R. Luria, *Cognitive Development: Its Cultural and Social Foundations* (Cambridge, MA: Harvard University Press, 1976).

129. Sylvia Scribner and Michael Cole, *The Psychology of Literacy* (Cambridge, MA: Harvard University Press, 1981).

130. Marshall McLuhan, *Understanding Media: The Extensions of Man* (New York: New American Library, 1964).

131. Finnegan, *Literacy and Orality*, 144.

132. Roger D. Abrahams, Review of *Xhosa Oral Poetry: Aspects of a Black South African Tradition* by Jeff Opland, *Poetics Today* 6, no. 3 (1985): 553–58, at 555–56.

133. Hountondji, *Struggle for Meaning*, 71.

134. Ibid., 189–90.

135. Ibid., 101.

136. Ibid., 102.

137. Ibid., 115.

138. Ibid., 72.

139. Immanuel Kant, "An Answer to the Question: What Is Enlighten-ment?" in *What is Enlightenment?: Eighteenth-Century Answers and Twentieth-Century Questions*, ed. and trans. James Schmidt, 58–64 (Berkeley: University of California Press, 1996), 58.

140. Hountondji, *African Philosophy*, 43.

141. Michel Foucault, *Power/Knowledge: Selected Interviews and Other Writings, 1972–1977*, ed. Colin Gordon (New York: Pantheon, 1980), 126.

142. The literature on these varying forms of knowledge is deep and var-ied. On *episteme* and *doxa*, see for example Pierre Bourdieu, *The Logic of Prac-tice*, trans. Richard Nice (Stanford, CA: Stanford University Press, 1990). On *metis*, see Marcel Detienne and Jean-Pierre Vernant, *Cunning Intelligence in Greek Culture and Society*, trans. Janet Lloyd (Chicago: University of Chicago Press, 1981) and James C. Scott, *Seeing Like a State: How Certain Schemes to Improve the Human Condition Have Failed* (New Haven, CT: Yale University Press, 1999). On *cosmopolitanism*, see Appiah, *Cosmopolitanism*.

143. Pierre Bourdieu, *Science of Science and Reflexivity*, trans. Richard Nice (Chicago: University of Chicago Press, 2004), 104.

144. John Guillory puts this particularly well: "Realism and antirealism espoused at the highest level of epistemological generality do not seem to me very useful positions to take in advance of specifying some way of talking about categories of objects, along with some particular object about which we would like to know. Consider what it would mean to establish in advance a realism or antirealism that would be equally adequate for all of the following objects: igneous rocks, God, adolescents, the color red, dementia praecox, poverty, a Sidney sonnet, desire, chaos, algorithms, dinosaurs, freedom, dis-ability, status, c sharp minor, capitalism, gamma rays, honor, the Renaissance, democracy, race, menopause, beauty, foreigners, the culture industry, na-tions, grammar, mitochondria, alienation, global warming, disciplines." See John Guillory, "The Name of Science, The Name of Politics," *Critical Inquiry* 29, no. 3 (Spring 2003): 526–41.

145. Steven Feierman, *Peasant Intellectuals: Anthropology and History in Tanzania* (Madison: University of Wisconsin Press, 1990).

146. See for example, James Ferguson, *Global Shadows: Africa in the Neoliberal World Order* (Durham, NC: Duke University Press, 2006), 101.

147. John S. Mbiti, *African Religions and Philosophy* (Nairobi: Heine-mann, 1992), 2–3.

148. Hountondji's anti-mythological commitments imply not just an affirmation of science but a full-fledged scientism. In *African Philosophy*, he argues: "If philosophy can also be of use, it is only by helping to liberate a genuine theoretical tradition on this continent, an open scientific tradition, master of its problems and of its themes, and also to the extent that it proves capable, once this tradition is established, of contributing in one way or another to its enrichment. That philosophy—that theoretical quest strictly hinged on science—will carry us a thousand miles away from the preoccupations which have inspired and shaped the myth of a so-called traditional African philosophy. It will get us far away from the metaphysical problems of the origins of the world, the meaning of life, the wherefore of death, human destiny, the reality of the beyond, the existence of God and all those insoluble problems which really belong to mythology, yet are the usual fodder of philosophical rumination." See Hountondji, *African Philosophy*, 99.

149. I do not propose these schools as mutually exclusive. They often overlapped. Many nationalists, for example, invented and advocated for "traditional African values" in the service of their nationalist goals.

150. Hountondji, *Struggle for Meaning*, 144.

151. Ibid., 145.

152. Ibid., 146.

153. Ibid., 145.

154. Hountondji, *African Philosophy*, 214.

155. Kwame Nkrumah, *Consciencism*, (London: Heinemann, 1964).

156. Hountondji, *African Philosophy*, 154.

157. Hountondji, *Struggle for Meaning*, 148.

158. "The whole existence of the structure consists of its effects, in short, that the structure, which is merely a specific combination of its peculiar elements, is nothing outside its effects"; Louis Althusser and Étienne Balibar, *Reading Capital* (London: NLB, 1970), 189.

159. Valentino Gerratano notes "the strange indulgence initially shown by Althusser to the historical-materialist content of Stalin's 'political science'"; Valentino Gerratana, "Althusser and Stalinism," *New Left Review* 1, nos. 101–2 (January–April 1977): 110–21.

160. Raymond Williams, *Problems in Materialism and Culture: Selected Essays* (London: Verso, 1980), 32.

161. Claude Levi-Strauss, *The Savage Mind* (Chicago: University of Chicago Press, 1966).

162. Note for example Gilles Deleuze's statement, made in the context of a dialogue with Foucault: "A theory is exactly like a box of tools. It has nothing to do with the signifier." See "Intellectuals and Power," in Michel Foucault, *Language, Counter-Memory, Practice: Selected Essays and Interviews*, ed.

Donald F. Bouchard, trans. Donald F. Bouchard and Sherry Simon (Ithaca, NY: Cornell University Press, 1977), 208.

163. Norman K. Denzin and Yvonna S. Lincoln, *Handbook of Qualitative Research*, 2nd ed. (Thousand Oaks, CA: Sage, 2000), 3.

164. Pamela Akinyi Wadende, *Chwuech Manimba: Indigenous Creative Education among Women of the Luo Community of Western Kenya* (PhD diss., Texas State University San Marcos, August 2011).

165. Ibid., 1.

166. This is not to imply that the historical meaning of *kit dak* architecture is ideal or unproblematic. I am attracted to the manner in which it seeks to reimagine space against the conformity of communalism and the hegemony of the corporation. However, it remains problematic insofar as it conceives of space in relatively static terms.

167. Wadende, *Chwuech Manimba*, 30.

168. Edward W. Said, *Representations of the Intellectual* (New York: Vintage Books, 1994), xviii.

169. John Hunwick, *West Africa, Islam, and the Arab World: Studies in Honor of Basil Davidson* (Princeton: Markus Wiener Publishers, 2006), 33.

170. Ibid.

171. On prophecy in the ancient East, see Martti Nissinen, ed., *Prophecy in Its Ancient Near Eastern Context: Mesopotamian, Biblical, and Arabian Perspectives* (Atlanta: Society of Biblical Literature, 2000). On African prophecy, see Joel E. Tishken, "The History of Prophecy in West Africa: Indigenous, Islamic, and Christian," *History Compass* 5, no. 5 (2007): 1468–82.

172. Abraham J. Heschel, *The Prophets* (New York: Harper Perennial Modern Classics, 2001), 17, 27.

173. Presbey, "H. Odera Oruka on Moral Reasoning."

174. William Blake, *William Blake*, ed. Michael Mason (Oxford: Oxford University Press, 1988), 22.

175. R. B. Y. Scott, *The Way of Wisdom in the Old Testament* (New York: Macmillan, 1971), 115.

176. The term "critic" derives from the Greek term *kritikos*—one who serves on a jury and delivers a verdict.

177. Compare this sense of crisis with the bourgeois insistence on "normalcy" and "security."

178. Heschel, *The Prophets*, 10.

179. Frederick Douglass, "West India Emancipation," in *Frederick Douglass: Selected Speeches and Writings*, ed. Philip S. Foner, abridged and adapted by Yuval Taylor, 358–68 (Chicago: Lawrence Hill Books, 1999), 367.

180. "Proverbs of Hell," in William Blake, *Selected Poetry*, ed. with an introduction by Michael Mason (Oxford: Oxford University Press, 1998), 76.

181. Theodor W. Adorno, *Critical Models: Interventions and Catchwords*, trans. Henry W. Pickford, introduction by Lydia Goehr (New York: Columbia University Press, 2005), 108.

182. Friedrich Nietzsche, *The Gay Science: With a Prelude in Rhymes and an Appendix of Songs*, trans. Walter Kaufmann (New York: Random House, 1974), 251.

183. This is the case with the forms of prophecy that have prevailed in the United States, starting with Puritan rhetorics. For a vigorous advocacy of these rhetorics, see James Darsey, *The Prophetic Tradition and Radical Rhetoric in America* (New York: New York University Press, 1997).

184. Interestingly, Martin Heidegger's brother, Fritz, was the town fool. See Geuss, *Politics and the Imagination*, 143.

185. Harriet Jacobs, *Incidents in the Life of a Slave Girl* (New York: The Modern Library, 2000), 234.

186. As James Clifford has pointed out, this chilly reception was not the most remarkable thing about the Nuer's encounter with Evans-Pritchard. The really intriguing question is why the Nuer did not kill Evans-Pritchard. See James Clifford, *On the Edges of Anthropology (Interviews)* (Chicago: Prickly Paradigm Press, 2003).

187. E. E. Evans-Pritchard, *The Nuer: A Description of the Modes of Livelihood and Political Institutions of a Nilotic People* (Oxford: Clarendon Press, 1940), 12–13.

188. Jean Comaroff and John L. Comaroff, "Occult Economies and the Violence of Abstraction: Notes from the South African Postcolony," *American Ethnologist* 26, no. 2 (1999): 279–303.

189. Ibid., 279.

190. Ibid., 283–84.

191. Ibid., 284.

192. Ed White challenges the pervasive "denial of the validity of conspiracy theories" by the "republican synthesis" school of historiographers and poststructuralist scholars of early America. See Ed White, "The Value of Conspiracy Theory." *American Literary History* 14, no. 1 (2002): 1–31.

193. Jean Baudrillard, "From The Precession of Simulacra," in *The Norton Anthology of Theory and Criticism,* ed. Vincent B. Leitch, 1732–41 (New York: Norton, 2001).

194. Note for example Walter Benjamin's beautiful essay on Karl Kraus, who he argues manifests a "strange interplay between reactionary theory and revolutionary practice." See "Karl Kraus," in Walter Benjamin, *Selected Writings*, vol. 2, *1931–1934*, ed. Michael W. Jennings, Howard Eiland, and Gary Smith, part 2, 431–58 (Cambridge, MA: Harvard University Press, 1999).

195. John A. Symonds, "Introduction," in Sophocles, *Oedipus Tyrannus*, ed. John A. Symonds, 1–48 (Kansas: Coronado Press, 1970).

196. Early meanings of "bohemia" also seem to indicate it may have been a reference to the Romani ethnic group. It is thus likely that bohemi- anism may have involved an appropriation of a way of life by a subgroup, much like U.S. hippies adopted or appropriated certain folkways that they deemed "Eastern."

197. *Sape* is a French colloquialism that roughly translates to "dress-ing with class." On the Congolese *sapeurs*, see Ch. Didier Gondola, "Dream and Drama: The Search for Elegance among Congolese Youth," *African Studies Review* 42, no. 1 (1999): 23–48. See also Daniele Tamagni's book of photogra- phy, *Gentlemen of Bacongo* (London: Trolley Books, 2009).

198. Oscar Wilde, as cited in Richard Gilman, *Decadence: The Strange Life of an Epithet* (New York: Farrar, Straus and Giroux, 1975), 127.

CHAPTER 3. RADICAL WORLD-BUILDING

1. To my mind, by far the most devastating and effective deconstruc- tion of aesthetic essentialism is Wayne Booth's *The Rhetoric of Fiction*.

2. Clive Bell, *Art* (New York: Capricorn, 1913), 17.

3. See Bernard Williams, *Moral Luck* (Cambridge: Cambridge Uni- versity Press, 1981).

4. See Edmund Gettier, "Is Justified True Belief Knowledge?" *Analysis* 23, no. 6 (1963): 121–23.

5. Christy Mag Uidhir has argued that pornography has a *manner in- specific* purpose whereas art has a *manner specific* purpose. Manner specificity is "for a purpose to be essentially constituted both by an action (or state of affairs) and a manner, such that the purpose is to perform that action (or bring about that state of affairs) in that particular manner" (194). Pornogra- phy is so constituted that its aims are to achieve sexual arousal by whatever manner possible. Pornography can therefore draw on the modalities of art- work, but such drawing upon is ancillary to its laser-like interest in gaining sexual arousal. Similar things can be said about advertisement. See Christy Mag Uidhir, "Why Pornography Can't Be Art," *Philosophy and Literature* 33, no. 1 (2009): 193–203.

6. Bell, *Art*.

7. R. G. Collingwood, *The Principles of Art* (Oxford: Clarendon Press, 1938), 38–41.

8. This is recounted by Edward Said in his *The World, the Text, and the Critic*, 32.

9. Miriam Bratu Hansen, "Benjamin's Aura," *Critical Inquiry* 34, no. 2 (Winter 2008): 336–75.

10. "The Work of Art in the Age of Mechanical Reproduction," in Walter Benjamin, *The Work of Art in the Age of Mechanical Reproduction*, ed. Hannah Arendt, trans. Harry Zohn, 217–51 (New York: Schocken, 1968).

11. Ibid.

12. *The Republic*, in Plato, *Plato: Complete Works*, 4.424b–c.

13. Immanuel Kant, *Critique of Judgment*, trans. Werner S. Pluhar (Indianapolis: Hackett Publishing Company, 1987), 76.

14. Ibid., 60.

15. Ibid., 31.

16. Ibid., 99.

17. Michael Wood, *Literature and the Taste of Knowledge* (Cambridge: Cambridge University Press, 2005), 11.

18. Joseph Conrad, *A Personal Record* (New York, Harper and Brothers Publishers, 1912), 115.

19. Said, *The World, the Text, and the Critic*, 90.

20. Ibid., 92.

21. Aesthetic knowledge is both "conscious" (involving a deployment of learned techniques) and "unconscious" (conveying a sensibility). And yet different traditions have tried to make it an either/or (that is, complete mastery of certain principles or completely unconscious). Depending on the tradition, the idea of craft in the making of artwork can either be too valorized or looked down upon. Sophocles is reputed to have said of Aeschylus that he created well without being aware of it. For his part, Euripides deemed Aeschylus's work inferior because good creation involved conscious awareness of technique. Or consider the veiled put-down involved in Henry James's description of Jane Austen as an instinctive novelist: "The key to Jane Austen's fortune with posterity has been in part the extraordinary grace of her facility, in fact of her unconsciousness: as if, at the most, for difficulty, for embarrassment, she sometimes, over her work-basket, her tapestry flowers, in the spare, cool drawing-room of other days, fell a-musing, lapsed too metaphorically, as one may say, into wool-gathering, and her dropped stitches, of these pardonable, of these precious moments, were afterwards picked up as little touches of human truth, little glimpses of steady vision, little master-strokes of imagination." See Henry James, *The Question of Our Speech: The Lesson of Balzac; Two Lectures* (New York: Houghton Mifflin, 1905), 63.

22. John Ruskin, *The Elements of Drawing and The Elements of Perspective* (London: J. M. Dent and Sons, 1907).

23. Booth, *The Rhetoric of Fiction*, 244.

24. It is arguable that stream of consciousness may often mislead insofar as it reiterates the Cartesian belief that thinking is a private activity that

"happens in the head." In this regard, the best cinema may disabuse us of this conceit. Robbed of the technique that novelists use of narrating the thoughts of their characters, filmmakers rightly dwell on bodily comportment (*habitus*) as a marker of what kind of thinking is going on. See Stanley Cavell's discussion of this in his insightful book, *Pursuits of Happiness: The Hollywood Comedy of Remarriage* (Cambridge, MA: Harvard University Press, 1981), 164.

25. Though, of course, this is how they are felt phenomenologically, not how it is actually.

26. In this regard, it will be recalled that Freud's sexism leads him to conceive of female genitalia as uncanny. This underscores how the uncanny itself may be a repression of the political unconscious of gender oppression.

27. The popular critic James Wood offers an example of a cramped fetishization of realism. Woods supposedly thinks that realism is superior to any other mode of narration because of its fidelity to "life," "human nature," and "consciousness." On the other hand, there is no dearth of postmodern criticism that sees realism as inherently problematic. Catherine Belsey, for example, has condemned realism claiming that it naïvely purports to offer a transparent window into reality and exerts a pernicious ideological effect by taking for granting an anterior reality. See Catherine Belsey, *Critical Practice* (London: Methuen, 1980).

28. See Jordan Elgrably, "The Art of Fiction No. 78: Interview with James Baldwin." *Paris Review* 91 (Spring 1984), available at http://www.the parisreview.org/interviews/2994/the-art-of-fiction-no-78-james-baldwin.

29. In our current context, the *anagnorisis* and the *epiphany* are almost surely signs of bad art (striking exceptions notwithstanding). This is particularly the case when used to signal narrative closure. The epiphany is a "knowledge-centric" form of the *deus ex machina*, a convenient exit for the author and the story's characters.

30. John Rawls, *Lectures on the History of Political Philosophy*, ed. Samuel Freeman (Cambridge, MA: Harvard University Press, 2007), 302.

31. As cited by Gabor Barabas, "Appendix A: On Translating the Poems of Radnoti," in *Miklos Radnoti: The Complete Poetry in Hungarian and English*, trans. Gabor Barabas (Jefferson, NC: McFarland & Company, Inc., Publishers, 2014), 230.

32. Stathis Gourgouris, *Does Literature Think? Literature as Theory for an Antimythical Era* (Stanford, CA: Stanford University Press, 2003), 2.

33. Kant, *Critique of Judgment*, 196.

34. Ibid., 182.

35. Ibid., 197–98.

36. Ibid., 186–87.

37. Samuel Taylor Coleridge, "The Statesman's Manual," in *The Complete Works of Samuel Taylor Coleridge: Aids to Reflection; Statesman's Manual*, ed. W. G. T. Shedd (New York: Harper & Brothers, 1884), 437.

38. Joseph Conrad, "Henry James: An Appreciation," in *Notes on Life and Letters* (New York: Doubleday, Page & Company, 1921), 17.

39. Even as subtle an exploration of art's distinctive claims to knowledge as Michael Wood's *Literature and the Taste of Knowledge* betrays this Romantic Platonism. Wood argues that "if the taste of words offers knowledge, if literature gives us a taste of knowledge, this can only be a taste, a sample, rather than an elaborate or plentiful meal. We are going to have to go elsewhere for the continuous main course" (10). Wood goes on to offer brilliantly insightful readings of literature's ability to yield knowledge, but the sentence above reiterates a longstanding Platonic yearning for an elusive (and likely chimerical) hope for the fullness of knowledge that always already exists elsewhere. See M. Wood, *Literature and the Taste of Knowledge*.

40. Victor Shklovsky, "Art as Technique," in *Russian Formalist Criticism: Four Essays*, ed. Lee T. Lemon and Marion J. Reis, 3–24 (Lincoln: University of Nebraska Press, 1965), 12.

41. Terry Eagleton, *Criticism and Ideology: A Study in Marxist Literary Theory* (London: Verso, 2006), 47.

42. The Frenchman Charles Batteux's book *The Fine Arts Reduced to a Single Principle* (1747) is often credited as an early legitimation of this distinction. Batteux famously argues that these diverse aesthetic practices neatly fit under a fine arts category because they are all aimed at the "imitation of beautiful nature."

43. Theodor W. Adorno, *The Culture Industry: Selected Essays on Mass Culture*, ed. and with an introduction by J. M. Bernstein (London: Routledge, 1991), 159.

44. Pierre Bourdieu, *The Rules of Art: Genesis and Structure of the Literary Field* (Stanford, CA: Stanford University Press, 1995), 3.

45. Alison Light, *Mrs. Woolf and the Servants: An Intimate History of Domestic Life in Bloomsbury* (New York: Bloomsbury Press, 2009).

46. Toni Morrison, *Playing in the Dark: Whiteness and the Literary Imagination* (New York: Vintage Books, 1993), 17.

47. Ibid., 70–76.

48. Terry Eagleton, *Criticism and Ideology*, 112.

49. John Guillory, *Cultural Capital*, 89.

50. Ibid.

51. See Catherine Gallagher, "The Rise of Fictionality," *The Novel*, vol. 1, ed. Franco Moretti (Princeton: Princeton University Press, 2006).

52. "Kitsch causes two tears to flow in quick succession. The first tear says: How nice to see children running on the grass! The second tear says:

How nice to be moved, together with all mankind, by children running on the grass!"; Milan Kundera, *The Unbearable Lightness of Being*, trans. Michael Henry Heim (New York: HarperCollins Publishers, 2005), 251.

53. Nicholas Brown, *Utopian Generations: The Political Horizon of Twentieth-Century Literature* (Princeton: Princeton University Press, 2005), 7.

54. Also note Toni Morrison on the whiteness of criticism: "Like thousands of avid but nonacademic readers, some powerful literary critics in the United States have never read, and are proud to say so, any African-American text. It seems to have done them no harm, presented them with no discernible limitations in the scope of their work or influence. I suspect, with much evidence to support the suspicion, that they will continue to flourish without any knowledge whatsoever of African-American literature. What is fascinating, however, is to observe how their lavish exploration of literature manages not to see meaning in the thunderous, theatrical presence of black surrogacy—an informing, stabilizing, and disturbing element—in the literature they do study. It is interesting, not surprising, that the arbiters of critical power in American literature seem to take pleasure in, indeed relish, their ignorance of African-American texts. What is surprising is that their refusal to read black texts—a refusal that makes no disturbance in their intellectual life—repeats itself when they read the traditional, established works of literature worthy of their attention. It is possible for example to read Henry James scholarship exhaustively and never arrive at a nodding mention, much less a satisfactory treatment, of the black woman who lubricates the turn of the plot and becomes the agency of moral choice and meaning in *What Maisie Knew*; Morrison, *Playing in the Dark*, 13. As if on cue, Michael Wood's erudite and learned engagement with Henry James's *What Maisie Knew* completely passes over matters of race. See M. Wood, *Literature and the Taste of Knowledge*.

55. In his book *The Broken Estate*, James Wood argues: "Nevertheless, the reality of fiction must also draw its power from the reality of the world. The real, in fiction, is always a matter of belief, and is therefore a kind of discretionary magic: it is a magic whose existence it is up to us, as readers, to validate and confirm. It is for this reason that many readers dislike actual magic or fantasy in novels. . . . Fiction demands belief from us, and that is demanding partly because we can choose not to believe. However, magic— improbable occurrences, ghosts, coincidences—dismantles belief, forcing on us miracles which, because they are beyond belief, we cannot choose not to believe. This is why almost all fiction is not magical, and why the great writers of magical tales are so densely realistic. The gentle *request* to believe is what makes fiction so moving. Joyce requests that we believe that Mick Lacy could sing the tune better than Stephen's father. . . . It is a belief that is requested, that we can refuse at any time, that is under our constant surveillance. This is surely the true secularism of fiction—why, despite its being a kind of magic, it

276 Notes to Pages 194–197

is actually the enemy of superstition, the slayer of religions, the scrutineer of falsity. Fiction moves in the shadow of doubt, knows itself to be a true lie, knows that at any moment it might fail to make its case. Belief in fiction is always belief 'as if.' Our belief is itself metaphorical—it only *resembles* actual belief, and is therefore never wholly belief"; James Wood, *The Broken Estate: Essays on Literature and Belief* (New York: Picador, 1999), xx. Wood's claim that *almost all* fiction is not magical is immediately implausible, which then raises the question of what he conceives to be "realism," "fiction," "magic," and "belief." He is only able to sustain his wildly idiosyncratic definitions by a commitment to rigorous cheating. When he encounters writers that he likes who are self-avowed political writers who draw on "magic" or the fantastical—writers like the communist José Saramago and the socialist Roberto Bolaño—he reads their works selectively, highlighting aspects of their books that he likes and explaining away their political goals and their unorthodox, a-realist forms.

56. This is true, even, of the work of Martha Nussbaum, which retains disturbing echoes of a *mission civilisatrice*.

57. Raymond Williams, *Culture and Society* (New York: Columbia University Press, 1983), 47.

58. Howard Jacobson as cited in Stephen Mulhall, *The Wounded Animal: J. M. Coetzee and the Difficulty of Reality in Literature and Philosophy* (Princeton: Princeton University Press, 2009), v.

59. B. Williams, *Ethics and the Limits of Philosophy*, 13–14.

60. Jacobson's notion that art transcends racism because it holds everything in suspense demonstrates a willful (and no doubt motivated) caricature of racism. European and U.S. racist regimes invest in racism precisely through "holding everything in suspense" in policies such as "color-blindness" and "laïcité."

61. This maneuver is also one that many scientists like to perform with science. Instead of simply critiquing the scientific practices that purported to establish the superiority of whites over other races as bad science, many who are invested in clinging to an essentialist conception of science dismiss these sciences as *pseudo-sciences*. These exercises in demarcation may be effective in ruling out certain people and theories from critical debate, but such effectiveness is at the cost of underwriting the false claim that there is an essence to scientific practice.

62. Antony Julius, *T. S. Eliot: Anti-Semitism and Literary Form* (Cambridge: Cambridge University Press, 1995), 33.

63. Ibid., 91.

64. G. W. F. Hegel, *Aesthetics: Lectures on Fine Arts*, trans. T. M. Knox, 2 vols. (Oxford: Clarendon Press, 1975).

65. John Dewey, *Art as Experience* (New York: Penguin Group, 1934), 347.

66. Ibid., 282.

67. Ibid., 58.

68. Barbara Ehrenreich, *Bright-Sided: How the Relentless Promotion of Positive Thinking Has Undermined America* (New York: Metropolitan Books, 2009).

69. Raymond Williams, *Modern Tragedy* (London: Chatto and Windus, 1966), 62. Ulrich Simon writes serenely that "disablement, genetic malformation, crippling diseases, may torment the victims and destroy their families, but they are not tragic"; Ulrich Simon, *Pity and Terror: Christianity and Tragedy* (London: Palgrave Macmillan, 1989), 37. See also C. S. Lewis, who rightly rejects the notion that tragedy represents what is truest about life, but takes for granted the belief that tragic art necessarily dramatizes the grandeur and splendor of suffering. Lewis writes: "The tragedian dare not present the totality of suffering as it usually is in its uncouth mixture of agony with littleness, all the indignities and (save for the pity) the uninterestingness, of grief. It would ruin his play. It would be merely dull and depressing. He selects from the reality just what his art needs; and what it needs is the exceptional"; C. S. Lewis, *An Experiment in Criticism* (Cambridge: Cambridge University Press, 1961), 78–79. Lewis presupposes that the common is uninteresting, which is a dubious assumption; moreover, his belief that there is something wrong with drama if it leaves audiences depressed is contestable.

70. Bernard Williams, *The Sense of the Past: Essays in the History of Philosophy*, ed. and with an introduction by Myles Burnyeat (Princeton: Princeton University Press, 2006), 55.

71. Ibid., 55.

72. Ibid., 56.

73. Ibid.

74. Ibid., 58.

75. Ibid., 59.

76. Friedrich Nietzsche, *The Birth of Tragedy*, trans. Walter Kaufmann (New York: Random House, 1967), 83.

CHAPTER 4. GEOGRAPHIES OF THE IMAGINATION

1. Ajume H. Wingo, "The Many-Layered Aesthetics of African Art," in *A Companion to African Philosophy*, ed. Kwasi Wiredu, 425–32 (Malden, MA: Blackwell Publishing Ltd., 2004).

2. Robert Farris Thompson, *Flash of the Spirit: African and Afro-American Art and Philosophy* (New York: Vintage Books, 1984).

3. Wingo, "The Many-Layered Aesthetics of African Art," 428.

4. Kofi Agawu, "Aesthetic Inquiry and the Music of Africa," in *A Companion to African Philosophy*, ed. Kwasi Wiredu, 404–14 (Malden, MA: Blackwell Publishing, 2004), 408.

5. Thompson, *Flash of the Spirit*, 7.

6. Ibid., 6.

7. Agawu, "Aesthetic Inquiry and the Music of Africa," 411.

8. Wingo, "The Many-Layered Aesthetics of African Art."

9. Agawu, "Aesthetic Inquiry and the Music of Africa," 407.

10. See Nkiru Nzegwu, "Art and Community: A Social Conception of Beauty and Individuality," in *A Companion to African Philosophy*, ed. Kwasi Wiredu, 415–24 (Malden, MA: Blackwell Publishing Ltd., 2004).

11. Hegel, *Hegel's Aesthetics*, 1:44–45.

12. For a fascinating discussion to which these brief remarks are indebted, see Geuss, *Politics and the Imagination*, 106.

13. As Chinua Achebe remarked of his childhood, early Christian converts in colonial Africa were contemptuous of indigenous art. See Chinua Achebe, *Hopes and Impediments: Selected Essays* (New York: Doubleday, 1988), 44.

14. In his book, *The Education of a British-Protected Child*, Achebe denounces this characterization as "blasphemous." He thinks it mistaken, he says, not because he was modest, but because it fails to appreciate the Igbo understanding of creativity as a communal enterprise. See Chinua Achebe, *The Education of a British-Protected Child: Essays* (New York: Anchor Books, 2009), 108.

15. Chinua Achebe, *Hopes and Impediments*, 45.

16. Ibid., 42.

17. Ibid., 44.

18. Ibid., 42.

19. See Said, *The World, the Text and the Critic*, 90–110. Said states: "Interestingly, the dramatic protocol of much of Conrad's fiction is the swapped yarn, the historical report, the mutually exchanged legend, the musing recollection. . . . Thus hearing and telling are the ground of the story, the tale's most stable sensory activities and the measure of its duration; in marked contrast, seeing is always a precarious achievement and a much less stable business" (94).

20. Francis Mulhern explains: "The phatic function of communication, in Roman Jakobson's classic definition, consists in monitoring and confirming the integrity of the communicative medium—as when, in a telephone conversation, a speaker says, 'Yes . . . yes,' meaning not 'I agree' or 'It is so' but 'I can hear

you'"; Francis Mulhern, "Inconceivable History: Storytelling as Hyperphasia and Disavowal," in *The Novel: Forms and Themes*, vol. 2, ed. Franco Moretti, 777–807 (Princeton: Princeton University Press, 2006), 779.

21. Ibid., 780.

22. The literary criticism of F. Abiola Irele, often hailed as the doyen of African literary criticism, betrays this hyperphatic desire. Abiola argues: "If there is anything distinctive about [the canon of African oral literature], it is what I'd like to call its organic mode of existence. In production, realization, and transmission, the text inheres in the physiology of the human frame and is expressed as voice, in gestures, and in immediate performance. The spoken word achieves here its plenitude as a total presence"; F. Abiola Irele, *The African Imagination: Literature in Africa and the Black Diaspora* (Oxford: Oxford University Press, 2001), 10.

23. Mulhern, "Inconceivable History," 792.

24. See for example Achebe's immensely controversial *There Was A Country: A Personal History of Biafra*. Achebe makes bracing and much needed critiques about the conduct of the war by the Nigerian ethnocracy. However, his critics are right that he resorts to *sotto voce* intimations of Igbo exceptional in relation to other Nigerian ethnic groups. Chinua Achebe, *There Was A Country: A Personal History of Biafra* (New York: Penguin, 2012).

25. Wole Soyinka, *Myth, Literature and the African World* (Cambridge: Cambridge University Press, 1976), 3.

26. Ibid., viii.

27. Ibid., 2–3.

28. Wole Soyinka, "Author's Note," in *Death and the King's Horseman*, ed. Simon Gikandi, 3 (New York: W.W. Norton, 2003).

29. Soyinka's heteronormative and masculinist assumptions are present everywhere in his work. For a discussion of Soyinka's novel *The Interpreters*, see Neville Hoad, *African Intimacies: Race, Homosexuality, and Globalization* (Minneapolis: University of Minnesota Press, 2007).

30. B. Williams, *Shame and Necessity*, 68.

31. J. M. Coetzee, "What is a Classic? A Lecture," in *Stranger Shores* (New York: Penguin Books, 2001), 1.

32. Ibid., 7.

33. Ibid., 7.

34. Ibid., 4.

35. Ibid., 5.

36. Ibid., 8.

37. Ibid., 9.

38. Ibid., 15.

39. Ibid., 16.

40. Matthew Arnold, "Dover Beach," in *Selected Poems of Matthew Arnold* (London: Macmillan, 1889), 165.

41. Egudu's notion that the essence of the African novel lies in its oral tradition is problematic, but it takes some effort to take this mistaken belief as one exclusively held by Africans. Figures as diverse as Conrad and Melville often sought desperately to retain an oral timbre in their writing.

Conclusion

1. Frederick Engels, "Ludwig Feuerbach and the End of Classical German Philosophy," available at https://www.marxists.org/archive/marx/works /1886/ludwig-feuerbach/foreword.htm.

2. As cited in Howard Eiland and Michael W. Jennings, *Walter Benjamin: A Critical Life* (Cambridge, MA: Harvard University Press, 2014), 662.

3. Carole Blair, Julie R. Brown, and Leslie A. Baxter, "Disciplining the Feminine," *Quarterly Journal of Speech* 80, no. 4 (1994): 383–409, at 383.

4. Audre Lorde, *Sister Outsider* (Trumansberg, NY: Crossing Press, 1981), 116.

5. Blair, Brown, and Baxter, "Disciplining the Feminine," 383–84.

6. "Criticism in short is always situated; it is skeptical, secular, reflectively open to its own failings. This is by no means to say that it is value-free. Quite the contrary, for the inevitable trajectory of critical consciousness is to arrive at some acute sense of what political, social, and human values are entailed in the reading, production, and transmission of every text. To stand between culture and system is therefore to stand close to—closeness itself having a particular value for me—a concrete reality about which political, moral, and social judgments have to be made, and, if not only made, then exposed and demystified"; Said, *The World, the Text, and the Critic*, 26.

7. "To lend himself, to project himself and steep himself, to feel and feel till he understands and to understand so well that he can say, to have perception at the pitch of passion and expression as embracing as the air, to be infinitely curious and incorrigibly patient, and yet plastic and inflammable and determinable, stooping to conquer and serving to direct—these are fine chances for an active mind, chances to add the idea of independent beauty to the conception of success"; Henry James, *Selected Literary Criticism*, ed. Morris Shapira (New York: McGraw-Hill, 1965), 136.

8. *Homo sum, humani nihil a me alienum puto* (I am human, and nothing of that which is human is alien to me), Publius Terentius Afer (better known as Terence).

9. Raymond Williams, *Culture and Materialism: Selected Essays* (London: Verso, 1980).

10. "Negative Capability, that is, when a man is capable of being in uncertainties, mysteries, doubts, without any irritable reaching after fact and reason"; John Keats, *The Complete Poetical Works and Letters of John Keats*, Cambridge Edition (Boston: Houghton, Mifflin, 1899), 277.

11. Gramsci, *Antonio Gramsci Reader*, 326.

12. "But, if constructing the future and settling everything for all times are not our affair, it is all the more clear what we have to accomplish at present: I am referring to *ruthless criticism* of all that exists, ruthless both in the sense of not being afraid of the results it arrives at and in the sense of being just as little afraid of conflict with the powers that be"; Karl Marx, "Letter from Marx to Arnold Ruge," *Deutsch-Französische Jahrbücher*, 1844. Available at https://www .marxists.org/archive/marx/works/1843/letters/43_09-alt.htm.

13. See Morrison, *Playing in the Dark*.

14. For insightful considerations of the zany, the interesting, and the cute, see Sianne Ngai, *Our Aesthetic Categories: Zany, Cute, Interesting* (Cambridge, MA: Harvard University Press, 2012).

15. See Guillory, *Cultural Capital*.

16. Walter Benjamin, "On the Concept of History," trans. Dennis Redmond, 3. Available at http://www.efn.org/~dredmond/Theses_on_History.pdf.

17. B. Williams, *The Sense of the Past*, 58.

BIBLIOGRAPHY

Abrahams, Roger D. "Review of *Xhosa Oral Poetry: Aspects of a Black South African Tradition* by Jeff Opland." *Poetics Today* 6, no. 3 (1985): 553–58.

Achebe, Chinua. *The Education of a British-Protected Child: Essays.* New York: Anchor Books, 2009.

———. *Hopes and Impediments: Selected Essays.* New York: Doubleday, 1988.

———. *There Was a Country: A Personal History of Biafra.* New York: Penguin, 2012.

Adorno, Theodor W. *Critical Models: Interventions and Catchwords.* Translated by Henry W. Pickford, introduction by Lydia Goehr. New York: Columbia University Press, 2005.

———. *The Culture Industry: Selected Essays on Mass Culture.* Edited and with an introduction by J. M. Bernstein. London: Routledge, 1991.

Agawu, Kofi. "Aesthetic Inquiry and the Music of Africa." In *A Companion to African Philosophy*, edited by Kwasi Wiredu, 404–14. Malden, MA: Blackwell Publishing, 2004.

Althusser, Louis, and Étienne Balibar. *Reading Capital.* London: NLB, 1970.

Anderson, Elizabeth. "Feminist Epistemology: An Interpretation and a Defense." *Hypatia* 10, no. 3 (1995): 50–84.

Ang, Ien. "Culture and Communication: Towards an Ethnographic Critique of Media Consumption in the Transnational Media System." In *What is Cultural Studies? A Reader*, edited by John Storey, 237–54. London: Arnold, 1996.

Antony, Louise. *Philosophers Without Gods: Meditations on Atheism and the Secular Life.* Oxford: Oxford University Press, 2007.

Appiah, Kwame Anthony. *Cosmopolitanism: Ethics in a World of Strangers.* New York: W. W. Norton, 2006.

———. "Foreword." In *The Struggle for Meaning: Reflections on Philosophy, Culture and Democracy in Africa*, by Paulin Hountondji, xi–xv. Athens: Ohio University Press, 2002.

———. *In My Father's House: Africa in the Philosophy of Culture.* New York: Oxford University Press, 1992.

Apter, Andrew. "'Que Faire?' Reconsidering Inventions of Africa." *Critical Inquiry* 19, no. 1 (Autumn 1992): 87–104.

Arendt, Hannah. "Martin Heidegger at Eighty." *The New York Review of Books,* October 21, 1971, 50–54.

Aristotle. *On the Soul.* Translated by W. S. Hett. Cambridge, MA: Harvard University Press, 1957.

Arnold, Matthew. "Dover Beach." In *Selected Poems of Matthew Arnold.* London: Macmillan, 1889.

Asante, Molefi Kete. *The Afrocentric Idea.* Philadelphia: Temple University Press, 1998.

Assmann, Jan. *The Mind of Egypt: History and Meaning in the Time of the Pharaohs.* Translated by Andrew Jenkins. Cambridge, MA: Harvard University Press, 2003.

Austin, John. *How to Do Things with Words.* Cambridge, MA: Harvard University Press, 1962.

Bakhtin, Mikhail. *The Dialogic Imagination: Four Essays.* Austin: University of Texas Press, 1981.

———. *Problems of Dostoevsky's Poetics.* Edited and translated by Caryl Emerson. Minneapolis: University of Minnesota Press, 1984.

Barabas, Gabor. "Appendix A: On Translating the Poems of Radnoti." In *Miklos Radnoti: The Complete Poetry in Hungarian and English,* translated by Gabor Barabas. Jefferson, NC: McFarland & Company, Inc., Publishers, 2014.

Batteux, Charles. *The Fine Arts Reduced to a Single Principle.* Translated by James O. Young. Oxford: Oxford University Press, 2015.

Baudrillard, Jean. "From The Precession of Simulacra." In *The Norton Anthology of Theory and Criticism,* edited by Vincent B. Leitch, 1732–41. New York: Norton, 2001.

Belcher, Wendy. "Medieval African and European Texts about the Queen of Sheba: Some Speculations about the Early Circulation of Ethiopian Discourse." *Newsletter of the UCLA Center for the Study of Women* (May 2006): 4–5.

Bell, Clive. *Art.* New York: Capricorn, 1913.

Belsey, Catherine. *Critical Practice.* London: Methuen, 1980.

Benjamin, Walter. "On the Concept of History," trans. Dennis Redmond. Available at http://www.efn.org/~dredmond/Theses_on_History.pdf.

———. *Selected Writings,* vol. 2, *1931–1934.* Edited by Michael W. Jennings, Howard Eiland, and Gary Smith. Cambridge, MA: Harvard University Press, 1999.

———. *Selected Writings,* vol. 4, *1938–1940.* Edited by Howard Eiland and Michael W. Jennings. Cambridge, MA: Harvard University Press, 2006.

———. *The Work of Art in the Age of Mechanical Reproduction.* Edited by Hannah Arendt. Translated by Harry Zohn. New York: Schocken, 1968.

Bernal, Martin. *Black Athena: The Afroasiatic Roots of Classical Civilization.* 3 vols. New Brunswick, NJ: Rutgers University Press, 1987.

Blair, Carole, Julie R. Brown, and Leslie A. Baxter. "Disciplining the Feminine." *Quarterly Journal of Speech* 80, no. 4 (1994): 383–409.

Blake, William. *William Blake*, ed. Michael Mason. Oxford: Oxford University Press, 1988.

———. *Selected Poetry.* Edited with an introduction by Michael Mason. Oxford: Oxford University Press, 1998.

Bledstein, Burton J. *The Culture of Professionalism: The Middle Class and the Development of Higher Education in America.* New York: W. W. Norton, 1976.

Booth, Wayne C. *The Rhetoric of Fiction.* 2nd ed. Chicago: University of Chicago Press, 1983.

———. *The Rhetoric of Rhetoric.* Oxford: Blackwell Publishing, 2004.

Bourdieu, Pierre. *Distinction: A Social Critique of the Judgement of Taste.* Translated by Richard Nice. London: Routledge, 1984.

———. *The Logic of Practice.* Translated by Richard Nice. Stanford, CA: Stanford University Press, 1990.

———. *Outline of a Theory of Practice.* Translated by Richard Nice. Cambridge: Cambridge University Press, 1977.

———. *The Political Ontology of Martin Heidegger.* Stanford, CA: Stanford University Press, 1991.

———. *The Rules of Art: Genesis and Structure of the Literary Field.* Stanford, CA: Stanford University Press, 1995.

———. *Science of Science and Reflexivity.* Translated by Richard Nice. Chicago: University of Chicago Press, 2004.

———. *Sketch for a Self-Analysis.* Translated by Richard Nice. Chicago: University of Chicago Press, 2004.

———. *Sociology in Question.* Translated by Richard Nice. London: Sage, 1993.

Boyd, Richard. "The Current Status of Scientific Realism." In *Scientific Realism*, edited by Jarrett Leplin, 41–82. Berkeley: University of California Press, 1984.

———. "How to Be a Moral Realist." In *Moral Discourse and Practice: Some Philosophical Approaches*, ed. Stephen Darwall, Allan Gibbard, and Peter Railton, 105–35. Oxford: Oxford University Press, 1997.

———. "Materialism Without Reductionism: What Physicalism Does Not Entail." In *Readings in Philosophy of Psychology*, vol. 1, edited by Ned Block, 67–106. Cambridge, MA: Harvard University Press, 1980.

———. "Scientific Realism and Naturalistic Epistemology." *PSA: Proceedings of the Biennial Meeting of the Philosophy of Science Association* 2 (1980): 613–62.

Brennan, Timothy. "Cosmo-Theory." *The South Atlantic Quarterly* 100, no. 3 (Summer 2001): 659–91.

Brown, Nicholas. *Utopian Generations: The Political Horizon of Twentieth-Century Literature.* Princeton: Princeton University Press, 2005.

Butler, Judith. *Bodies That Matter: On the Discursive Limits of Sex.* London: Routledge, 1993.

———. *Excitable Speech: A Politics of the Performative.* New York: Routledge, 1997.

———. "Gender as Performance." In *A Critical Sense: Interviews with Intellectuals,* edited by P. Osborne, 109–25. London: Routledge, 1996.

Caffentzis, George C. "On the Scottish Origin of 'Civilization.'" In *Enduring Western Civilization: The Construction of the Concept of Western Civilization and Its "Others,"* edited by Silvia Federici, 13–36. Westport, CT: Praeger, 1995.

Calvin, John. *Institutes of the Christian Religion.* Edited by John T. McNeill, translated by Ford Lewis Battles. Philadelphia: Westminster John Knox, 1960.

Carroll, Sean. "Guest Post: Terry Rudolph on Nature versus Nurture." August 27th, 2012. Available at http://blogs.discovermagazine.com/cosmic variance/2012/08/27/guest-post-terry-rudolph-on-nature-versus-nurture /#.WULLBevyu70.

Cavell, Stanley. *Pursuits of Happiness: The Hollywood Comedy of Remarriage.* Cambridge, MA: Harvard University Press, 1981.

Clarke, T. J. "Origins of the Present Crisis." *New Left Review* 2 (March–April 2000): 85–96.

Clifford, James. *On the Edges of Anthropology (Interviews).* Chicago: Prickly Paradigm Press, 2003.

Cloud, Dana L. "The Null Persona: Race and The Rhetoric of Silence in the Uprising of '34." *Rhetoric and Public Affairs* 2, no. 2 (1999): 177–209.

Coetzee, J. M. "What is a Classic? A Lecture." In *Stranger Shores.* New York: Penguin Books, 2001.

Coleridge, Samuel Taylor. "The Statesman's Manual." In *The Complete Works of Samuel Taylor Coleridge: Aids to Reflection; Statesman's Manual,* edited by W. G. T. Shedd. New York: Harper & Brothers, 1884.

Collingwood, R. G. *The Principles of Art.* Oxford: Clarendon Press, 1938.

Comaroff, Jean, and John L. Comaroff. "Occult Economies and the Violence of Abstraction: Notes from the South African Postcolony." *American Ethnologist* 26, no. 2 (1999), 279–303.

Conrad, Joseph. "Henry James: An Appreciation." In *Notes on Life and Letters.* New York: Doubleday, Page & Company, 1921.

———. *A Personal Record.* New York, Harper and Brothers Publishers, 1912.

Cooper, John M. *Pursuits of Wisdom: Six Ways of Life in Ancient Philosophy from Socrates to Plotinus.* Princeton: Princeton University Press, 2012.

Darsey, James. *The Prophetic Tradition and Radical Rhetoric in America*. New York: New York University Press, 1997.

Davidson, Donald. "A Coherence Theory of Truth and Knowledge." In *Truth and Interpretation: Perspectives on the Philosophy of Donald Davidson*, edited by Ernest LePore, 307–19. Oxford: Basil Blackwell, 1986.

Debord, Guy. *The Society of the Spectacle*. Detroit: Black & Red, 1970.

Deleuze, Gilles. *Spinoza: Practical Philosophy*. Translated by Robert Hurley. San Francisco: City Light Books, 1988.

Denzin, Norman K., and Yvonna S. Lincoln. *Handbook of Qualitative Research*. 2nd ed. Thousand Oaks, CA: Sage, 2000.

Derrida, Jacques. *Limited Inc*. Evanston, IL: Northwestern University Press, 1988.

———. *Positions*. Translated by Alan Bass. Chicago: University of Chicago Press, 1981.

———. "The Purveyor of Truth." In *The Purloined Poe: Lacan, Derrida, and Psychoanalytic Reading*, translated by Alan Bass, edited by John P. Muller and William J. Richards, 173–212. Baltimore: Johns Hopkins University Press, 1988.

———. *Writing and Difference*. Translated by Alan Bass. Chicago: University of Chicago Press, 1978.

Detienne, Marcel, and Jean-Pierre Vernant. *Cunning Intelligence in Greek Culture and Society*. Translated by Janet Lloyd. Chicago: University of Chicago Press, 1981.

Dewey, John. *Art as Experience*. New York: Penguin Group, 1934.

Dotson, Kristie. "How is this Paper Philosophy?" *Comparative Philosophy* 3, no. 1 (2012): 3–29.

Douglass, Frederick. "West India Emancipation." In *Frederick Douglass: Selected Speeches and Writings*, edited by Philip S. Foner, abridged and adapted by Yuval Taylor, 358–68. Chicago: Lawrence Hill Books, 1999.

Dunne, Joseph. *Back to the Rough Ground*. Notre Dame, IN: University of Notre Dame Press, 1993.

Durkheim, Emile. *The Rules of Sociological Method: And Selected Texts on Sociology and Its Method*. Edited by Steven Lukes. Translated by W. D. Halls. New York: Free Press, 1982.

Eady, Cornelius. *Brutal Imagination*. New York: G. P. Putnam's Sons, 2001.

Eagleton, Terry. *Criticism and Ideology: A Study in Marxist Literary Theory*. London: Verso, 2006.

Ehrenreich, Barbara. *Bright-Sided: How the Relentless Promotion of Positive Thinking Has Undermined America*. New York: Metropolitan Books, 2009.

Ehrenreich, Barbara, and John Ehrenreich. "The New Left: A Case Study in Professional-Managerial Class Radicalism." *Radical America* 11, no. 3 (May–June 1977): 7–22.

Eiland, Howard, and Michael W. Jennings. *Walter Benjamin: A Critical Life.* Cambridge, MA: Harvard University Press, 2014.

Elgrably, Jordan. "The Art of Fiction No. 78: Interview with James Baldwin." *Paris Review* 91 (Spring 1984). Available at http://www.theparisreview.org /interviews/2994/the-art-of-fiction-no-78-james-baldwin.

Engels, Frederick. "Ludwig Feuerbach and the End of Classical German Philosophy." Available at https://www.marxists.org/archive/marx/works/1886 /ludwig-feuerbach/foreword.htm.

Evans-Pritchard, E. E. *The Nuer: A Description of the Modes of Livelihood and Political Institutions of a Nilotic People.* Oxford: Clarendon Press, 1940.

Eze, Emmanuel Chukwudi. "The Color of Reason: The Idea of 'Race' in Kant's Anthropology." In *Postcolonial African Philosophy: A Critical Reader,* edited by Emmanuel Chukwudi Eze, 103–40. Cambridge, MA: Blackwell, 1997.

Fabian, Johannes. *Out of Our Minds: Reason and Madness in the Exploration of Central Africa.* Berkeley: University of California Press, 2000.

Fears, Darryl. "Exonerations Change How Justice System Builds a Prosecution." *Washington Post,* May 3, 2007. Available at http://www.washington post.com/wp-dyn/content/article/2007/05/02/AR2007050202304.html.

Feierman, Steven. *Peasant Intellectuals: Anthropology and History in Tanzania.* Madison: University of Wisconsin Press, 1990.

Ferguson, James. *Global Shadows: Africa in the Neoliberal World Order.* Durham, NC: Duke University Press, 2006.

Finnegan, Ruth. *Literacy and Orality: Studies in the Technology of Communication.* New York: Basic Blackwell, 1988.

Fiske, John. "Moments of Television: Neither the Text nor the Audience." In *Remote Control: Television, Audiences, and Cultural Power,* edited by Ellen Seiter et al., 56–78. London: Routledge, 1989.

Fodor, Jerry. "Special Sciences, or The Disunity of Science as a Working Hypothesis." In *Readings in Philosophy of Psychology,* vol. 1, edited by Ned Block, 120–33. Cambridge, MA: Harvard University Press, 1980.

Foucault, Michel. *The Foucault Reader.* Edited by Paul Rabinow. New York: Pantheon Books, 1984.

———. *Language, Counter-Memory, Practice: Selected Essays and Interviews.* Edited by Donald F. Bouchard, translated by Donald F. Bouchard and Sherry Simon. Ithaca, NY: Cornell University Press, 1977.

———. *Power/Knowledge: Selected Interviews and Other Writings, 1972–1977.* Edited by Colin Gordon. New York: Pantheon, 1980.

Gadamer, Hans-Georg. *Truth and Method.* New York: Seabury Press, 1975.

Gallagher, Catherine. "The Rise of Fictionality." In *The Novel,* vol. 1, edited by Franco Moretti, 336–63. Princeton: Princeton University Press, 2006.

Garfinkel, Alan. *Forms of Explanation: Rethinking the Questions in Social Theory.* New Haven, CT: Yale University Press, 1981.

Geuss, Raymond. "Goals, Origins, Disciplines." *Arion* 17, no. 2 (2009): 1–24.

———. *Politics and the Imagination.* Princeton: Princeton University Press, 2010.

———. "Richard Rorty at Princeton: Personal Recollections." *Arion* 15, no. 3 (2008): 85–100.

Gerratana, Valentino. "Althusser and Stalinism." *New Left Review* 1, nos. 101–2 (January–April 1977): 110–21.

Gettier, Edmund. "Is Justified True Belief Knowledge?" *Analysis* 23, no. 6 (1963): 121–23.

Gilman, Richard. *Decadence: The Strange Life of an Epithet.* New York: Farrar, Straus and Giroux, 1975.

Goffman, Erving. *The Goffman Reader.* Edited with introductory essays by Charles Lemert and Ann Branaman. Oxford: Blackwell, 1997.

———. *The Presentation of Self in Everyday Life.* New York: Doubleday Anchor, 1956.

Goldman, Alvin. "The Need for Social Epistemology." In *The Future for Philosophy*, edited by Brian Leiter, 182–207. Oxford: Oxford University Press, 2004.

Gondola, Ch. Didier. "Dream and Drama: The Search for Elegance among Congolese Youth." *African Studies Review* 42, no. 1 (1999): 23–48.

Goody, Jack. *The Domestication of the Savage Mind.* New York: Cambridge University Press, 1977.

Gourgouris, Stathis. *Does Literature Think? Literature as Theory for an Antimythical Era.* Stanford, CA: Stanford University Press, 2003.

Graff, Harvey. "The Legacies of Literacy." *Journal of Communication* 32, no. 1 (1982): 12–26.

Gramsci, Antonio. *The Antonio Gramsci Reader: Selected Writings 1916–1935.* Edited by David Forgacs. New York: New York University Press, 2000.

Guillory, John. *Cultural Capital: The Problem of Literary Canon Formation.* Chicago: University of Chicago Press, 1993.

———. "The Name of Science, The Name of Politics." *Critical Inquiry* 29, no. 3 (Spring 2003): 526–41.

———. "The Sokal Affair and the History of Criticism." *Critical Inquiry* 28, no. 2 (Winter 2002): 470–508.

Hadot, Pierre. *What Is Ancient Philosophy?* Translated by Michael Chase. Cambridge, MA: Harvard University Press, 2002.

Hall, Stuart. "Encoding/Decoding." In *Culture, Media, Language: Working Papers in Cultural Studies 1972–79*, edited by Stuart Hall, Andre Lowe, and Paul Willis, 128–38. London: Hutchingson, 1986.

Hansen, Miriam Bratu. "Benjamin's Aura." *Critical Inquiry* 34, no. 2 (Winter 2008): 336–75.

Haslanger, Sally. "Changing the Culture and Ideology of Philosophy: Not by Reason (Alone)." *Hypatia* 23, no. 2 (2008): 210–23.

Havelock, E. A., and J. P. Hershbell. *Communication Arts in the Ancient World.* New York: Hastings House, 1978.

Hays, Richard. "Salvation by Trust? Reading the Bible Faithfully," *The Christian Century,* February 26, 1997, 218–23. Available at http://www.religion-online .org/article/salvation-by-trust-reading-the-bible-faithfully/.

Hegel, G. W. F. *Aesthetics: Lectures on Fine Arts.* Translated by T. M. Knox. 2 vols. Oxford: Clarendon Press, 1975.

Heidegger, Martin. *Being and Time.* Translated by J. Macquarrie and E. Robinson. Oxford: Basil Blackwell, 1962.

———. *The Heidegger Reader.* Edited with introduction by Gunter Figal, translated by Jerome Veith. Bloomington: Indiana University Press, 2009.

———. "Only a God Can Save Us: Der Spiegel's Interview with Martin Heidegger," in *The Heidegger Controversy: A Critical Reader,* ed. Richard Wolin, trans. Maria P. Alter and John D. Caputo, 91–116. Cambridge, MA: MIT Press, 1993.

Heschel, Abraham J. *The Prophets.* New York: Harper Perennial Modern Classics, 2001.

Hoad, Neville, *African Intimacies: Race, Homosexuality, and Globalization.* Minneapolis: University of Minnesota Press, 2007.

Hountondji, Paulin. *African Philosophy: Myth and Reality.* Translated by Henri Evans. Bloomington: Indiana University Press, 1983.

———. *The Struggle for Meaning: Reflections on Philosophy, Culture and Democracy in Africa.* Translated by John Conteh-Morgan. Athens: Ohio University Press, 2002.

Hunwick, John. *West Africa, Islam, and the Arab World: Studies in Honor of Basil Davidson.* Princeton: Markus Wiener Publishers, 2006.

Husserl, Edmund. *The Crisis of European Science and Transcendental Phenomenology: An Introduction to Phenomenological Philosophy.* Translated by D. Carr. Evanston, IL: Northwestern University Press, 1970.

———. *Ideas.* Translated by W. R. Boyce-Gibson. New York: Macmillan, 1962.

Irele, F. Abiola. *The African Imagination: Literature in Africa and the Black Diaspora.* Oxford: Oxford University Press, 2001.

Irigaray, Luce. "Wonder: A Reading of Descartes' *The Passions of the Soul.*" In *Feminist Interpretations of Rene Descartes,* edited by Susan Bordo, translated by Carolyn Burke and Gillian C. Gill, 105–14. University Park: Pennsylvania State University Press, 1999.

Jacobs, Harriet. *Incidents in the Life of a Slave Girl.* New York: The Modern Library, 2000.

James, Henry. *The Question of Our Speech: The Lesson of Balzac; Two Lectures.* New York: Houghton Mifflin, 1905.

———. *Selected Literary Criticism.* Edited by Morris Shapira. New York: McGraw-Hill, 1965.

———. *What Maisie Knew.* Oxford: Oxford University Press, 1980.

Julius, Antony. *T. S. Eliot, Anti-Semitism and Literary Form.* Cambridge: Cambridge University Press, 1995.

Kant, Immanuel. "An Answer to the Question: What Is Enlightenment?" In *What Is Enlightenment?: Eighteenth-Century Answers and Twentieth-Century Questions,* edited and translated by James Schmidt, 58–64. Berkeley: University of California Press, 1996.

———. *Critique of Judgment.* Translated by Werner S. Pluhar. Indianapolis, IN: Hackett Publishing Company, 1987.

———. *Critique of Pure Reason.* Translated by Norman Kemp-Smith. London: Macmillan, 1929.

———. *Prolegomena.* Translated by Paul Carus. Chicago: Open Court, 1902.

Keats, John. *The Complete Poetical Works and Letters of John Keats.* Cambridge Edition. Boston: Houghton, Mifflin, 1899.

Keefer, Michael H. "The Dreamer's Path: Descartes and the Sixteenth Century." *Renaissance Quarterly* 49, no. 1 (Spring 1996): 30–76.

Kitcher, Philip. "1953 and All That: A Tale of Two Sciences." *The Philosophical Review* 93, no. 3 (1984): 335–73.

———. "The Trouble with Scientism: Why History and the Humanities Are also a Form of Knowledge." *The New Republic,* May 4, 2012. Available at https://newrepublic.com/article/103086/scientism-humanities-knowledge-theory-everything-arts-science.

Kittay, Eva F. *Love's Labor: Essays on Equality, Dependence and Care.* London: Routledge, 1999.

Kresse, Kai. "'Philosophy Must Be Made Sagacious': An Interview with Prof. Henry Odera Oruka, 16th August 1995 at the University of Nairobi." In *Sagacious Reasoning: Henry Odera Oruka in Memoriam,* edited by Anke Graness and Kai Kresse, 251–60. Frankfurt: Peter Lang, 1997.

Krugman, Paul. "How Did Economists Get It So Wrong?" *New York Times,* September 2, 2009.

Kundera, Milan. *The Unbearable Lightness of Being.* Translated by Michael Henry Heim. New York: HarperCollins Publishers, 2005.

Laudan, Larry. "The Demise of the Demarcation Problem." In *Physics, Philosophy and Psychoanalysis: Essays in Honor of Adolf Grünbaum,* edited by Robert S. Cohen and Larry Laudan, 111–27. Dordrecht: D. Reidel Publishing, 1983.

Lefkowitz, Mary. *Not Out of Africa: How Afrocentrism Became an Excuse to Teach Myth as History.* New York: Basic Books, 1996.

Levi-Strauss, Claude. *The Savage Mind.* Chicago: University of Chicago Press, 1966.

Lewis, C. S. *An Experiment in Criticism.* Cambridge: Cambridge University Press, 1961.

Lewontin, Richard C. "Is Nature Probable or Capricious?" *BioScience* 16, no. 1 (1966): 25–27.

Light, Alison. *Mrs. Woolf and the Servants: An Intimate History of Domestic Life in Bloomsbury.* New York: Bloomsbury Press, 2009.

Lippi-Green, Rosina. *English with an Accent: Language, Ideology and Discrimination in the United States.* London: Routledge, 1997.

Lobkowicz, Nicholas. *Theory and Practice: History of a Concept from Aristotle to Marx.* Notre Dame, IN: University of Notre Dame Press, 1967.

Locke, John. *An Essay Concerning Human Understanding.* Edited by A. C. Fraser. New York: Dover, 1959.

Lorde, Audre. *Sister Outsider.* Trumansberg, NY: Crossing Press, 1981.

Luria, A. R. *Cognitive Development: Its Cultural and Social Foundations.* Cambridge, MA: Harvard University Press, 1976.

MacIntyre, Alasdair. *After Virtue: A Study in Moral Theory.* Notre Dame, IN: University of Notre Dame Press, 1981.

Mafeje, Archie. "Africanity: A Commentary by Way of Conclusion." *CODESRIA Bulletin,* nos. 3–4 (2001): 14–16.

Marx, Karl. "Letter from Marx to Arnold Ruge." *Deutsch-Französische Jahrbücher,* 1844. Available at https://www.marxists.org/archive/marx/works/1843/letters/43_09-alt.htm.

Massad, Joseph. "The 'Post-Colonial' Colony: Time, Space, and Bodies in Palestine/Israel." In *The Pre-Occupation of Postcolonial Studies,* edited by Hamid Naficy, Fawzia Afzal-Khan, and Kalpana Seshadri, 311–46. Durham, NC: Duke University Press Books, 2000.

Mbiti, John S. *African Religions and Philosophy.* Nairobi: Heinemann, 1992.

McLuhan, Marshall. *Understanding Media: The Extensions of Man.* New York: New American Library, 1964.

Merrick, Teri. "Teaching Philosophy: Instilling Pious Wonder or Vicious Curiosity?" *Christian Scholar's Review* 34, no. 4 (Summer 2010): 401–20.

Morrison, Toni. *Playing in the Dark: Whiteness and the Literary Imagination.* New York: Vintage Books, 1993.

Mudimbe, V. Y. *The Idea of Africa.* Bloomington: Indiana University Press, 1994.

———. *The Invention of Africa: Gnosis, Philosophy, and the Order of Knowledge.* Bloomington: Indiana University Press, 1988.

Mulhall, Stephen. "Realism, Modernism and the Realistic Spirit: Diamond's Inheritance of Wittgenstein, Early and Late." *Nordic Wittgenstein Review* 1, no. 1 (2012): 7–33.

———. *The Wounded Animal: J. M. Coetzee and the Difficulty of Reality in Literature and Philosophy.* Princeton: Princeton University Press, 2009.

Mulhern, Francis. "Inconceivable History: Storytelling as Hyperphasia and Disavowal." In *The Novel: Forms and Themes*, vol. 2, edited by Franco Moretti, 777–807. Princeton: Princeton University Press, 2006.

Ngai, Sianne. *Our Aesthetic Categories: Zany, Cute, Interesting.* Cambridge, MA: Harvard University Press, 2012.

Nietzsche, Friedrich. *Beyond Good and Evil: Prelude to a Philosophy of the Future.* Translated by Helen Zimmern. New York: Macmillan, 1907.

———. *The Birth of Tragedy.* Translated by Walter Kaufmann. New York: Random House, 1967.

———. *The Gay Science: With a Prelude in Rhymes and an Appendix of Songs.* Translated by Walter Kaufmann. New York: Random House, 1974.

———. *On the Genealogy of Morality.* Edited by Keith Ansell-Pearson, translated by Carol Diethe. Cambridge: Cambridge University Press, 1994.

———. *The Will to Power.* Edited by Walter Kaufmann, translated by Walter Kaufmann and R. J. Hollingdale. New York: Random House, 1968.

Nissinen, Martti. *Prophecy in Its Ancient Near Eastern Context: Mesopotamian, Biblical, and Arabian Perspectives.* Atlanta: Society of Biblical Literature, 2000.

Nkrumah, Kwame. *Consciencism.* London: Heinemann, 1964.

Norman, Arthur M. Z. "Daniel's the Tragedie of Cleopatra and Antony and Cleopatra." *Shakespeare Quarterly* 9, no. 1 (1958): 11–18.

Nussbaum, Martha C. *Upheavals in Thought: The Intelligence of Emotions.* Cambridge: Cambridge University Press, 2001.

Nzegwu, Nkiru. "Art and Community: A Social Conception of Beauty and Individuality." In *A Companion to African Philosophy*, edited by Kwasi Wiredu, 415–24. Malden, MA: Blackwell Publishing Ltd., 2004.

Ochieng-Odhiambo, F. "The Evolution of Sagacity." *Philosophia Africana* 5, no. 1 (2002): 19–32.

Ochieng, Omedi. "The Epistemology of African Philosophy: Sagacious Knowledge and the Case for a Critical Contextual Epistemology." *International Philosophical Quarterly* 48, no. 3 (2008): 337–60.

———. *Groundwork for the Practice of the Good Life: Politics and Ethics at the Intersection of North Atlantic and African Philosophy.* New York: Routledge, 2016.

Ong, Walter J. *Orality and Literacy: The Technologizing of the Word.* New York: Methuen, 1982.

Oruka, H. Odera. *Sage Philosophy: Indigenous Thinkers and Modern Debate on African Philosophy.* Nairobi: African Center for Technology Studies, 1991.

————. *Trends in Contemporary African Philosophy*. Nairobi: Shirikon Publishers, 1990.

Pippin, Robert. "*Critical Inquiry* and Critical Theory: A Short History of Nonbeing." *Critical Inquiry* 30, no. 2 (Winter 2004): 424–28.

Plato. *Plato: Complete Works*. Edited with introduction and notes by John M. Cooper. Indianapolis, IN: Hackett Publishing Company, 1997.

Plantinga, Alvin. "Theism and Mathematics," *Theology and Science* 9, no. 1 (2011): 27–33.

————. *Where the Conflict Really Lies: Science, Religion and Naturalism*. New York: Oxford University Press, 2011.

Presbey, Gail. "H. Odera Oruka on Moral Reasoning." *The Journal of Value Inquiry* 34, no. 4 (December 2000): 517–28.

Protagoras. *The Older Sophists*. Edited by Rosamund Kent Sprague. Indianapolis, IN: Hackett Publishing Company, 2001.

Putnam, Hilary. *Ethics Without Ontology*. Cambridge, MA: Harvard University Press, 2004.

————. *Mind, Language and Reality: Philosophical Papers*. Vol. 2. Cambridge: Cambridge University Press, 1975.

Rawls, John. *Lectures on the History of Political Philosophy*. Edited by Samuel Freeman. Cambridge, MA: Harvard University Press, 2007.

Rée, Jonathan. "Passions of a Prussian." *Lingua Franca: The Review of Academic Life* 11, no. 5 (July 2001): 53–66.

Ricoeur, Paul. *Time and Narrative*. Chicago: University of Chicago Press, 1988.

Rosen, Michael. *Hegel's Dialectic and Its Criticism*. Cambridge: Cambridge University Press, 1982.

Ruskin, John. *The Elements of Drawing and The Elements of Perspective*. London: J. M. Dent and Sons, 1907.

Ryle, Gilbert. *The Concept of Mind*. New York: Barnes & Noble, 1949.

Said, Edward W. *Representations of the Intellectual*. New York: Vintage Books, 1994.

————. *The World, the Text, and the Critic*. Cambridge, MA: Harvard University Press, 1983.

Schwartzman, Lisa H. *Challenging Liberalism: Feminism as Political Critique*. University Park: Pennsylvania State University Press, 2006.

Scott, James C. *Seeing Like a State: How Certain Schemes to Improve the Human Condition Have Failed*. New Haven, CT: Yale University Press, 1999.

Scott, R. B. Y. *The Way of Wisdom in the Old Testament*. New York: Macmillan, 1971.

Scribner, Sylvia, and Michael Cole. *The Psychology of Literacy*. Cambridge, MA: Harvard University Press, 1981.

Shapin, Steven. *A Social History of Truth*. Chicago: University of Chicago Press, 1994.

Shklovsky, Victor. "Art as Technique." In *Russian Formalist Criticism: Four Essays*, edited by Lee T. Lemon and Marion J. Reis, 3–24. Lincoln: University of Nebraska Press, 1965.

Simpson, David. *Situatedness, or, Why We Keep Saying Where We're Coming From.* Durham, NC: Duke University Press, 2002.

Simon, Ulrich. *Pity and Terror: Christianity and Tragedy.* London: Palgrave Macmillan, 1989.

Soyinka, Wole. "Author's Note." In *Death and the King's Horseman,* ed. Simon Gikandi, 3. New York: W. W. Norton, 2003.

———. *Myth, Literature and the African World.* Cambridge: Cambridge University Press, 1976.

Symonds, John A. "Introduction." In Sophocles, *Oedipus Tyrannus*, edited by John A. Symonds, 1–48. Kansas: Coronado Press, 1970.

Tamagni, Daniele. *Gentlemen of Bacongo.* London: Trolley Books, 2009.

Thompson, Robert Farris. *Flash of the Spirit: African and Afro-American Art and Philosophy.* New York: Vintage Books, 1984.

Tishken, Joel E. "The History of Prophecy in West Africa: Indigenous, Islamic, and Christian." *History Compass* 5, no. 5 (2007): 1468–82.

Uidhir, Christy Mag. "Why Pornography Can't Be Art." *Philosophy and Literature* 33, no. 1 (2009): 193–203.

Vickers, Brian. *In Defense of Rhetoric.* Oxford: Oxford University Press, 1988.

Wadende, Pamela Akinyi. *Chwuech Manimba: Indigenous Creative Education among Women of the Luo Community of Western Kenya.* PhD diss., Texas State University San Marcos, August 2011.

Wander, Philip. "The Third Persona: An Ideological Turn in Rhetorical Theory." In *Contemporary Rhetorical Theory: A Reader,* edited by John Louis Lucaites, Celeste Michelle Condit, and Sally Caudill, 357–79. New York: Guilford Press, 1999.

Weisberg, Michael. "Three Kinds of Idealization." *Journal of Philosophy* 104, no. 12 (2007): 639–59.

White, Ed. "The Value of Conspiracy Theory." *American Literary History* 14, no. 1 (2002): 1–31.

Whorf, Benjamin. "The Relation of Habitual Thought and Behavior to Language." In *Language, Culture, and Personality: Essays in Memory of Edward Sapir,* edited by Leslie Spier, 75–93. Menasha, WI: Sapir Memorial Publication Fund, 1941.

Wilder, Craig Steven. *Ebony and Ivy: Race, Slavery, and the Troubled History of America's Universities.* New York: Bloomsbury Press, 2013.

Williams, Bernard. *Ethics and the Limits of Philosophy.* Cambridge, MA: Harvard University Press, 1985.

———. *Moral Luck.* Cambridge: Cambridge University Press, 1981.

————. *Philosophy as a Humanistic Discipline.* Edited by A. W. Moore. Princeton, NJ: Princeton University Press, 2006.

————. *The Sense of the Past: Essays in the History of Philosophy.* Edited and with an introduction by Myles Burnyeat. Princeton: Princeton University Press, 2006.

————. *Shame and Necessity.* Berkeley: University of California Press, 1993.

Williams, Raymond. *Culture and Materialism: Selected Essays.* London: Verso, 1980.

————. *Culture and Society.* New York: Columbia University Press, 1983.

————. *Modern Tragedy.* London: Chatto and Windus, 1966.

————. *Problems in Materialism and Culture: Selected Essays.* London: Verso, 1980.

Wingo, Ajume H. "The Many-Layered Aesthetics of African Art." In *A Companion to African Philosophy*, edited by Kwasi Wiredu, 425–32. Malden, MA: Blackwell, 2004.

Wittgenstein, Ludwig. *Tractatus Logico-Philosophicus.* Translated by C. K. Ogden. London: Routledge & Kegan Paul, 1922.

Wood, James. *The Broken Estate: Essays on Literature and Belief.* New York: Picador, 1999.

Wood, Michael. *Literature and the Taste of Knowledge.* Cambridge: Cambridge University Press, 2005.

INDEX

OMEDI OCHIENG

is assistant professor of communication at Denison University.
He is the author of a number of books and articles,
including *Groundwork for the Practice of the Good Life:*
Politics and Ethics at the Intersection of North Atlantic
and African Philosophy.

CPSIA information can be obtained
at www.ICGtesting.com
Printed in the USA
LVHW02*1914050718
582805LV00009B/193/P

9 780268 103293